Yoga Psychology
(A Handbook of Yogic Psychotherapy)

Yoga Psychology
A Handbook of Yogic Psychotherapy

Kamakhya Kumar

Foreword by
Ganesh Shankar Giri

Prologue by
J.P.N. Mishra

DK PRINTWORLD
Publishers of Indian Traditions

Cataloging in Publication Data — DK
[Courtesy: D.K. Agencies (P) Ltd. <docinfo@dkagencies.com>]

Kumāra, Kāmākhyā, 1975- author.

Yoga psychology : a handbook of yogic psychotherapy / Kamakhya Kumar ; foreword by Ganesh Shankar Giri ; prologue by J.P.N. Mishra. – 2nd impression.

pages cm

Includes verses in Sanskrit (Devanagari and roman).
Includes bibliographical references and index.
ISBN 9788124607114 (HB)
ISBN 9788124607121 (PB)

1. Yoga. 2. Yoga – Psychological aspects. 3. Yoga – Therapeutic use. 4. Psychotherapy. I. Title.

LCC BL1238.52.K86 2021 | DDC 294.5436 23

First published in India, 2013
Second impression published in 2021
ISBN 13: 978-81-246-0711-4 (HB)
ISBN 13: 978-81-246-0712-1 (PB)

Printed and published by:
D.K. Printworld (P) Ltd.
Regd. Office: Vedaśrī, F-395, Sudarshan Park
(Metro Station: ESI Hospital)
New Delhi – 110015
Phones: (011) 2545 3975, 2546 6019
E-mail: indology@dkprintworld.com
Website: www.dkprintworld.com

Foreword

It is a special task of joy to write a foreword to a book that can bring happiness to those yoga students, yoga lovers and yoga aspirants who want to understand the Yoga-Psychology well.

Great truths are universally relevant, and consequently defy every: attempt at definition. Same is the case with yoga and psychology. Yoga being the union of the individual soul with the supreme soul is universal in appeal. Yoga, as spiritual union, signifies the soul's union with god. The practice of yoga then is a process of self-discovery and therefore yoga is not a practice for achieving outward results like poise, muscular co-ordination, or the development of artistic or intellectual skills. Likewise psychology is not merely a practice of achieving mental health through psychotherapy rather it is the science of mind unveiling the secrets of the different stages of mind like conscious, unconscious and superconscious mind.

Yoga, as union, implies perfect harmony of body–mind and spirit. On a physical level, it implies glowing health on mental level, it implies the harmonious integration of the personality and the corresponding elimination of psychological "complexes", and on the soul level, yoga implies union of the little self with the greater self, of the ego with the vastness of cosmic-awareness, and, as stated earlier, of the individual soul with its infinite source: God.

Maharṣi Patañjali in his *Yogā-Sūtras* says: "Yoga is the inhibition (*nirodha*) of the modifications (*vr̥tti*) of the mind." Now that yoga is the inhibition or cessation of mental waves, it is of course essential to understand the mind first which we have in psychology. Therefore without proper knowledge or understanding of mind we can't understand the happening like the inhibition of mental waves which occur during the higher practice of yoga like *samādhi*. In *asamprajñāta samādhi* there is the complete or total end of the mind. It is the state of mind where occurs the divine union of the individual soul with the supreme soul. That is why this Samādhi is also known as the seedless (*nirbīja samādhi*). Therefore for a better understanding of such divine phenomena it is of course essential to understand the science of mind and the psychology of yoga first. This is what the book presents in detail.

The book advocates a holistic view of Yoga-Psychology. It beautifully blends yogic knowledge along with its psychology for a better understanding of yoga. I do hope the readers will not only find the book interesting and stimulating, but also respond to it through personal experience and enjoyment.

Ganesh Shankar Giri
Department of Yogic Science
Doctor Harisingh Gour Central University,
Sagar (Madhya Pradesh)

Prologue

YOGA is a science common to all and the whole humanity in its true nature of efficacy, results and applications. We all can derive satisfaction from it in our own way, that too, without any preoccupied notion and ill effects. There are three dimensions of yoga: yoga and objective body; yoga and subjective mind; and yoga and consciousness. In fact, these are not three separate dimensions, they are three facets of the same super science. It is the only science which has the message for the body, the mind and the consciousness, and all three work together without ringing the bell. Most of the times, integral components of yoga practices yield these effects through the operational mechanism, known as mind–body–consciousness, although the outcome is denoted merely as bodily changes. Only by understanding the psychological phenomena well, a researcher can explain the scientific principles behind the multifaceted effects of yogic practices.

The linkage between the mind and body, particularly in reference to yogic sciences, was widely accepted in the ancient wisdom and oriental learning, but later developed an artificial dichotomy between these two components. Modern medical science focuses only on body as something which is apart from the mind. However psychosomatic linkages have now got its due importance by both modern medical practitioners and therapists of Indian tradition. It has now been proved by scientific researches beyond doubt that yoga practices brings in better equilibrium in the autonomic function and metabolic rate at one hand, and neurohumoral functions at the other, so that the state of both physical and mental well-being is achieved. This itself reflects that physiological and psychological conditionings go hand-in-hand and operate simultaneously.

The ultimate aim and goal of yogic sciences is not only to attain optimum physical and mental health but also to eliminate the level of unconsciousness of an individual practising it. The pathway of mechanism for attaining such goals may be vivid but one thing is very clear that for attaining such goals one has to understand, follow and nourish the body and mind simultaneously. In that way psychology of yoga has its own importance. Its basic principles need to be documented in terms modern physiology and psychology. In fact, it is the need of the hour.

Kamakhya Kumar is a scholar of yoga. He has not only studied the fundamental principles based on the original texts, but also has applied it while treating the patients suffering from various psychosomatic disorders. He has a long experience of teaching and research in the field of yogic physiology and psychology. In this *Yoga Psychology* book he has explained all the relevant aspects of psychotherapy based on yogic principles. Various techniques of yogic psychotherapy like prayer, *mantra sādhanā*, spiritual counselling, *yajña, saṅkīrtana, svādhyāya* and *vrata anuṣṭhāna*, are well elaborated. All these techniques so far were found scattered here and there, and needed patent and scientific explanations. Kumar has done be an commendable work and I hope it will be an utmost useful monograph for students, scholars and practitioners.

I wish him all success in his sacred endeavour of serving the heritage of yoga.

J.P.N. Mishra

Contents

Introduction

THE importance of yoga is in its amenability in rendering the entire content of the human psychology in terms of consciousness. No doubt scriptures produced world over have contributed to the moderation of human psychology so as to check its inherent violent nature throughout the ages. If there had not been check of this nature in the form of scriptural prescriptions, man would have left the world in havoc. Today man is faced with the practical utilities of science which have negated the utility, appeal and value of these scriptures. In this process of evaluation, modern psychology has played an important role. Physical science would have abstained itself from entering the domain of spirituality had not psychology attacked the inherent consciousness and sided with physical sciences exclusively to explain the phenomenon of consciousness as a by-product of the physical form, like the Cārvākas. Man, finding himself defenceless, took resort to faith and declared it as inviolable but this inviolability has also been shaken and sooner or later it, too, has given way to thorough analysis for its tenability. In this exercise, faith does not seem to have any bright future on account of its sheer non-rationality.

Herein lies the advantage of Vedic yoga since its entire structure is based on consciousness as the basic stuff of creation in all its forms and varieties. Vedic seers, by means of deep meditation, were able to see through everything, howsoever gross and mightily tangible it was, as a formation of consciousness. This has been the finding of not one or two seers, but of many seers, living over a million sq. km of the Indian soil for thousands of years in isolated groups, sequestered from one another by considerable distance, and hurdled by rivers, forests and wild animals. Despite all these points of distraction, their common concurrence on consciousness as the essential stuff of creation is astounding and much more than the modern physicist's discovery regarding convertibility of matter into energy. While the physicist's discovery boosted the effort of the psychologist to create a psychology with matter as its basic stuff, the Vedic seers left the entire legacy of consciousness as the same sort of stuff to think of the possibility of formulating a psychology of the psyche.

When we study the present situation, we find that the modern psychology reigning between the tension of opposites — the real and the ideal. The real is our past animal nature, pulling us back to itself in the form of instinctive drives, while the ideal is our effort to make adjustment in the mode of fulfilment of our instinctive drives so as to conform to the social norms of the day. The animal nature is self-seeking while the ideal conforms to the social norms, requiring moving beyond sheer self-interest so as to concede to the requirements of others involved in the given situation, be they members of family, neighbours, classmates, colleagues, or any sort of people who have an interest to be shared with. It is only around this point that the modern psychology is moving under different denominations — behavioural, transactional, industrial, educational, marital, psychoanalytical — to name just a few. The interaction of the opposites creates tension while the psychologist is seeking to remove the same through adjustments and readjustments. The adjustments and readjustments are tried upon under the presumption that both the real and the ideal have a common origin, the physical. Thus, a modern psychologist removes, sets and resets psychological factors as per requirements of given situations and he has nothing to think about beyond these adjustments and readjustments. On account of having adopted the norm of physical sciences, the modern psychology envisages the human life as a machine to be kept on working properly unmindful of any aim or objective before it in any sense. If a living being, particularly a human, begins to be treated as a machine, how can it be expected to have an objective of its own apart from its amenability to exploitation by its owner?

If the human conscience is left with anything alive in it that seeks fulfilment, it can be fulfilled through Vedic yoga and can have the joy of that fulfilment in abundance without turning to anywhere else. This is due to its basic postulate of consciousness as the source and essence of everything. According to it even the instinctive life can be explained in terms of consciousness as its source and basis. Explanation for it is to be found in concentricity of consciousness, i.e. consciousness in the form of individual consciousness. It needs to be understood that consciousness is prone as much to concentricity as to extensity, as has been said by Kṣemarāja in his commentary on *Spanda-Kārikā*:

> The creative power of consciousness is always engaged in exercising her energy in enjoying the taste of manifestation and yet her energy is never depicted. She is the wave of the ocean of consciousness, the volitional power of the consciousness.

The methods of yoga can be pursued without recourse to any dogma, and they require the same rigour as science insists, namely, observation, experimentation and verification by repeatable experience. Yoga can be looked upon as the experiential basis for philosophical speculations and conclusions, and if rightly used, it can be a bridge between philosophy and science.

Yoga claims that it has developed methods, which can deal with the supra-physical as rigorously and as objectively as modern science deals with physical phenomena. Yoga claims that its methods can deal both with the physical and supra-physical, and, if needed and encouraged it could develop an integral science of both the physical and supra-physical and their interrelationship.

Our ancient literature and the Indian philosophy are pregnant with yogic sciences. Unfortunately for non-Sanskrit-knowing people, the literature of yoga is not largely available in English. The general teachings of yoga are to be found in the Upaniṣads and the *Bhagavad-Gītā*; those, in many translations, are within your reach, but they are general, not special; they give you the main principles, but do not tell you about the methods in any detailed manner.

The special literature of yoga is, first of all, many of the minor Upaniṣads, "the hundred-and-eight" as they are called. Then comes the enormous mass of literature called Tantra. These books have an evil significance in the ordinary English ear, but not quite rightly. The Tantras are very useful books, very valuable and instructive; all occult science is to be found in them. But they are divisible into three classes: those that deal with white magic, those that deal with black magic, and those that deal with what we may call grey magic, a mixture of the two. Now magic is the word which covers the methods of deliberately bringing about super-normal physical states by the action of the will.

Through the sound practice of yoga, one can attain a disease-free body as well as keen intellect. *Yogaśikhopaniṣad* mentions that this body is the abode of Śiva, hence, a *yogī* considers the body as a temple and keeps it healthy for further development of consciousness.

Today life has become more competitive, fast and individualistic, and as such more stressful. This has given rise to a lot of psychosocial problems reflected in interpersonal irritations to the breaking up of conjugal life, families and society at large. The social scenario as highlighted in the media is full of violence, corruption and crimes of all sorts. Can yoga work as an effective intervener in controlling or containing these social maladies which are threatening the very existence of human society? Psychologists agree that these problems are rooted in the human psyche. So, along the line of the United Nations Organization's (UNO) emblem, we must resolve to "fight them in the minds of men", and instead of giving sermons and preaching to others it must start from oneself. From this viewpoint, yoga is a valuable instrument.

So far we discuss the objectives, theories and principles of yoga, it is a science because of its practices and applications. Yoga believes in the basic reality of individual differences and so no yogic practice can be effective for all. As per predispositions of human personality, some people are dynamic and action-oriented for whom *haṭha-yoga* and *karma-yoga* would be more effective. Similarly, for emotional persons *bhakti-yoga*, for intellectual persons *jñāna-yoga*, and for intuitive/introvert people *rāja-yoga* can be most beneficial and effective. However, instead of placing a person under a specific personality type it is more scientific to provide the appropriate package of yogic practices for an individual, keeping in mind his specific needs and personality make-up.

Re-emerging yogic science on the basis of its theoretical models, practical approach and exploratory studies has given high hopes of being an effective intervener for the promotion of health, subjective well-being and desired societal transformation. It is very rich in management techniques and practices, which may be applied in different fields of life demanding stress management, confidence building, and promotion of mental and spiritual health. It is a fruitful field for fundamental and applied research and teaching at higher levels by behavioural scientists, particularly psychologists. Now it is high time that the indigenous knowledge of yoga and yoga psychology is suitably incorporated as a subject of study, research and service in the universities and institutes, running professional courses.

1

Introduction to Yoga

Yoga: Its Meaning and Definitions

YOGA is the art of right living. It is based on the tenets of "simple living and high thinking". Yoga is a way of life, an integrated system of education for the body, mind and inner spirit. This art of right living was perfected and practised in India thousands of years ago but, since yoga deals with the universal truth, its teachings are as valid today as they were in ancient times.

Practitioners of yoga believe in a reality beyond the means of our senses (as the powers of these senses have limits, and thus they limit what we can know). What is currently beyond the means of my everyday perception is the concept of the Ultimate Reality, otherwise known as *Ātman/Brahman, sat-cit-ānanda* — which is single and complete — I'd imagine that unity with this ultimate reality would be enlightenment and therefore our highest good — no more of the suffering of relative existence and boundless love, strength and compassion.

Many schools of yoga believe that this state is utterly blissful. Thus yoga is a practical aid, not a religion, and its techniques may be practised by Buddhists, Christians, Hindus, Jains, Muslims, and atheists alike. Yoga is in union with all.

Literally the word *yoga* means "union", the union of the finite with the infinite. This shows that yoga has different meanings at different places. The word yoga is derived from the Sanskrit root *yuj* (to join, to use, to concentrate one's attention on) meaning to bind, join, attach and yoke to direct and concentrate one's attention on, to use and apply.

Etymologically the word *yoga* is derived from the Sanskrit root *yugira* meaning to write, to combine or to integrate. Gradually the word *yoga* has three different meanings with different views.

Yugira yoge: Grammatically the word *yoga* has been derived from the Sanskrit root *Yugira*. *Yugira yoge* means union. The word *yoga* has been used in this sense in Vedic Saṁhitās. The union of *citta* and soul is *yoga*. This is the meaning of *yugira yoge*.

Yuja samadhau: The word *yoga* derived from the Sanskrit root *yuj* — *yuja samadhau* stands for *dhyāna* or *samādhi*. While interpreting the word *yoga* in his commentary (*Bhāṣya*) on various Upaniṣads and the *Gītā*, Śaṅkarācārya considered the word *yoga* as derivative of the root *yuj* meaning *samādhi*.

Maharṣi Vyāsa in his commentary, *Bhāṣya*, on Patañjali's *Yoga-Sūtras* and Yājñavalkya on *Sarva-Darśana Saṁgraha* in the context of Patañjali's Yoga Darśana interpret the word *yoga* as *samādhi*.

Yuja saṁyamane: Grammatically the word *yoga* is used as the meaning "to control the senses".

Philosophically, the word *yoga* means union with the supreme spirit. What unites us with the supreme spirit is yoga.

Technically, the word *yoga* has been used to refer to the system of philosophy propounded by the Sage Patañjali, about, the second century BCE but in general, yoga may be called a method by which one can remove "ignorance", the cause of manifold, and thus attain union with the supreme self.

Yoga is a Sanskrit word which means union. From this root is derived the English word "yoke". The union implied here is an eternal truth. It is not something to be achieved by artifice, such as couples uniting in wedlock or nations uniting on the strength of peace treaties. Yoga signifies the essential unity that is the basis of life. In the highest sense, yoga as spiritual union signifies the soul's union with God.

Thus yoga means:

> Union, balance, and a harmonious state of mind; bridging the different aspects of life; connecting the individual consciousness with the supreme consciousness; the union of the two — the lover and the beloved, the seeker and God, Śiva and Śakti, *iḍā* and *piṅgalā*, the sun and the moon, active and passive.

Maharṣi Patañjali defined yoga as:

योगश्चित्तवृत्तिनिरोधः।।

yogaścitta vṛtti nirodhaḥ । — *Pātañjala Yoga-Sūtras* 1.2

> Yoga is restraining the mind-stuff (*citta*) from taking various forms (*vṛttis*). Yoga is the science by which we stop *citta* from assuming, or becoming transformed into, several faculties.

As the reflection of the moon on the sea is broken or blurred by the waves, so is the reflection of the *Ātman* the true self, broken by the mental waves. Only when the sea is stilled to mirror-like calmness can the reflection of the moon be seen, and only when the "mind stuff", the *citta*, is controlled to absolute calmness, is the self to be recognized. According to *Kaṭha Upaniṣad:*

> यदा पञ्चावतिष्ठन्ते ज्ञानानि मनसा सह।
> बुद्धिच न विश्चेष्टति तामाहुः परमां गतिम्॥
>
> *yadā pañcāvatiṣṭhante jñānāni manasā saha* ।
> *budhiśca na viceṣṭati, tam āhuḥ paramāṁ gatim* ॥
>
> तां योगमिति मन्यन्ते स्थिरामिन्द्रियधारणाम्।
> अप्रमत्तस्तदा भवति योगो हि प्रभवाप्ययौ॥
>
> *tāṁ yogam iti manyante sthirām indriyadhāraṇām* ॥
> *apramattas tadā bhavati yogo hi prabhav āpyayau* ॥
>
> —*Kaṭha Upaniṣad*, III.iii.10-11

> The highest state is that, when the five senses of knowledge, together with the *manas* (the lower mental faculty) cease from their normal activities and the *buddhi* (pure intellect) itself doesn't stir. They consider being the state of yoga, this firm holding back of the senses, when one is completely undistracted. Yoga, verily, is beginning and end (birth and death).

The *Yoga-Vāsiṣṭha* defines yoga as a device that makes one reach the other shore of the stream of sorrow. It is indeed true that a *yogī* is a person who is eternally free of cravings and sorrows. He overcomes ignorance for good for forever.

Sri Aurobindo says the meaning of the word *yoga* is to join our eternal consciousness with our true self — the divine within ourselves; which is one everywhere.

We find yoga defined at different places in the *Gītā*. First, yoga is equanimity in success and failure. Second, yoga is skill and efficiency in action. Third, yoga is the supreme secret of life. Fourth, yoga is the giver of untold happiness.

Another definition given in *Śrīmadbhagavad-Gītā* is yoga is serenity. Yet another definition given in the same text is yoga is the destroyer of pain. Many more definitions of yoga are given in *Gītā*.

योगस्थः कुरु कर्माणि सङ्गं त्यक्त्वा धनञ्जय।
सिद्ध्यसिद्ध्योः समो भूत्वा समत्वं योग उच्यते।।

yogasthaḥ kuru karmāṇi saṅgaṁ tyaktvā dhanañjaya ।
siddhy-aśiddhyoḥ samo bhūtvā samatvaṁ yoga ucyate ।।
— 2.48

O, Arjuna perform your duties well, established in the yogic way of life, without any attachment. Treat success and failure alike, such equanimity is called yoga.

बुद्धियुक्तो जहातीह उभे सुकृतदुष्कृते।
तस्माद्योगाय युज्यस्व योगः कर्मसु कौशलम्।।

buddhi-yukto jahātīha ubhe sukṛta-duṣkṛte ।
tasmād yogāya-yujyasva yogaḥ karmasu kauśalam ।।
— 2.50

Endued with this evenness of mind, one frees oneself in this life, alike from vice and virtue; devote yourself therefore, to this yoga. Yoga is the very dexterity of work. It is skill and effectiveness in action.

तं विद्याद् दुःखसंयोगवियोगं योगसञ्ज्ञितम्।।

taṁ vidyād duḥkha-saṁyoga-viyogaṁ yoga-sañjñitam ।।
— 6.23

That state which is free from the contact of sorrow, is called yoga.

Yoga through repeated experiments throughout its history of more than 5,000 years came to the conclusion that consciousness is the most fundamental essence of creation at macrocosmic as well as microcosmic levels. This viewpoint has been formed not through pronouncements of a single individual but is the result of profound investigation by a number of seers and sages of the Vedas, independently through *tapas* since aeons. What they did through their *tapas* was not only introspection but by diving deep within themselves and saw however everything tangible was explicable in terms of consciousness. This consciousness pervaded not only in their psychic being but also in their vitality, physicality, also the entire cosmos and each manifestation pervaded by it.

Introspection is only an outer façade of their approach, just a beginning. Mind for them is a tool of understanding and whatever dawned before the introspecting mind could not be sheer physical. The seer turned his consciousness within, with the result that he was able to reach the root of consciousness lying in his self-transcendence.

On reaching that state, he found out consciousness as all in all in transcendence as well as in immanence. In transcendence it remained in its pure form and in immanence it assumed all possible forms the world consists of. Thus, while the *puruṣa* of Patañjali and that of introspecting psychologists remained confined to his individual being as totally exclusive of the universal, the Vedic seer rose in transcendence beyond the universal. He realized in him the individual and the universal as two phases of the transcendent with which he came to identify himself by virtue of his sharing in the transcendent consciousness.

This is also evident from multitude seers who produced huge archetypal ideas, myths, legends and principles that are common with less possibility of mutual give and take in most of the cases. This uniformity in their experience has no explanation except for the commonness of the psychic ground happening to have been struck by them so large in number and with so many spans of time amongst them in terms of both space and time. On analysis of Jung's *Theory of Archetypes*, one finds that it is quite possible for people belonging to different nationalities and ages to produce similar archetypal images but in no case quite identical. The similarity in such cases is due to inherence of the collective unconscious in common within the whole mankind, the dissimilarity is due to the possibility of variations in the composition of that unconscious itself, as it is formed out of varying experiences of mankind throughout the globe right from its animal ancestry.

This was the one of the extraordinary event in the history of mankind since it involved so much absorption on the part of the aspirant of knowledge so as to become completely coincident to the very object of knowledge. In fact, we cannot deny that the more deeply we get ourselves involved in intricacies of the composition of an object, the better we understand it. It is only through such an involvement with the area of research that scientists have come to understand so much of life and the world at the physical level.

Now at the end of their investigation from this standpoint, they are beginning to realize the extent to which consciousness contributes in determining the shape of things not only on the commonsense but also on the scientific. This is evident from the fact that when a scientist starts his investigation into the shape of the ultimate constituent of matter with the presupposition that it may be something like a particle, it appears to him like that and when he starts the same with the probability of it being wave-like, it appears exactly as such in before him. This experimentation on the scientific level bears out not only the supremacy of consciousness *vis-à-vis* matter but also its creativity in shaping its notion of the physical.

When we ponder over the creative capability of consciousness as working within us, we find it hard to resist the conclusion that this capability must have its source in corresponding creativity of consciousness in its pure form. If this creativity of consciousness can handle and mould matter anyway it chooses, as we learn from the experiments of scientists, we are left with no option but to affirm that consciousness must have come to have evolved these capabilities on the human level by virtue of being the real source of matter. This is what the Vedic seers contend through their admission of the origin of the physical in pure consciousness as *Ātman* and *Brahman* representing it in its concentricity and extensity, respectively. Thus organic and inorganic are only manifestation of consciousness which is both transcendent and immanent.

The importance of yoga is in its amenability to rendering the entire content of the human psychology in terms of consciousness. No doubt scriptures produced world over have contributed to the moderation of human psychology so as to check his inherent violent nature throughout the ages. If there had not been check of this nature in the form of scriptural prescriptions, man would have left the world in havoc. Today man is faced with the practical utilities of science which has negated the utility, appeal and value of these scriptures. In this process of evaluation, modern psychology has played an important role. Physical science would have abstained itself from entering the domain of spirituality had not psychology attacked the inherent consciousness and sided with physical sciences exclusively to explain the phenomenon of consciousness as a by-product of the physical form, like the Cārvākas. Man, finding himself defenceless, took resort to faith and declared it as inviolable but this inviolability has also been shaken and sooner or later it, too, has given way to thorough analysis for its tenability. In this exercise, faith does not seem to have any bright future on account of its sheer non-rationality.

Herein lies the advantage of Vedic yoga since its entire structure is based on consciousness as the basic stuff of creation in all its forms and varieties. Vedic seers, by means of deep meditation, were able to see through everything, howsoever gross and mightily tangible it was as a formation of consciousness.

Traditions of Yoga

Yoga has two origins, one from Vedas and the other from Tantras. Tantras developed a philosophy and a set of practices, which in the tāntric tradition, are known as *yogācāra*, conduct for people who practise Tantra through yoga. The Vedic tradition describes yoga in the form of the Upaniṣads. Each Upaniṣad represents a line of learning, a tradition, a *paramparā*. Yoga became the process encompassing the body and the mind leading to the experience of spirit. This is how the Vedic and tāntric traditions viewed yoga in ancient India.

In the present scenario there are only two established schools of yoga: the southern school and the northern school. Yoga as taught and practised by *ṛṣi*s, *muni*s and *tapasvī*s in the Gangetic belt, the Narmadā belt and the Himalayan belt belongs to the northern school. The southern school represents the yoga practised and envisioned by the southern group of *sādhu*s and saints, renunciates and recluses, mystics, and *siddha*s.

Today the main propagators of the southern school of yoga are T. Krishnamacharya, the teacher of Deshikachar and B.K.S. Iyengar. The southern school believes in attaining total physical perfection. *Haṭha-yogī*s also believe in this principle.

The northern school is more meditative, having as its basis the *Yoga-Sūtras* of Patañjali. In the *Yoga-Sūtras*, the emphasis is on mind management, thought management, and *haṭha-yoga* finds very little mention. Patañjali's yoga is recognized as the northern school of yoga.

In the northern school of yoga there are different *paramparās* (traditions or cultures). There is even a tradition of *haṭha-yogīs*. There is a tradition of *kriyā-yogīs*, a tradition of *kuṇḍalinī yogīs*; there are not only *raja-yogīs* but also *jñāna-yogīs* and *bhakti-yogīs*. All these *yogīs* have one thing in common: Yoga, a practice and discipline through which it becomes possible to strengthen one's nature, to realize the human spirit, and to awaken the inherent potential to become a balanced, perfect human being. Human being can attain perfection in one thing, in all the expressions of life. To attain this end many branches developed in the northern school of yoga.

Fifty years ago, the philosophical side of yoga was known to a few people, but nobody knew the practical side. It was believed that yoga was meant for enunciates, *sādhus* and *saṁnyāsīs* who had renounced everything and had left the pursuits of the world for a life of contemplation, meditation, reflection, introversion and isolation; that it was a way to salvation which an ordinary person in society could not adopt without renouncing some major attachments, desires, ambitions and efforts in life. Yoga was known as a philosophy only, as a form of discipline which could be utilized to strengthen one's spirit, mind, body and life. The theoretical knowledge was brought to the public by Swami Vivekananda, Sri Aurobindo, Ramaṇa Maharṣi, Baba Ram Das, Swami Sivananda, Shriram Sharma Acharya and others in the bygone century.

There are over a hundred different schools of yoga. Some of the most well known are the following:

- *Jñāna-yoga*: The path of wisdom; considered the most difficult path.
- *Bhakti-yoga*: The practice of extreme devotion in one-pointed concentration upon one's concept of God.
- *Karma-yoga*: All movement, all work of any kind is done with the mind centred on a personal concept of God.
- *Rāja-yoga*: Called the "royal path", because it incorporates exercises and breathing practice with meditation and study, producing a well-formed individual.
- *Haṭha-yoga*: The physical movements and postures, plus breathing techniques. This is what most people associate with yoga practice.

- *Tantra-yoga*: A way of showing the unseen consciousness in form through specific words, diagrams and movements. One of the diagrams that is used to show the joining of the physical and spiritual bodies is two triangles superimposed upon one another. The downward-pointing triangle represents the physical body, or the female aspect having to do with work, action and movement; the upward-pointing triangle represents the spiritual body of support, energy and vastness.
- *Kashmir Śaivism*: This yoga system states that everything in the universe has both male and female qualities. In Kashmir Śaivism, these male and female principles form an equal partnership, so interdependent that they cannot be separated. The attraction between them produces the ultimate union of opposites, creating the immense complexity of the universe that we enjoy and celebrate. Unlike other philosophies, Kashmir Śaivism is based in emotion rather than intellect. In fact, Śaivism says that intellectual understanding by itself will never lead us to the realization of the summit of yoga. The system's great exponents teach that the egotistical intellect blocks our ability to fully experience our individual power.

Jñāna-Yoga

The word *jñāna* (*gyāna*) literarily means knowledge and wisdom, thus it is known as yoga of knowledge or wisdom. What is that knowledge? It is the understanding or experience of the self. To know the self through knowledge or wisdom is *jñāna-yoga*.

This path of yoga deals directly with the highest of all human desires — the desire to know the Truth — and it gives an explanation of what Truth means and shows the practical way of realizing it. Truth is not the subject to change, death, decay and destruction. It never changes at any time; it was never born and will never die. It is self-existent and does not depend on anything. *Jñāna-yoga* is the science that provides a systematized and organized method of study in order to fulfil this desire to know the Truth.

The Truth or Reality is only *ātman* the knowledge of self, which is Ultimate. To know that and to know the importance of that *ātman* Lord Kr̥ṣṇa says in the *Gītā* 2.20:

न जायते म्रियते वा कदाचिन्नायं भूत्वा भविता वा न भूयः।
अजो नित्यः शाश्वतोऽयं पुराणो न हन्यते हन्यमाने शरीरे।।

na jāyate mriyate vā kadācin nāyaṁ bhūtvā bhavitā vā na bhūyaḥ ।
ajo nityaḥ śāśvato 'yaṁ purāṇo na hanyate hanyamāne śarīre ।।

It is never born, nor does it die. It is unborn, eternal, changeless, ever-Itself. It is not killed when the body dies.

When the aspirant becomes aware of this Ultimate Truth he starts realizing the self and starts following the path of *jñāna-yoga* and ultimately gets liberated from all worldly bondage of *karma*. In this sense Lord Kṛṣṇa again says in the *Gītā* 2.51:

कर्मजं बुद्धियुक्ता हि फलं त्यक्त्वा मनीषिणः।
जन्मबन्धविनिर्मुक्ताः पदं गच्छन्त्यनामयम्।।

karmajaṁ buddhi-yuktā hi phalaṁ tyaktvā manīṣiṇaḥ ।
janma-bandha-vinirmuktāḥ padaṁ gacchanty anāmayam ।।

The aspirant of *jñāna-yoga* after knowing the Ultimate Truth possessed of this evenness of mind and abandoning the fruits of their actions, freed for ever from the fetters of birth and go to that state which is beyond all evil that is *mokṣa*.

Hence all the *sādhanā* in which the intellect or knowledge is used as an object is *jñāna-yoga*; as the holy *Gītā* describes *jñāna-yoga* with the name of Sāṁkhya Yoga, but basically the *sādhanā* of Vedānta is known as *jñāna-yoga*. In Vedānta, the knowledge is the main path of yoga; through which the aspirant becomes one with *Brahman*.

According to the principle of *jñāna-yoga*, the *ātman* is *ānanda-svarūpa* (as blissful), *jñāna-svarūpa* (knowledge form), *sat* (truth), *nitya* (forever), *śuddha* (pure) and *buddha* (intellect). In the real sense the *ātman* is *Brahman* itself. Only *Brahman* is the reality, there is no existence except it.

Brahman is self-focused, endless, uninterrupted, unborn, conscious and blissful. As the fire is one and reflects in different forms in several places, the same is the case with *Brahman*, it is one but appears in the form of soul of every creatures and it is beyond all of them.

According to *jñāna-yoga*, knowledge of unity of *jīva* (the individual being) and *Brahman* (the Supreme Being) brings the aspirant to the state of *mokṣa* (liberation). In other words, the knowledge of *Brahman* and liberation from all the worries is *mokṣa* itself.

According to this tradition, knowledge is possible only when the oneness of *jīva* and *Brahman* has been achieved. It has been said that the aspirant of higher level knowledge gets to know that reality only through listening to the *śrutivākya* (the sayings of *Brahman*). He becomes able to remove the difference between *jīva* and *Brahman*. According to Vedānta, this reality is possible only through knowledge.

The practice of *jñāna-yoga* is divided into two paths: *antaraṅga* practice and *bahiraṅga* practice. *Bahiraṅga* (external) practice includes *viveka, vairāgya, ṣaṭsampatti* and *mumukṣutva*; whereas the *antaraṅga* (internal) practice includes *śravaṇa, manana* and *nididhyāsana*.

VIVEKA *(*DISCRIMINATION*)*

The *sādhaka* (practitioner) has to develop and cultivate the ability to recognize what is impermanent, temporary and fleeting in life as the *sādhaka* experiences the fact — what is of everlasting value and pointing to the eternal. The practitioner becomes able to discriminate the superficial and the essential; as well as the illusory reality on the surface and the absolute reality in the inner, the deep dimension of existence. In this way the person tries to scrutinize, analyse and evaluate constantly the experiences, inclinations, decisions and actions.

VAIRĀGYA *(*DISPASSION*)*

In the practice of *vairāgya* the practitioner has to guard his mind against becoming possessed, infatuated and even slightly getting disturbed by passions, springing from the sensual desires. Later on he has to stop all the disturbances like attachment to things that bring sensual satisfaction. The opposite of *vairāgya* is *rāga* (passion), meaning originally colouring, which indicates that passions are, in fact, obstructions to the mind which do not allow clear vision. To achieve the clarity of mind (which is essential for final knowledge and wisdom) attachments and passions must be avoided and abolished.

ṢAṬSAMPATTI *(*SIX ATTAINMENTS*)*

This discipline includes a sixfold instruction of self-education for success on the path of yoga:

- *Śama:* The cultivation of tranquillity of the mind.
- *Dama:* Self-control in action.
- *Uparati:* Means to eradicate the eagerness to possess.

- *Titikṣā:* To have patience.
- *Śraddhā:* Confidence (in the meaning of faith).
- *Samādhāna:* Intentness of the mind.

MUMUKṢUTVA (LONGING FOR LIBERATION)

This fourth *sādhanā* of Vedānta is very important. It should be understood as the intense desire to get the higher level of consciousness, i.e. *samādhi*. The *sādhaka* (aspirant) should develop a positive desire for liberation. Its development is supported by the previous endeavours as the advanced ability to discriminate the unsatisfactory superficial reality and the safety-promising, spiritual dimension of higher experience. This practice leads towards ultimate reality (*Brahman*).

In *jñāna-yoga,* in the practice of *antaraṅga,* the first one is *śravaṇa* which means hearing. The practitioner has to go first through an extensive and intensive study, for which he should go to his *guru* (the spiritual teacher or master) and should listen to the lessons on (about) *Brahman*. In ancient time it was done in *āśrama*s (the traditional school of Vedānta or Yoga), nowadays it includes thorough studies of the traditional doctrines of the Vedāntic texts or Upaniṣads. This gives to the mind of the aspirant the right direction, outlook and material for the second stage, which is *manana*.

Manana starts with intellectual analysis of the material gained by studying the texts. In the analysis of the material gained by knowledge of the world of sensual and emotional experience and on the level of speculative thinking, ultimate knowledge cannot be found. Absolute truth lies beyond them. When the practitioner firmly arrives at this conclusion, he is able to enter the path of meditation which brings him to the final stage of training, which is *nididhyāsana*.

Nididhyāsana can be translated as constant meditation. This stage of training makes it clear to the *sādhaka* that the process of opening a new channel to reality over and above the senses and the intellect is not a matter of mental exercises during meditational session only, but that it is also equally necessary to introduce a kind of meditational attitude towards one's life so that eventually the mind is in a state of meditation even when dealing with the business of everyday life. As this capacity is developed and deepened, the *yogī*'s intuition and spiritual vision grow until he reaches the final vision of truth, which brings the aspirant at the final achievement of liberation (*mokṣa*).

Bhakti-Yoga

Bhakti-yoga is the easiest and natural way for God-realization. It is deeply concerned with our life. This path of devotion is for everyone. Anybody can practise it. Even the vilest man can start with it and gradually improvement will take place. The *Nārada Bhakti-Sūtra* defines *bhakti* in the second verse as follows:

> सा त्वस्मिन् परम प्रेमरूपा।।२।।
>
> *sā tvasmin parama-premarūpā*।
>
> *Bhakti* is the supreme love for Him (God).

The object of real devotion is only God and nothing else. This love should be pure and powerful; there should not be any kind of selfish idea associated with it. Therefore one should not expect anything like wealth, prosperity or any worldly object from God — not even the happiness.

The *Bhagavad-Gītā* discusses the *bhakti-yoga* as an easier path of yoga. It says that when a devotee's love for God reaches its climax, his love for God is known as the yoga of devotion. The devotee wants nothing in return; and when he loves God in such a way his love takes the form of yoga which is called the yoga of devotion (*bhakti-yoga*).

In the verse 22 of the eighth chapter Lord Kr̥ṣṇa reflects the yoga of devotion when he says:

> पुरुषः स परः पार्थ भक्त्या लभ्यस्त्वनन्यया।
> यस्यान्तःस्थानि भूतानि येन सर्वमिदं ततम्।।
>
> *puruṣaḥ sa paraḥ pārtha bhaktyā labhyas tv ananyayā*।
> *yasyāntaḥ sthāni bhūtāni yena sarvam idaṁ tatam*।।
>
> O Arjuna! that eternal unmanifest supreme *Puruṣa*, in whom all beings reside and by whom all this is pervaded, is attainable only through exclusive devotion.

Verse 26 of the ninth chapter highlights how a devotee with his pure love wins the heart of the Lord.

> पत्रं पुष्पं फलं तोयं यो मे भक्त्या प्रयच्छति।
> तदहं भक्त्युपहृतमश्नामि प्रयतात्मनः।।

patraṁ puṣpaṁ phalaṁ toyaṁ yo me bhaktyā prayacchati ।
tad ahaṁ bhakty-upahṛtam aśnāmi prayatātmanaḥ ।।

Whosoever offers to me with love a leaf, a flower, a fruit or even water, I appear in person before that disinterested devotee of sinless mind and delightfully partake of that article offered by him with love.

When we go through verse 17 of the twelfth chapter we find what Lord Kṛṣṇa himself says about devotion:

यो न हृष्यति न द्वेष्टि न शोचति न काङ्क्षति।
शुभाशुभपरित्यागी भक्ति मान्यः स मे प्रियः।।

yo na hṛṣyati na dveṣṭi na śocati na kāṅkṣati ।
śubhāśubha-parityāgī bhaktimān yaḥ sa me priyaḥ ।।

He who neither rejoices nor hates, nor grieves, nor desires and who renounces both good and evil actions and is full of devotion, is dear to me.

The final aim of *bhakti* is the communion of individual consciousness with supreme or universal consciousness. But before we come to this stage, there are different stages of *bhakti* which act at the deeper level of mind to transform the mental structure, the mental conditioning. Goswāmī Tulsī Dās explains the nine steps of *bhakti* in Araṇya Kāṇḍa of *Śrīrāmacaritamānasa* in a very specific form as:

नवधा भगति कहउँ तोहि पाहीं।
सावधान सुनु धरु मन माहीं।।

प्रथम भगति संतन्ह कर संगा।
दूसरि रति मम कथा प्रसंगा।।४।।

navadhā bhagati kahauṁ tohi pāhīṅ ।
sāvadhāna sunu dharu mana māhīṅ ।।

prathama bhagati saṅtanha kara saṅgā ।
dūsari rati mama kathā prasaṅgā ।।३४.४।।

Satsaṅga (associate with truth or the company of truthful person) is considered to be the first form of *bhakti*. Being near a saint and having their *satsaṅga*, instruction and guidance can be one form of *bhakti*. Another form of the same *bhakti* can be taken as analysing the truth and spiritual life; but whatever it is the main emphasis is on one's being in the company of truth.

Now, if we also define this psychologically, the truth here represents a quality which is gained after attaining discernment. If there is no discernment, there can be no discovery of truth. So, in order to experience truth one needs to have the power, the force of discrimination.

One can attain this form of *bhakti* through *sādhanā*, whether that *sādhanā* is being in the company of a person who is enlightened, absorbing his or her vibrations and allowing the inner mind to experience it, or whether that *sādhanā* is self-analysis, trying to develop the faculty of discernment through a meditative process or way of life. According to their level of life and consciousness, everyone has to give his own definition to *satsaṅga* (being in the company of truth).

The second form of *bhakti* is *kathā prasaṅga*, in colloquial language listening to *līlā*s (story of divine beings). These *līlā*s about enlightened beings can help inspire us to accept a different lifestyle, mentality and mode of behaviour. However, it also has a psychological meaning. It is the nature of the mind to involve itself in constant gossip and criticism. The moment one stops the mind gossiping and criticizing, it becomes calm, peaceful and fixed, it begins to experience a different kind of personal nature, which has no attraction towards the world of senses and objects. That is the experience of *śūnyatā* (the void) awareness of a different quality manifesting.

गुर पद पंकज सेवा तीसरि भगति अमान।
चौथि भगति मम गुन गन करइ कपट तजि गान।।

gura pada paṅkaja sevā tīsari bhagati amāna ।
cauthi bhagati mama guna gana karai kapaṭa taji gāna ।।

The third form of *bhakti* is *amāna* (becoming egoless). In order to be egoless it is necessary to have *vairāgya* and live in world, but not be of the world. In fact, the entire philosophy of the *Bhagavad-Gītā* is based on this very principle — one should do his own work, should perform own *dharma*, carry out all obligations, but should not think that he is the indispensable one. One should not have any attachment. One may be attached to something, whether to a person, or to the results of an action. Wherever there is even the slightest inkling of attachment, there is a connection with ego. Possessiveness, desire and ambition are all involved in attachment. To be egoless is to give a different vision of life where we are able to experience the state of non-being.

The fourth form of *bhakti* is *japa*. *Japa* literally means continuous repetition of a mantra or God's name. It is constant remembrance that, the individual self, who lives in this body, and the cosmic self, which pervades the entire universe, are one. In *japa*, the essence has to be realized. A raindrop and water in the river or ocean are two different things, but they are composed of the same essence or matter. *Japa* is the process of identifying with the divine or cosmic nature. It is a method by which a person who has attained *viveka* and *vairāgya* can disassociate the individual self from the manifest dimension and link with the cosmic dimension:

मंत्र जाप मम दृढ़ बिस्वासा।
पंचम भजन सो बेद प्रकासा।।

mantra jāpa mama dr̥ḍha bisvāsā |
pañcama bhajana so beda prakāsā ||

The fifth form of *bhakti* is *bhajana* — incorporating the transcendental, humanitarian and unconditioned qualities into everyday life. The qualities which we express in our lives are conditioned qualities which give some restrictions and motivations in them. The real language of living is in expressing these qualities — cosmic, divine and human, which are not conditioned, but are free from every kind of mental or manifest impression. When one is free from the attractions and repulsions of life, love is experienced. So, removing the conditions which we create in the expression of a quality is the fifth form of *bhakti*.

छठ दम सील बिरति बहु करमा।
निरत निरंतर सज्जन धरमा।।

chaṭha dama sīla birati bahu karamā |
nirata niraṅtara sajjana dharamā ||

सातवँ सम मोहि मय जग देखा।
मोतें संत अधिक करि लेखा।।

sātavam̐ sama mohi maya jaga dekhā |
moteṅ saṅta adhika kari lekhā ||

The sixth form of *bhakti* is the total involvement in *sajjana dharma*, i.e. manifesting in one's life the qualities which are divine and human while following one's *dharma*. Generally, when we live a quality in our life, we tend to isolate ourselves from the *dharma* belonging to the realm of the body, the realm of the mind and emotions, and also from the *dharma* governing the spiritual dimension. It sounds easy, but we find it very difficult to combine the principles of spirituality and awareness with the normal, external environment and lifestyle. Instead of feeling the rejection and repulsion inside, instead of identifying with a personal desire, live life from moment to moment by accepting situations as they come up, and follow *dharma* accordingly.

The seventh form of *bhakti* is *seeing the spark of life and divinity in each and everyone.* There should be no distinction between one and another. There should be no concept of high and low, but there is identification. Seeing the divinity within self as well as other beings, whether animate or inanimate, is the highest form of compassion where the individual self is totally eradicated (*kapūta*).

आठवँ जथालाभ संतोषा।
सपनेहुँ नहिं देखइ परदोषा।।२।।

āṭhavaṁ jathālābha santoṣā।।
sapanehuṁ nahiṅ dekhai paradoṣā।।35.2।।

नवम सरल सब सन छलहीना।
मम भरोस हियँ हरष न दीना।।

navama sarala saba sana chalahīnā।
mama bharosa hiyaṁ haraṣa na dīnā।।

The eighth form of *bhakti* is *contentment*, not seeing fault in other beings. One who does not struggle, or fight, who does not see any kind of fault in other people, but who lives and flows with life, is content. If there is acceptance of the natural law then there will be no criticism. Everyone is following His law, to develop the acceptance is one of the important forms of *bhakti*.

The ninth form of *bhakti* is *ātma-nivedana* (*total surrender, total fusion or total merger*). *Ātma* means self and *nivedana* means to offer. It happens when even the last vestige of individual identity is dissolved in cosmic awareness. At that level the body becomes God. The state of *ātma-nivedana* is not very easy to attain. If faith becomes powerful and takes that real experience where the existence ceased to this world this will be the state of *ātma-nivedana*.

नव महुँ एकउ जिन्ह कें होई।
नारि पुरुष सचराचर कोई।।३।।

nava mahuṁ ekau jinha keṅ hoī ।
nāri puruṣa sacarācara koī ।।35.3।।

The nine forms of *bhakti* is not only for the fulfilment of only the requirement but these can lead to discrimination and ultimately the final state, i.e. *samādhi* the goal of yoga.

Bhakti is of two types — *parā* and *aparā*. As we go on, in the preparatory stage, we unavoidably stand in need of many concrete helps to enable us to get on, indeed, the mythological and symbological parts of all religions.

When *bhakti* has reached its peak, it is called the *parā*, no more is there any fear of hideous manifestations of fanaticism. In the words of Swami Vivekananda: "The one great advantage of *bhakti* is that it is the easiest and the most natural way to reach the great divine."

Karma-Yoga

Karma comes from the Sanskrit root *kr̥* which means to do. *Karma* literary means action, which everyone performs in this world, whether consciously or unconsciously. The human beings have a natural tendency to perform something. The *Gītā* (3.5) says:

न हि कश्चित्क्षणमपि जातु तिष्ठत्यकर्मकृत्।
कार्यते ह्यवशः कर्म सर्वः प्रकृतिजैर्गुणैः।।

na hi kaścit kṣaṇam api jātu tiṣṭhaty akarma-kr̥t ।
kāryate hy avaśaḥ karma sarvaḥ prakr̥tijair guṇaiḥ ।।

No person can stop his activity at any time even for a moment, because the entire humanity has been forced by the Nature to perform action.

Karma is the expression of the rule of perfect justice within us. It is the law of the cosmos reflected in the microcosm. There is nothing arbitrary or punitive about it. It is a universal law and an inevitable fact. All the phenomena of Nature are governed by one important law, the universal law of causation, which is also known by the name "the law of *karma*". The law of causation is a universal law that keeps up the inner harmony and the logical order of the universe. Man's deeds are subject to this law.

No success can be attained without understanding the law of *karma*. The three aspects of the law of *karma* should clearly be grasped. The first is the *sañcita karma*, the sum total and stored actions, good or bad in the innumerable past lives that we have left behind. The whole of it is recorded and preserved. The second is *prārabdha karma*, the inevitable *karma*. It is that portion of our *karma* which is assigned to us to be worked out in a single life in relation to men and things we met and experienced in previous lives. The third form is that of *kriyamāna karma*. It is that *karma* which is in the course of making. It is that which preserves our free-will with certain limitations and ensures our future success.

One cannot do anything with past *karma*s unless he is fully enlightened. With knowledge of the divine, the enlightened ones create the fire of knowledge that burns all the bondages created by past *karma*s. That is possible but unless one has that ability, he has to reap the consequences of his past *karma*s.

From birth to death the human beings perfom *karma* because of the bondage of the law of *karma*. These *karma*s are the causative factor behind the bondage of a person. Now the question arise — if *karma* binds us and without doing *karma* one cannot stop himself, then how can one be liberated or is there no chance? The answer is — as the *karma* is the causative factor of bondage, it can liberate the aspirant because it is the causative factor of liberation also. The second question arises what type of *karma* bounds us and what kind of *karma* liberates us? Lord Kṛṣṇa replies Arjuna in the *Gītā* 16.24 as:

तस्माच्छास्त्रं प्रमाणं ते कार्याकार्यव्यवस्थितौ।
ज्ञात्वा शास्त्रविधानोक्तं कर्म कर्तुमिहार्हसि।।

tasmāc chāstraṁ pramāṇaṁ te kāryākārya-vyavasthitau।
jñātvā śāstra-vidhānoktaṁ karma kartum ihārhasi।।

Which *karma* should be performed and which one should not, to distinguish it there is no reference in any text, you should act after knowing the view of authorized text.

One should perform *karma* according to the need of the situation; the main thing is that one should be aware of his *kartavya* (duty). One should perform his duty without any expectation. In this context the *Gītā* 3.9 says:

> यज्ञार्थात्कर्मणोऽन्यत्र लोकोऽयं कर्मबन्धनः।
> तदर्थं कर्म कौन्तेय मुक्तसङ्गः समाचर॥
>
> *yajñārthāt karmaṇo 'nyatra loko 'yaṁ karma-bandhanaḥ* ।
> *tad arthaṁ karma kaunteya mukta-saṅgaḥ samācara* ॥
>
> The world is bound by actions other than those performed for the sake of *yajña*, therefore O son of Kuntī! you perform action for *yajña* only. Here the *yajña* means the action done for the sake of others or of selfless motive. The *karma* performed for others without any expectation, does not bind the aspirant. This selfless action is called *karma-yoga*.

In the first stage of the *sādhanā* of *karma-yoga* the aspirant performs his action with the feeling of duty. Through the attachment to *karma* or the result of *karma* the person gets bound with *karma*. Hence any obstacle in the path of *karma* hurts the performer because the performer is attached to the fruits of *karma*. When the aspirant gives up the attachment to the result, he becomes a *karma-yogī*.

> युक्तः कर्मफलं त्यक्त्वा शान्तिमाप्नोति नैष्ठिकीम्।
> अयुक्तः कामकारेण फले सक्तो निबध्यते॥
>
> *yuktaḥ karma-phalaṁ tyaktvā śāntim āpnoti naiṣṭhikīm* ।
> *ayuktaḥ kāma-kāreṇa phale sakto nibadhyate* ॥
>
> — *Gītā* 5.12
>
> The aspirant of *karma-yoga* performs the *karma* for the realization without expectation whereas the *sakāma puruṣa* (general performer) binds them with the desire of result. Hence the *karma-yogī* does not attach himself to the success or failure. Without expectation the mind becomes desireless and then he becomes free from attachments with the world. It leads him to liberation.

The question arises now — without expectation can the performer become inspirationless? The answer is "no". Hence the real inspiration will be with the desireless performer. To perform the duty without any obstruction the aspirant needs some codes of conduct, which seem to be very difficult but with the help of a *guru* it becomes easy for the *karma-yogī*. In the practice of *karma-yoga* the aspirant needs a *guru*, in whom he has full faith. It is also important here that the aspirant should have strength of resolution and full dedication to his *guru*. The faith and resolution make the path of *yoga* smooth.

Mantra-Cūḍāmanyopniṣad says that the disciple should have the following features in him: pure mind, good character, faith in *guru*, dedication to the path, and he should be an optimist. With all these virtues the aspirant of *karma-yoga* becomes closer to God. He becomes able to perform the *karma* and offer it to God, which is the theme of *karma-yoga*. Lord Kṛṣṇa says the same thing in the *Gītā* 9.27 as:

> यत्करोषि यदश्नासि यज्जुहोषि ददासि यत्।
> यत्तपस्यसि कौन्तेय तत्कुरुष्व मदर्पणम्।।
>
> *yat karoṣi yad aśnāsi yaj juhoṣi dadāsi yat* ।
> *yat tapasyasi kaunteya tat kuruṣva mad-arpaṇaṁ* ।।
>
> O son of Kuntī! (O Arjuna!) whatever action you perform like *yajña, tapa* or *dāna,* offer it to me and then you will be free from the bondage of their results.

Karma-yoga in real sense makes one get the freedom which is the goal of human beings. Every unselfish action takes us towards the goal. Most of the human beings in this world follow the path of *karma-yoga* consciously or unconsciously. Those who know that the path of *karma* is like worship of the Lord, perform their actions skilfully, selflessly and lovingly.

It is an effective and valid path of *yoga* to experience the total self. One who is in control of the self and who is devoid of desire is a true renunciate. A true renunciate easily attains enlightenment through this path.

Rāja-Yoga

The word *rāja-yoga* is found in many of the Upaniṣads. It may be regarded as the master of all the yogic practices. All the yogic practices lead to *samādhi*, but the speciality of this path is that it starts from *samādhi*. Sine *samādhi* comes in every path, it has been considered to be the complimentary practice of yoga or the greatest path of yoga.

The importance of *rāja-yoga* has been accepted widely. The great *haṭha-yogī* Svātmārāma says in *Haṭha-Yoga-Pradīpikā* as:

> केवलं राजयोगाय हठविद्योपदिश्यते।।
>
> *kevalaṁ rājayogāya haṭhavidyopadiṣyate* ।
>
> The lession of *haṭha-yoga* is only for the attainment of *rāja-yoga*.

There are various definitions of *rāja-yoga*. *Yoga Svarodaya* defines it as:

> यथाकाशे भ्रमण वायुराकाशे व्रजते स्वयम्।
> तथाकाशे मनोलैन राजयोग क्रियामतम्।।
>
> *yathākāśe bhramaṇa vāyurākāśe vrajate svayam*
> *tathākāśe manolaina rāja-yoga kriyāmatam*
>
> Just as the air passing through sky never appears, likewise to establish the mind in *śūnya* (no object) is *rāja-yoga*.

Yogaśikhopaniṣad defines *rāja-yoga* as:

> रजो वसति जन्तुनां देवी तत्त्वं समावृतं।
> रजसो रेतसो योगाद्राजयोग इति स्मृतः।।137।।
>
> *rajo vasati jantūnāṁ devī-tattvaṁ samāvr̥taṁ* ।
> *rajaso retaso yogād-rāja-yoga iti smr̥taḥ* ।।137।।
>
> The *rāja* form of *kuṇḍalinī* when merges with the *retas* form of Śiva or the union of *ātma-tattva* (individual self) with *brahma-tattva* (the supreme self) is *rāja-yoga*.

A careful observation of the above-mentioned definitions shows that the establishment of the self in *Brahman* is *raja-yoga*. In this state the practitioner becomes one with *Brahman*; the dualism destroys and this is the aim of any path of yoga. For the practitioner the world disappears; and he gets rid of all miseries of the world and is established in the self.

The practitioner of *rāja-yoga* has been divided into three types — *uttama* (the advance practitioner); *madhyama* (the medium); and *adhama* (the beginners). This categorization also differentiates the practice of the individual.

The *uttama* type of practitioner needs a special type of package for the attainment that is *abhyāsa* and *vairāgya*. Maharṣi Patañjali has also given the same instruction to them in his *Yoga-Sūtras* 1.12:

अभ्यासवैराग्याभ्यां तन्निरोधः।।

abhyāsa vairāgyābhyāṁ tannirodhaḥ।

There are two methods for stopping the flow of the *cittavṛttis*. First is *abhyāsa* (continuous practice) and the second one is *vairāgya* (detachment) from all the *rāga* and *dveṣa* (liking and disliking).

The next thing is *Īśvarapraṇidhāna*. It has been said that the advance practitioner can attain *samādhi* through *Īśvarapraṇidhāna* only. In this context Maharṣi Patañjali says in his *Yoga-Sūtras* 2.45:

समाधिसिद्धिरीश्वरप्रणिधानात्।।४५।।

samādhi siddhirīśvara prāṇidhānāt

One can attain success in *samādhi* by complete resignation/ surrender to God. Here the word *samādhi* is not exactly that; it is a state of trance. In this state the aspirant loses the body awareness and becomes able to start with deeper awareness.

Hence the aspirant is here of high quality, he need not to practise the other steps; he can start from *samādhi* onwards. Such *yogīs* already have completed their *sādhanā* in their past lives.

The second type of practitioner — *madhyama* — has been instructed to practise *kriyā-yoga*. This type of aspirant needs a few more hard practices as he also has past-life practice but of lower form. Thus for such practitioners Patañjali describes *kriyā-yoga* in his *Yoga-Sūtras* 2.1:

तपःस्वाध्यायेश्वरप्रणिधानानि क्रियायोगः।।१।।

tapaḥ svādhyāyeśvarapraṇidhānāni kriyāyogaḥ

Tapa (penance), *svādhyāya* (self-study) and *Īśvarpraṇidhāna* (faith in God) constitute *kriyā-yoga*. *Tapa* literarily means to burn; here *tapaḥ* means the *sādhanā* of optimum level where all the past *karma* burns and the aspirant illuminates the imperfection.

The aspirant of *madhyama* class needs to develop the mastery over summer–winter, pain–pleasure, and contempt–respect, etc. The mind then becomes able to be stable in all the stages. While doing *tapa*, aspirant starts studying the self, the inner self (*svādhyāya*), and it leads towards his surrender to God (*Īśvarapraṇidhāna*). These three things lead the aspirant to *samādhi*.

The beginners (*adhama sādhaka*) those who have not started the *sādhanā* are suggested to adopt *aṣṭāṅga-yoga* (eightfold path). Maharṣi Patañjali says in his *Yoga-Sūtras* 2.29:

यमनियमासनप्राणायामप्रत्याहारधारणाध्यानसमाध्योऽष्टावङ्गानि।।

yamaniyamāsanaprāṇāyāmapratyāhāradhāraṇā dhyānasamādhyo 'ṣṭāvaṅgāni।।

Yama, niyama, āsana, prāṇāyāma, pratyāhāra, dhāraṇā, dhyāna and *samādhi* are the steps of *aṣṭāṅga-yoga*. They need to practice all the steps as their body and mind both need a preparation and suppleness for *samādhi*.

In the practice of *rāja-yoga* the aspirant requires the practice to attain *samādhi* according to his level. Somewhere *rāja-yoga* is also known as *dhyāna-yoga*, because ultimately the aspirant has to reach that state where *samādhi* is easier to attain. In this context *dhāraṇā*, *dhyāna* and *samādhi* come in series and are called *saṁyama* together.

त्रयमेकत्र संयमः।।

trayamekatra saṁyamaḥ।। — *Pātañjala Yoga-Sūtras* 3.4

When *dhāraṇā* (concentration), *dhyāna* (meditation) and *samādhi* become one this state is called *saṁyama* (discipline). This discipline is necessary no doubt, but at the same time regularity, too, is essential for the aspirant.

Now the question arises if every *sādhaka* (aspirant) has to reach *samādhi* then what is the difference among them? There are different levels of *samādhi* too, which has been suggested to different levels of *sādhaka*.

We have the description the four kinds of *rāja-yogī* in ancient texts. They are — *prathama kalpita, madhu bhūmika, madhu pratīka* and *atikrānta bhānanīya*. Among these *prathama kalpita* is said to be the newly arrived, and the *sādhaka*s need to practise the *savitarka samādhi*. The second type of *yogī*s are said to be at a better level, the *madhu bhūmika*; they need to have the practice of *nirvitarka samādhi*. The third type of *rāja-yogī*s, known as *madhu pratīka*s, are said to be better than both of the earliar types and need to practise the *asmitānugata samādhi*. The best type of *sādhaka* or *atikrānta bhānanīya yogī* has already attained the mastery over *ṛtambharā-prajñā* and over *asmitānugata samādhi*. Through the regular practice of that he experiences *asamprajñāta samādhi*.

When a *sādhaka* becomes able to govern the *cittavṛtti* (mental fluctuation) of mind and attain *ṛtambharā-prajñā*, he becomes one with his *kāraṇa prakṛti* (the subtle self) and *ātman* gets liberated and thus attains *kaivalya* (the ultimate reality).

Thus it can be said that *rāja-yoga* is the only practice of yoga which is open for all and easier to adopt also. Only through the practice of *rāja-yoga, ātman* gets to know the real self.

Introduction to Pātañjala Yoga

Only an intellectual discussion over the *Yoga-Sūtras* of Patañjali is not enough. Sage Patañjali didn't discover them for mind game. These *sūtra*s have been authored to understand the practical process of uplifting the levels of consciousness to search the possibilities of mind and ultimately go beyond them. *Yoga-Sūtras* are basically practice oriented. They discuss not only the *samādhi* intellectually, but do also give the practical knowledge and tools.

Statue of Maharṣi Patañjali

Several *sūtra*s explains those facts, which are beyond the worldly experiences. *Yoga-Sūtras* cannot be understood at mental level but the aspirants of yoga who practise it get help to understand the vast depth of mind and *prāṇa*. They understand it with experience. These *sūtra*s help the practitioners to reflect the path and to proceed carefully. Thus to understand them intellectually is neither possible nor relevant. As on the long route, the path of yoga, the *Yoga-Sūtras* plays the same role.

Yoga-Sūtras contains 195 verses; *sūtra* literally means thread. Here in *Yoga-Sūtras*, this thread has been used to arrange the knowledge systematically like a garland, which is a complete philosophy itself.

The text authored by Patañjali, commonly known as Yoga-Darśana, means philosophy of Yoga came from Sanskrit root *dṛś* which literally means to see. Here in *Yoga-Sūtras* the word *darśana* has been used only due to its ability to throw light on the path of yoga. It can be stated that *Yoga-Sūtras* develops the internal spiritual vision to see the invisible wisdom. *Yoga-Sūtras* can be taken as best, appropriate and quite scientific text among all the yogic texts authored till date. It has been divided into four chapters — Samādhi Pāda, Sādhanā Pāda, Vibhūti Pāda and Kaivalya Pāda.

Samādhi Pāda contains fifty-one *sūtra*s which focus on the following points: Definition of yoga; aim of yoga; *vr̥tti*s; how to overcome the *vr̥tti*s, i.e. *abhyāsa* and *vairāgya*; the objects of *samādhi*; *Īśvarapraṇidhāna*; *citta-vikṣepa*; how to remove *citta vikṣepa*; *citta prasādana* and its method as well as *sabīja* and *nirbīja samādhi*.

Sādhanā Pāda contains fifty-five *sūtra*s and they reflect the following subjects: *kriyā-yoga*, its practice and results, *pañca kleśa*s and the process to destroy them; *dr̥śya* (*prakr̥ti*) and *draṣṭra* (*puruṣa*), their qualities, union and the process of overcoming them as well as to achieve the *viveka-jñāna*; and the importance of yoga practice. This chapter also covers the *bahiraṅga-yoga*, the first five steps of *aṣṭāṅga-yoga*, i.e. *yama*, *niyama*, *āsana*, *prāṇāyāma* and *pratyāhāra*. These five steps of *aṣṭāṅga-yoga* and their benefits for the aspirants are clearly mentioned in Sādhanā Pāda of *Yoga-Sūtras*.

Vibhūti Pāda also contains fifty-five *sūtra*s and this chapter focuses on the rest three steps of *aṣṭāṅga-yoga* — commonly called *antaraṅga yoga*, i.e. *dhāraṇā*, *dhyāna* and *samādhi*. It also mentions the *nirbīja samādhi* and the *bahiraṅga sādhanā* to attain the state of *saṁyama*. After that, the *pāda* reflects the subject on the results of *citta*; it also mentions all the objects related to *prakr̥ti* and its results. This chapter also mentions different *saṁyama*s and later on it discusses *viveka-jñāna*, i.e. *kaivalya*.

Kaivalya Pāda, containing thirty-four *sūtra*s, mentions the five ways to achieve *siddhi*s and their results, as well as the results of meditation, i.e. overcoming the *saṁskāra* and the secrets of *yogī*'s *karma*. This chapter also discusses the *karma* done by normal persons, their types and the results. Later on, the chapter delves on the subject of *viveka-jñāna* and ultimately what is *dharmamedha samādhi* and the state of *kaivalya*.

The speciality of this text is that all the *sūtra*s (verses) are arranged systematically by Sage Patañjali and each one of them is to fulfil some specific purpose at that point. Maharṣi steps over from one to next *sūtra* and from one chapter to next chapter very wisely. Every word of these *sūtras* is meaningful and significant at its place.

All the technical words have been defined clearly in next *sūtra* so that the aspirant cannot face any misconception. Though several Sanskrit words having different and vast meanings in *Yoga-Sūtras,* the reader or practitioner gets the solution easily because of the clarification available in the next *sūtra.* At the level of clarity and consisted form, this text is almost unique. For some of the regions Maharṣi has made this text short so that the aspirant can remember the *sūtras* and there will be less chance of misconception. From the beginning to the end *Pātañjala-Yoga-Sūtras* is filled with knowledge and wisdom.

Aṣṭāṅga-Yoga

All spiritual activities are aimed at liberating the soul from the clutches of illusory name, form and identity and its reunion with its source — the universal consciousness. *Aṣṭāṅga* (eightfold) *yoga* is one of the most authentic paths of *sādhanā* to achieve this end.

All the powers of mind like imagination, observation, decision-making, control, memory and wisdom are activated by the prāṇic energy. Vivacity of senses is also possible by prāṇic energy only. All the intricate autonomous functions of the body and its organs are carried on without any conscious control of our own by this mysterious life-force — the prāṇic energy.

यमनियमासनप्राणायामप्रत्याहारधारणाध्यानसमाधयोऽष्टावङ्गानि ।

yama-niyama-āsana-prāṇāyāma-pratyāhāra-dhāraṇā-dhyāna samādhayo 'ṣṭāvaṅgāni ।

— *Pātañjala Yoga-Sūtras* 2.29

To control and consciously utilize this life-force for self-upliftment, purity and tranquillity of mind and emotions are essential. To achieve this end, *yama* and *niyama* are the two essential initial disciplines prescribed by *aṣṭāṅga-yoga* of Maharṣi Patañjali in his *Yoga-Sūtras* 2.30 and 2.32:

अहिंसासत्यास्तेयब्रह्मचर्यापरिग्रहाः यमाः ।।३०।।

शौचसंतोषतपःस्वाध्यायेश्वरप्रणिधानानि नियमाः ।।३२।।

ahiṁsāsatyāsteyabrahmacaryāparigrahā yamāḥ।।30।।

śaucasantoṣatapaḥsvādhyāyeśvarapranidhānāni niyamāḥ।।32।।

Non-violence, truth, non-stealing, celibacy and renunciation are called *yama*s, and cleanliness, contentment, austerity, study of scriptures (spiritual texts) and unwavering surrender to the will of God are called *niyama*s. By following these disciplines the body becomes charged with energy, mind becomes cleansed and quiet, and the *sādhaka* is bestowed with will, zeal and faith to rapidly progress in his *sādhanā* of self-awareness and self-realization.

स्थिरसुखमासनम्।।

sthirasukham āsanam। — *Pātañjala Yoga-Sūtras* 2.46

Along with *yama*s and *niyama*s, the practice of *āsana*s (yogic postures) is the third essential step so that one is able to sit in one posture for long hours without any uneasiness of body and mind.

तस्मिन् सति श्वासप्रश्वासयोर्गतिविच्छेदः प्राणायामः।।

tasmin sati śvāsa-praśvāsa-yor-gati-vicchedaḥ prāṇāyāmaḥ।
— *Pātañjala Yoga-Sūtras* 2.49

The fourth step in this eight-step ladder of *aṣṭāṅga-yoga* is *prāṇāyāma* (control of breath). Normally the prāṇic energy in our ignorant state wildly dances to the tunes of passions and unbridled animal urges. Practice of *prāṇāyāma* helps in calming down and controlling these wayward and wild movements of the mind.

स्वविषयासम्प्रयोगे चित्तस्वरूपानुकार इवेन्द्रियाणां प्रत्याहारः।।

svaviṣayāsamprayoge cittasvarūpānukāra ivendriyāṇāṁ pratyāhāraḥ।।
— *Pātañjala Yoga-Sūtras* 2.54

देशबन्धश्चित्तस्य धारणा।।१।।
तत्र प्रत्ययैकतानता ध्यानम्।।२।।

deśa-bandhaś cittasya dhāraṇā।
tatra pratyayaikatānatā dhyānam।।
— *Pātañjala Yoga-Sutras* 3.1-2

Higher practices of *prāṇāyāma* are dangerous with an impure and disorganized mind and can even lead to acute mental disorders hence advanced stages of *prāṇāyāma* should always be practised together with the fifth, sixth and seventh steps of *aṣṭāṅga-yoga sādhanā,* i.e. *pratyāhāra* (withdrawal of senses), *dhāraṇā* (concentration) and *dhyāna* (meditation). Without purification and control of the mind the *prāṇa sādhanā* remains a mere breathing exercise. It is beneficial to body health, but it is not prāṇic yoga.

सर्वार्थतैकाग्रतयोः क्षयोदयौ चित्तस्य समाधिपरिणामः।।

sarvārthataikāgratayoḥ kṣayodayau cittasya samādhi-pariṇāmaḥ ।।
— *Pātañjala Yoga-Sūtras* 3.11

One has to learn the process of consciously focusing this energy for achieving the desired result. However the ultimate aim of the *prāṇa sādhanā* is the liberation of the enslaved individual being (*prāṇa*) from the prison of the false ego identity and its merger–union with the cosmic prāṇic being of eternal life, light and love — *samādhi* — the eighth and the final step of *aṣṭāṅga-yoga sādhanā*. Persons endowed with abundance of this prāṇic energy are reckoned as truly great.

Introduction to Haṭha-Yoga

Normally people understand *haṭha-yoga* as doing yogic postures and attaining them forcefully, whether it takes a lot of energy or makes the practitioner exerted. But it is definitely not the case. The word *haṭha* has been used in yogic texts and ancient literature in a different meaning. It has been defined as:

हकारेण तु सूर्यः स्यात्सकारेणेन्दुरुच्यते।
सूर्याचन्द्रमसोरेक्यं हठ इत्याभिधीयते।।

ha-kāreṇa tu sūryaḥ syāt-sa-kāreṇ-endur-ucyate ।
sūryā-candramas-orekyaṁ haṭha itya-ābhidhīyate ।।
— *Yogaśīkhopaniṣad* 133

The word *haṭha* is made up of two *bīja mantras*: *ha* and *ṭha;* where *ha* represents Sun or *piṅgalā nāḍī* and *ṭha* represents Moon or *iḍā nāḍī*. Basically the union of these two *nāḍī*s is called *haṭha-yoga*. The another meaning of these two *bīja mantra*s can be understood as follows: *ṭha* represents *prāṇa*, the vital energy, and *ha* represents mental energy. So *haṭha-yoga* means the union of the prāṇic and mental forces.

When *iḍā* and *piṅgalā* unite together, the *prāṇa* starts flowing into *suṣumnā* and the dormant power *kuṇḍalinī,* which is lying in the *mūlādhāra cakra*, rises and enters *suṣumnā* and passing through all the six *cakra*s reaches the highest peak *brahmarandhra* or *sahasrāra*, and attain the oneness. This is the union of Śakti and Śiva or *ātman* and *parmātman*, this process destroys the ignorance of the aspirant and illuminates his heart and soul. Thus the process of this union is called *haṭha-yoga*.

The aim of *haṭha-yoga* is to have the mastery over body and mind. The main objective is to create an absolute balance of the interacting activities and processes of the physical body, mind and energy. When this balance is established the impulses generated give a call of awakening to the central force which is responsible for the evolution of human consciousness.

Haṭha-Yoga-Pradīpikā is one of the most authentic textbooks on *haṭha-yoga*, written in CE 1200 by Swami Svātmārāma, a great yoga *guru* who formulated the principles of *haṭha-yoga* and systematically explained various techniques, its effects on body, mind and states of consciousness. This is a comprehensive text on *āsana*s, *prāṇāyāma*, cleansing techniques, *mudrā*s (mental attitude or gestures), *bandha*s (energy locks), *nāda* (sound), meditation and many more guidelines for following the path of yoga.

Swami Svātmārāma was the follower of Nātha tradition, (followers of Ādi Nātha or Lord Śiva), taught by great *guru*s like Gorakhanātha and then Matsyendranātha. This is the tradition of sages who live in caves or Himalayas and renounce material life adopting *saṁnyāsa*.

Whereas *Gheraṇḍa Saṁhitā* 1.9, another text on *haṭha-yoga*, explains the process in seven steps in details as:

शोधनं दृढता चैव स्थैर्य धैर्य च लाघवम्।
प्रत्यक्षं च निर्लिप्तं च घटस्य सप्तसाधनम्।।

śodhanaṁ dṛḍhatā caiva sthairya dhairya ca lāghavam ।
pratyakṣam ca nirliptaṁ ca ghaṭasya sapta-sādhanam ।।

These are the following seven steps: *śodhanam* (purification), *dṛḍhatā* (suppleness of body), *sthairya* (stillness of body), *dhairyam* (patience), *lāghavam* (lightness of body), *pratyakṣam* (facing the troubles) and *nirliptam* (detachment) of *ghaṭastha sapta sādhana* (seven steps of the perfection of body) which should be practised by the aspirant of *haṭha-yoga*.

How to attain this perfection, for that Maharṣi Gheraṇḍa explains the *saptāṅga yoga* (seven steps of yoga) as:

षट्कर्मणा शोधनं च आसनेन भवेद्दृढम्।
मुद्रया स्थिरता चैव प्रत्याहारेण धीरता।।

प्राणायामाल्लाघवं च ध्यानात्प्रत्यक्षमात्मनः।
समाधिना निर्लिप्तं च मुक्तिरेव न संशयः।।

saṭkarmaṇā śodhanaṁ ca āsanena bhaved dr̥ḍham ।
mudrayā sthiratā caiva pratyāhāreṇa dhīratā ।।

prāṇāyāmāl lāghavaṁ ca dhyānāt-pratyakṣamātmanaḥ ।
samādhinā nirliptaṁ ca muktireva na saṁśayaḥ ।।
— *Gheraṇḍa Saṁhitā*, 1.10-11

The practice of *ṣaṭkarma* purifies the body, *āsana*s make the body strong, *mudrā*s bring stillness in the body; through the practice of *pratyāhāra* one can get the patience, *prāṇāyāma* makes the body of *sādhaka* (aspirant) light and by the practice of *samādhi* the mind gets detached; there is no doubt about it. The above-mentioned seven steps of yoga should be understood in detail.

Haṭha-yoga is also known as the science of purification as it includes six types of cleansing process. In order to purify the mind it is necessary for the body as a whole to undergo a process of absolute purification. This purification or *ṣaṭkarma* is of six types: *dhauti, basti, neti, nauli, trāṭaka* and *kapālabhāti*.

After the practice of *ṣaṭkarma* the practice comes in *haṭha-yoga* is *āsana*. Hence *Pātañjala Yoga-Sūtras* defines *āsana* as *sthiram sukham āsanam* (stillness and comfortable posture are called *āsana*) but in *haṭha-yoga* it is a specific position which opens the energy channels and psychic centres. When *prāṇa* (energy) flows freely, the body also becomes supple. Stiffness of the body is due to blockages and accumulation of wastes.

It is said that it should be of eighty-four lakh types but it doesn't seem practical. We find the description of eighty-four types of *āsana*s. Maharṣi Gheraṇḍa describes thirty-two types of *āsana*s. Among them *padmāsana, siddhāsana, svastikāsana, vajrāsana* and *paścimottānāsana* are common. *Siddhāsana* is said to be the best for *sādhanā*, as *siddhāsana* blocks the downfall of energy, it is useful for spiritual awakening.

Thereafter the practice comes in *haṭha-yoga* is *mudrā*. *Mudrā* is the specific gesture of the body. *Haṭha-Yoga-Pradīpikā* discusses ten *mudrās* whereas *Gheraṇḍa Saṁhitā* mentions twenty-five types of *mudrās*. *Jālandhara bandha, mūla bandha, uḍḍīyāna bandha, mahā bandha, mahā-mudrā, khecarī* and *viparītakaraṇī-mudrā* are common among them.

Haṭhayogic texts give a lot of importance to the practice of *prāṇāyāma*. It is very clearly said that for the perfection in *sādhanā* of *haṭha-yoga, prāṇāyāma* should be practised after *āsanas*. Texts describe *aṣṭakumbhaka* (eightfold practice of *prāṇāyāma*), i.e. *sūrya-bhedī, ujjayī, bhastrikā, bhrāmarī, śītalī, sītkāri, mūrchā* and *plavinī*. Through the practice of *prāṇāyāma* body becomes lightweighted, all the *nāḍīs* become purified and the mind becomes stable.

Now comes the practice of *dhāraṇā, dhyāna* and *samādhi*, which is the asset of any *sādhanā*. Practice of *dhyāna* (meditation) is of four types as mentioned in *haṭha-yoga* — *padastha, piṇḍastha, rūpastha* and *rūpātīta*. There is a description of two types of specific meditation — *saguṇa* and *nirguṇa dhyāna*. Practice of *dhyāna* leads to self-realization and through the regular practice of that *dhyāna* the mind becomes detached and it is the state of *samādhi*. The aspirant can attain *mokṣa* or *kaivalya*. Swami Svātmārāma explains the aim of *haṭha-yoga* in *Haṭha-Yoga-Pradīpikā* 1.2 as:

केवलं राजयोगाय हठविद्योपदिश्यते।।

kevalaṁ rājayogāya haṭhavidyopadiśyate ।

The lesson of *haṭha-yoga* is only for the attainment of *rāja-yoga* or the ultimate reality.

The same thing is repeated at the end of the text as follows:

सर्वे हठलयोपाया राजयोगस्य सिद्धये।।

sarve haṭhalayopāyā rājayogasya siddhaye ।
— *Haṭha-Yoga-Pradīpikā* 4.103

All the practices and clues given in *haṭha-yoga* are only for the attainment of *rāja-yoga*.

ṢAṬ-KARMA

Haṭha-yoga, as described in the early yoga Upaniṣads, was made up of the *ṣaṭ-karmas*, and is a very precise and systematic science. *Ṣaṭ* means "six" and *karma* means "action"; the *ṣaṭ-karmas* consist of six purification practices as mentioned earliar. The aim of *haṭha-yoga* and, therefore, of the *ṣaṭ-karma*s is to create harmony between the two major prāṇic flows, *iḍā* and *piṅgalā*, thereby attaining physical and mental purification and balance.

All *ṣaṭ-karma* techniques purify not only the physical body but effect its subtle components, to ensure safe and successful progression along the spiritual path. Therefore, even if you were attracted by *āsana*, *prāṇāyāma*, or meditation in the beginning, very soon you will understand that without the inner purification you cannot go far. It is no wonder that the *yogī*s who have attained perfection consider *ṣaṭ-karma* with great esteem. The six *kriyā*s, according to *Gheraṇḍa Saṁhitā* and *Haṭha-Yoga-Pradīpikā*, are *dhauti, basti, neti, nauli, trāṭaka*, and *kapālabhāti*.

धौतिर्वस्तिस्तथा नेतिः लौलिकी त्राटकं तथा।
कपालभातिश्चैतानि षट्कर्माणि समाचरेत्।।

धौतिर्बस्तिस्तथा नेतिस्त्राटकं नौलिकं तथा।
कपालभातिश्चैतानि षट्कर्माणि प्रचक्षते।।

dhautir-vastis-tathā netiḥ, laulikī trāṭakaṁ, tathā ।
kapāla-bhātiś-caitāni, ṣaṭ-karmāṇi samācaret ।।
— *Gheraṇḍa Saṁhitā* 1.12

dhautir-bastis-tathā netis-trāṭakaṁ naulikaṁ tathā ।
kapāla-bhātiś-caitāni ṣaṭ-karmāṇi pracakṣate ।।
— *Haṭha-Yoga-Pradīpikā* 2.22

Maharṣi Gheraṇḍa explains the *ṣaṭ-karma* in detail very systematically. The first *ṣaṭ-karma* is *dhauti*. This means to clean and in *Gheraṇḍa Saṁhitā* it is said to be of four types: *antaradhauti, dantadhauti, hṛddhauti* and *mūlaśodhana*.

Antaradhauti literally means cleansing of internal organs. It is of four types again — *vātasāra, vārisāra, vahnisāra* and *bahiṣkṛta*. *Danta-dhauti* means dental cleansing, which is also of four types: *dantamūla, jihvāmūla, karṇarandhra* and *kapālarandhra*. *Hṛddhauti* means cleansing of heart region and it is of three types: *daṇḍa dhauti, vamana dhauti* and *vastra dhauti*. The fourth *dhauti* is *mūlaśodhana*, which is the cleansing of anal region.

The second process is *neti*. It should be understood as the nasal passage cleansing. Basically it is of two types: *jala neti* and *sūtra neti* according to *Gheraṇḍa Saṁhitā*. Somewhere there is the description of *dugdha neti* and *ghṛta neti* also.

The next cleansing process is *basti*. It is the cleansing of lower abdomen or rectum only. It is of two types according to Maharṣi Gheraṇḍa: *jala basti* and *pavana basti*.

Later the practice comes is *nauli*. It is the movement of abdominal muscles and it is of three types: *dakṣiṇa nauli, vāma nauli* and *madhya nauli*.

Trāṭaka is the cleansing of eyes. According to *Gheraṇḍa Saṁhitā* it is of two types: *bāhya* and *ābhyantara*.

The last process is *kapālabhāti* and it is also of three types: *vātakrama, sītakrama* and *vyutkrama*.

Practice of *ṣaṭ-karma* mentioned above is not necessary for all aspirants; it is for those who need the inner cleansing. This means the aspirant doesn't have balanced three *doṣa*s (*vāta*, *pitta* and *kapha*), or *sapta dhātu*s are not in balance. The practice of *ṣaṭ-karma* brings a balance among them.

The *ṣaṭ-karma*s are also used to balance the three humours in the body: *kapha* (mucous); *pitta* (bile); and *vāta* (wind). According to both Āyurveda and *haṭha-yoga*, an imbalance of the humours will result in illness. These practices are also used before *prāṇāyāma* and other higher yoga practices in order to purify the body of toxins and to ensure safe and successful progression along the spiritual path. These powerful techniques should never be learned from books or taught by inexperienced people. According to the tradition only those instructed by a *guru* may teach others. It is essential to be personally instructed as to how and when to perform them according to individual needs.

The *ṣaṭ-karma*s are the first step and the important practices in *haṭha-yoga*. They are said to cleanse the body internally. As *aṣṭāṅga-yoga* emphasizes on *yama* and *niyama*, *haṭha-yoga* emphasizes on cleaning process that is *kriyā*s. In belief that a healthy and clean body can only have healthy and clean mind.

When the different systems of the body have been purified of toxins, a harmony in the energy channels (*nāḍī*s) is created, the overall result is that energy can flow freely through the body, thereby attaining emotional purification and balances the brain works much more effectively. When all components of the body are well balanced, the mind becomes more stable.

ĀSANA

Svātmārāma the author of *Haṭha-Yoga-Pradīpikā* defines *āsana* as: *kuryāt tad āsanaṁ sthairyam ārogyaṁ cāṅga-lāghavam*. This implies that *āsana*s should result in stability and absence of disease, as well as contributing to lightness of the body and feeling of well-being. Following practices are basically for the physical fitness, though they have their spiritual effects and other haṭha yogic benefits.

According to *Gheraṇḍa Saṁhitā*, *ṣaṭ-karma* is the first step of *haṭha-yoga*, but according to *Haṭha-Yoga-Pradīpikā*, *āsana* is the first step of *haṭha-yoga*:

हठस्य प्रथमांगत्वादासनं पूर्वमुच्यते ।
कुर्यात्तदासनं स्थैर्यमारोग्यं चांगलाघवम् ।। 1.17 ।।

haṭhasya prathamāṅgatvād āsanaṁ pūrvam ucyate ।
kuryāt tad āsanaṁ sthairyam ārogyaṁ cāṅga-lāghavam ।।
— *Haṭha-Yoga-Pradīpikā* 1.17

Before everything, *āsana* is spoken of the first step of *haṭha-yoga*. Having done *āsana* one gets steadiness of body and mind, he will be free from every disease and a feeling of lightness in the body can be experienced by the practitioner.

आसनानि समस्तानि यावन्तो जीवजन्तवः।
चतुरशीति लक्षाणि शिवेन कथितानि च।।

āsanāni samastāni yāvanto jīva-jantavaḥ ।
caturaśīti lakṣāṇi śivena kathitāni ca ।।
— *Gheraṇḍa Saṁhitā* 2.1

Gheraṇḍa Saṁhitā describes, as per the kinds of animals and creatures, eighty-four lakh types of *āsana*s, among them thirty-two are important.

तेषां मध्ये मर्त्यलोके द्वात्रिंशदासनं शुभम्।

teṣāṁ madhye martya-loke dvātriṁśad āsanaṁ śubham ।
— *Gheraṇḍa Saṁhitā* 2.2

Haṭha-Yoga-Pradīpikā describes fifteen *āsana*s. Which are mainly: *svastikāsana, gomukhāsana, vīrāsana, kūrmāsana, kukkuṭāsana, uttāna-kūrmāsana, dhanurāsana, matsyendrāsana, paścimottānāsana, mayūrāsana, śavāsana, siddhāsana, padmāsana, siṁhāsana* and *bhadrāsana*. These *āsana*s can be divided basically into two types, first type of *āsana*s are for making the body supple and the second type of *āsana*s are to support the meditation.

*Āsana*s are not just physical exercises: they have biochemical, psycho-physiological and psycho-spiritual effects. The cells of the body have their own intelligence and memory. Through practice of different *āsana*s blood circulation is improved, the hormone system is balanced, the nervous system is stimulated and toxins are eliminated, so that the cells, sinews and nerves are kept at their peak level. Physical, mental, and spiritual health and harmony are attained.

सिद्धं पद्मं तथा भद्रं मुक्तं वज्रं च स्वस्तिकम्।
सिंहं च गोमुखं वीरं धनुरासनमेव च।।

मृतं गुप्तं तथा मात्स्यं मत्स्येन्द्रासनमेव च।
गोरक्षं पश्चिमोत्तानमुत्कटं सङ्कटं तथा।।

मयूरं कुक्कुटं कूर्मं तथा चोत्तानकूर्मकम्।
उत्तानमण्डुकं वृक्षं मण्डुकं गरुडं वृषम्।।

शलभं मकरं चोष्ट्रं भुजङ्गं योगमासनम्।
द्वात्रिंशदासनान्येव मर्त्ये सिद्धिप्रदानि च।।

siddhaṁ padmaṁ tathā bhadraṁ muktaṁ vajraṁ ca svastikam ।
siṁhaṁ ca gomukhaṁ vīraṁ dhanurāsanam eva ca ।।

mr̥taṁ guptaṁ tathā mātsyaṁ matsyendrāsanam eva ca ।
gorakṣaṁ paścimottānam-utkaṭaṁ saṅkaṭaṁ tathā ।।

mayūraṁ kukkuṭaṁ kūrmaṁ tathā ca-uttāna-kūrmakam ।
uttāna-maṇḍukaṁ vr̥kṣaṁ maṇḍukaṁ garuḍaṁ vr̥ṣam ।।

śalabhaṁ makaraṁ ca-uṣṭraṁ bhujaṅgaṁ yogam-āsanam ।
dvātriṁśad-āsana-any eva martye siddhi-pradāni ca ।।

— *Gheraṇḍa Saṁhitā* 2.3-6

Gheraṇḍa Saṁhitā mentions thirty-two types of *āsana*s which are as follows: *siddhāsana, padmāsana, bhadrāsana, muktāsana, vajrāsana, svastikāsana, siṁhāsana, gomukhāsana, vīrāsana, dhanurāsana, mr̥tāsana* or *śavāsana, guptāsana, matsyāsana, matsyendrāsana, gorakṣāsana, paścimottānāsana, utkaṭāsana, saṅkaṭāsana, mayūrāsana, kukkuṭāsana, kūrmāsana, uttāna-kūrmāsana, vr̥kṣāsana, maṇḍūkāsana, uttāna-maṇḍūkāsana, garuḍāsana, vr̥ṣāsana, śalabhāsana, makarāsana, bhujaṅgāsana* and *yogāsana*.

Importance of *āsana* can be understood as they are for the health and balance of the body; have a deeper purpose: to diffuse the consciousness uniformly throughout the body, so that duality between senses, nerves, cells, mind, intelligence and consciousness is eradicated, and the whole being is in harmony. When the nervous, circulatory, respiratory, digestive, endocrine and genito-excretory systems are cleansed through *āsana*s, *prāṇa* moves unobstructed to the remotest cells and feeds them with a copious supply of energy.

According to haṭhayogic texts, *āsana*s are the bases for advancement in yoga. The practical aspect of *āsana* has been described in last chapter of the same book, which will support the aspirant as a guide.

PRĀṆĀYĀMA

The word *prāṇāyāma* is made up of two words: *prāṇa* and *āyāma*. *Prāṇa* is the vital energy and *āyāma* means expansion of the prāṇic energy. Swami Svātmārāma in *Haṭha-Yoga-Pradīpikā* talks about *prāṇāyāma* as the way to awaken the *kuṇḍalinī*, regular practice of *prāṇāyāma* can lead to spiritual awakening and self-realization. He describes various types of *prāṇāyāma*, which has different effects on the body, mind and spirit.

Prāṇāyāma has been mentioned as *kumbhaka* in haṭhayogic texts. It is the fourth step of the *aṣṭāṅga-yoga* described by Patañjali. The credit for making the practice of *prāṇāyāma* popular as a discipline in its own right and as a means for maintaining the health of the body and mind goes to the followers of *haṭha-yoga*. They gave it a place of great importance among the practices of *haṭha-yoga*.

अथातः संप्रवक्ष्यामि प्राणायामस्य सद्विधिम्।
यस्य साधनमात्रेण देवतुल्यो भवेन्नरः॥

athātaḥ saṁpravakṣyāmi prāṇāyāmasya sad-vidhim ।
yasya sādhana-mātreṇa deva-tulyo bhaven-naraḥ ॥
— *Gheraṇḍa Saṁhitā* 5.1

Gheraṇḍa says that the practice of *prāṇāyāma* leads the aspirant to the level of God. Authors of *haṭha-yoga* describe various techniques of *prāṇāyāma*, emphasizing the utility of each of them. There are instructions to practise them separately and comfortably.

सूर्यभेदनमुज्जायी सीत्कारी शीतली तथा।
भस्त्रिका भ्रामरी मूर्च्छा प्लाविनीत्यष्टकुंभकाः॥

sūrya-bhedanam-ujjāyī sītkārī śītalī tathā ।
bhastrikā bhrāmarī mūrcchā plāvinīty-aṣṭa-kumbhakāḥ ।।
— *Haṭha-Yoga-Pradīpikā* 2.44

Haṭha-Yoga-Pradīpikā explains eight types of *prāṇāyāma*s and their effects, but cautions that just as a trainer of lions, tigers or elephants studies their habits and moods and treats them with kindness and compassion, and then puts them through their paces slowly and steadily, the practitioner of *prāṇāyāma* should study the capacity of his lungs and make the mind passive in order to tame the incoming and outgoing breath. If the animal trainer is careless, the animals will maim him. In the same way, a wrong practice of *prāṇāyāma* will sap the energy of the practitioner.

सहितः सूर्यभेदश्च उज्जायी शीतली तथा।
भस्त्रिका भ्रामरी मूर्च्छा केवली चाष्टकुम्भकाः।।

sahitaḥ sūrya-bhedaś ca ujjāyī śītalī tathā ।
bhastrikā bhrāmarī mūrcchā kevalī ca-aṣṭa-kumbhakāḥ ।।
— *Gheraṇḍa Saṁhitā* 5.46

In *Haṭha-Yoga-Pradīpikā* and *Gheraṇḍa Saṁhitā*, *prāṇāyāma*s are mentioned as *aṣṭakumbhaka*, i.e. eight types of *prāṇāyāma*. But both the text having their own *aṣṭa kumbhaka*, though some of them are common.

MUDRĀ–BANDHA

Bandha means lock and *mudrā* means seal. The human system has many apertures or outlets. By locking and sealing these, the divine energy known as *kuṇḍalinī* is awakened and finds its union with *puruṣa* in the *sahasrāra cakra*.

In order to follow the technique of *prāṇāyāma*, it is necessary to know something about *mudrā*s and *bandha*s. *Mudrā* denotes positions which close the body apertures, and where the fingers are held together with special hand gestures.

Bandha also means bondage, joining together, fettering or catching hold. It also refers to a posture in which certain organs or parts of the body are gripped, contracted and controlled. When electricity is generated, it is necessary to have transformers, conductors, fuses, switches and insulated wires to carry the power to its destination; otherwise the current would be lethal.

When *prāṇa* is made to flow in the *yogī*'s body by the practice of *prāṇāyāma*, it is equally necessary for him to employ *bandha*s to prevent the dissipation of energy and to carry it to the right places without damage. "Without the *bandha*, the *prāṇāyāma* practice, and the flow of *prāṇa* can injure the nervous system.

महामुद्रा नभोमुद्रा उड्डीयानं जलन्धरम्।
मूलबन्धो महाबन्धो महाबेधश्च खेचरी।।1।।

विपरीतकरी योनिर्वज्रोणि शक्तिचालनी।
ताडागी माण्डुकी मुद्रा शाम्भवी पञ्चधारणा।।2।।

अश्विनी पाशिनी काकी मातङ्गी च भुजङ्गिनी।
पञ्चविंशतिमुद्राश्च सिद्धिदा इह योगिनाम्।।3।।

mahā-mudrā nabho-mudrā uḍḍīyānaṁ jalandharam ।
mūlabandho mahā-bandho mahā-bedhaś-ca khecarī ।।1।।

viparītakarī yonir-vajroṇi śakti-cālanī ।
tāḍāgī māṇḍukī mudrā śāmbhavī pañca-dhāraṇā ।।2।।

aśvinī pāśinī kākī mātaṅgī ca bhujaṅginī ।
pañcaviṁśati-mudrāś-ca siddhidā iha yogināṁ ।।3।।

— *Gheraṇḍa Saṁhitā* 3.1-3

Mahā-mudrā, nabho-mudrā, uḍḍīyāna, jālandhara, mūla-bandha, mahā-bandha, mahā-vedha, khecarī, viparītakaraṇī, yoni, vajrolī, śakti-cālanī, tāḍāgī, māṇḍūkī, śāmbhavī, aśvinī, pāśinī, kākī, mātaṅgī and *bhujaṅginī*, are the twenty-five *mudrā*s, which gives perfections to the *yogī*s.

Out of the several *mudrā*s mentioned in haṭhayogic texts, *jālandhara, uḍḍiyāna* and *mūla bandha* are essential to *prāṇāyāma*. They help to distribute energy and prevent its waste through hyper-ventilation of the body. They are practised to arouse the sleeping *kuṇḍalinī* and direct its energy up through the *suṣumṇā* channel during *prāṇāyāma*. Their use is essential for experiencing the state of *samādhi*.

2

Introduction to Psychology

Psychology: Meaning and Definitions

THERE are two origins of psychology; one is philosophy and the other is physiology. The discussions on these subjects date back as far as the early Greek thinkers like Aristotle and Socrates. The word psychology is derived from the Greek word *psyche*, meaning "soul" or "mind". Psychology is both applied and academic, and a science, which studies the human mind and behaviour. Latest research in psychology seeks to understand as well as explain thought, emotion and behaviour. Applications of psychology include mental health, self-help, performance enhancement, ergonomics and many other areas affecting our life.

Defining psychology is not an easy task because of both the wide scope of its concerns as well as the philosophical differences among its practitioners. Psychology can be normally defined as the study of the human mind and behaviour. Psychologists may define the word, something like: psychology is "the science of the problems of human being".

Some intellectuals keep psychology in the arts section but some others take it as a science. Scientific theories are important tools for the organization of observed facts. To some people, the word theory simply means someone's unsupported and unfounded notion of how things ought to be done or a set of abstract principles that does not work in practical situations. However, *theory* has quite a different meaning, in science theories are general principles which summarize many observations and predict what can be expected to happen in new situations. As summaries and predictors of events, scientific theories should not be thought of as "right" or "wrong" but merely as more or less useful in helping to summarize what has been observed and in making predictions about what is to be expected when new observations or experiments are done. As new data are obtained, theories are subject to modification, or old theories may eventually be scrapped in favour of new ones which do a better job of summarizing and predicting than did the old theories. Many of the arguments among scientists are over the modification and scrapping of theories as new data are gathered.

One of the definitions states that psychology is the study of behaviour. Behaviour includes anything a person or animal does and it can be observed in some way. Behaviour, unlike mind or thoughts or feelings, can be observed, recorded and studied. No one ever saw or heard a mind, but we can see and hear behaviour. We can see and measure what a person does and hear, and record what a person says (this is vocal behaviour). From what is done and said, psychologists can and do make inferences about the feelings, attitudes, thoughts, and other mental processes behind the behaviour. In this way, internal mental events can be studied as they manifest themselves through what people do — their *behaviour.* Thus, it is through behaviour that we can actually study and come to understand internal mental processes that would otherwise be hidden from us. When we define *psychology* as "the science of behaviour", we are not excluding mind; we are saying that what a person does — his or her *behaviour* — is the avenue through which internal mental events can be studied.

Psychology is a science dealing with mental phenomena and processes. Psychologists study emotions, perceptions, intelligence, consciousness, and the relationship between these phenomena and processes and the work of the glands and muscles. Psychologists are also interested in diseased or disordered mental states, and some psychologists provide therapy for individuals.

There are some misconceptions about psychology, as it is the scientific study of human and animal behaviour with the object of understanding why living beings behave as they do. People often confound psychology with psychiatry, which is a branch of medicine dedicated to the cure of mental disorders. As almost any science, its discoveries have practical applications. As it is a rather new science, applications are sometimes confused with the science itself. It is easier to distinguish what is "pure" and "applied" in older disciplines: everybody can separate physics and mathematics from engineering, or anatomy and physiology from medicine.

In general, psychology is concerned with how people perceive the world around them as well as how they react to it, how they grow and how they learn, and how they relate to others and function in groups.

Sensation, Perception and Extrasensory Perception

Although intimately related, sensation and perception play two complimentary but different roles in how we interpret our world. Sensation refers to the process of sensing our environment through touch, taste, sight, sound and smell. This information is sent to our brains in raw form where perception comes into play. Perception is the way we interpret these sensations and therefore make sense of everything around us.

SENSATION

Sensations can be defined as *the passive process of bringing information from the outside world into the body and to the brain.* The process is passive in the sense that we do not have to be consciously engaging in a "sensing" process. Perception can be defined as *the active process of selecting, organizing, and interpreting the information brought to the brain by the senses.*

Vision, hearing, taste, smell, and touch are the so-called five senses. But the number of human senses is closer to ten than five. In addition to touch, the skin contains separate warmth, cold and pain senses. Furthermore, sense-organs in the muscles, tendons and joints tell us about the position of our limbs and the state of tensions in the muscles. They serve the sense called *kinesthesis.* The *vestibular sense* informs us about the movement and stationary position of the head; it is the key sense in maintaining balance.

Each sensory system is a kind of channel, consisting of a sensitive element (*the receptor*), nerve fibres leading from this receptor to the brain or spinal cord, and the various relay stations and processing areas within the brain. When a sensory channel is stimulated we have a sensation that is characteristic of that channel. For instance, whether the eye is stimulated by light or by pressure on the eyeball, we have a visual experience.

In order to know about the world around (and within) us, physical energy must be changed into activity within the nervous system. The process of converting physical energy into nervous system activity is called *transduction*. Transduction occurs at the *receptors* — cells which are specialized for the most efficient conversion of one kind of energy in general, during the transduction process, receptor cells convert physical energy into an electric voltage, or potential, called the *receptor potential*. In some sensory systems, the receptor potential, called the receptor potential itself directly triggers the nerve impulses that travel to the brain or spinal cord. In other sensory systems, the receptor potential leads to further electrical events, which in turn trigger nerve impulses. Whether it is the receptor potential itself or some other voltage, the electrical event that triggers nerve impulses is known as the *generator potential*.

For a given event in the environment, thousands of nerve impulses are generated and conducted to the central nervous system. Since these impulses travel along many different nerve fibres at slightly different times, they form a pattern of input to the central nervous system that is the basis of our sensory experience of the event. Thus, beginning with the transduction process at the receptor, physical energy results in a pattern of nerve impulses in the central nervous system. In other words, the physical energy is changed into a code made up of a pattern of nerve firings. The firing patterns that correspond to events in the environment are known as *afferent codes* (the word *afferent* in this context means "in-put"). As you will see later in this chapter, some progress has been made in deciphering the afferent codes corresponding to certain sensory experiences.

PERCEPTION

Perception refers to the way the world looks, sounds, feels, tastes or smells. In other words, *perception* can be defined as whatever is experienced by a person. However, for much of what we perceive, the sensory-input patterns provide only the raw material for experience. For example, when we perceive the visual riches of an art museum, people's faces, television, or a conversation, active processes work on the sensory input to transform it into what we actually experience. Thus *perception* — our experience of the world — arises from sensory input plus the ways we process the sensory information.

An *illusion* is not a trick or a misperception; it is a perception. We call it an *illusion* simply because it does not agree with our other perceptions. For instance, our perception of the line lengths in the Muller-Lyer illusion does not agree with the perception we would have if there were no arrows. The presence of the arrows in the figure causes us to process the sensory input in such a way that we perceive the lines as unequal in length. But what did you perceive? Perceptual processes have done their work to produce the illusion. A simpler version of this horizontal–vertical illusions demonstrates that our perception often depends on processes that go far beyond the raw material of the sensory input. The rest of this chapter is about perceptual processes (most of them visual) that transform sensory inputs into what we actually experience.

At any given moment, our sense-organs are bombarded by a multitude of stimuli, yet we perceive only a few of them clearly. Were you aware of the background noises in your environment until you read this sentence? Yet input from the ears was coming in all the time. *Attention* is the term given to the perceptual processes that select certain inputs for inclusion in our conscious experience, or awareness, at any given time.

Aristotle (384–322 BCE) is credited with the traditional classification of the five sense-organs: sight, smell, taste, touch and hearing. As far back as the 1760s, the famous philosopher Immanuel Kant proposed that our knowledge of the outside world depends on our modes of perception. In order to define what is "extrasensory" we need to define what is "sensory". Each of the five senses consists of organs with specialized cellular structures that have receptors for specific stimuli. These cells have links to the nervous system and thus to the brain. Sensing is done at primitive levels in the cells and integrated into sensations in the nervous system. Sight is probably the most developed sense in humans, followed closely by hearing.

The eye is the organ of vision. It has a complex structure consisting of a transparent lens that focuses light on the retina. The retina is covered with two basic types of light-sensitive cells — rods and cones. The cone cells are sensitive to colour and are located in the part of the retina called the fovea, where the light is focused by the lens. The rod cells are not sensitive to colour, but have greater sensitivity to light than the cone cells. These cells are located around the fovea and are responsible for peripheral vision and night vision. The eye is connected to the brain through the optic nerve. The point of this connection is called the "blind spot" because it is insensitive to light. Experiments have shown that the back of the brain maps the visual input from the eyes.

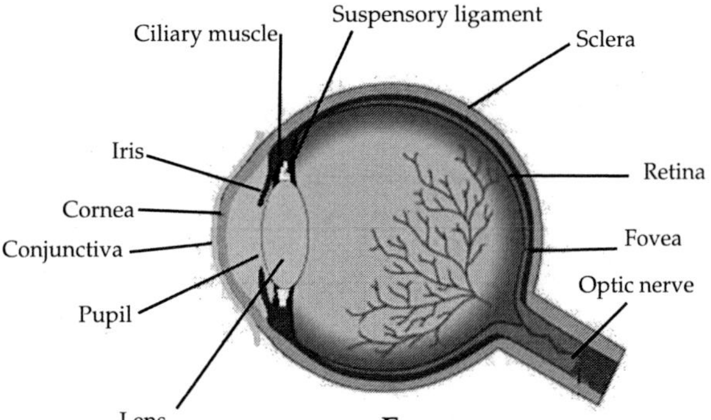

Eye

The brain combines the input of our two eyes into a single three-dimensional image. In addition, even though the image on the retina is upside–down because of the focusing action of the lens, the brain compensates and provides the right-side-up perception. Experiments have been done with subjects fitted with prisms that invert the images. The subjects go through an initial period of great confusion, but subsequently they perceive the images as right-side-up.

The range of perception of the eye is phenomenal. In the dark, a substance produced by the rod cells increases the sensitivity of the eye so that it is possible to detect very dim light. In strong light, the iris contracts reducing the size of the aperture that admits light into the eye and a protective obscure substance reduces the exposure of the light-sensitive cells. The spectrum of light to which the eye is sensitive varies from the red to the violet. Lower electromagnetic frequencies in the infra-red are sensed as heat, but cannot be seen. Higher frequencies in the ultraviolet and beyond cannot be seen either, but can be sensed as tingling of the skin or eyes depending on the frequency. The human eye is not sensitive to the polarization of light, i.e. light that oscillates on a specific plane. Bees, on the other hand, are sensitive to polarized light, and have a visual range that extends into the ultraviolet. Some kinds of snakes have special infra-red sensors that enable them to hunt in absolute darkness using only the heat emitted by their prey. Birds have a higher density of light-sensing cells than humans do in their retinas, and therefore, higher visual acuity.

Colour blindness or "Daltonism" is a common abnormality in human vision that makes it impossible to differentiate colours accurately. One type of colour blindness results in the inability to distinguish red from green. This can be a real handicap for certain types of occupations. To a colour-blind person, a person with normal colour vision would appear to have extrasensory perception. However, we want to reserve the term "extrasensory perception" for perception that is beyond the range of the normal. Another common misconception is that colour blindness can be corrected with contact lenses. This is not the case.

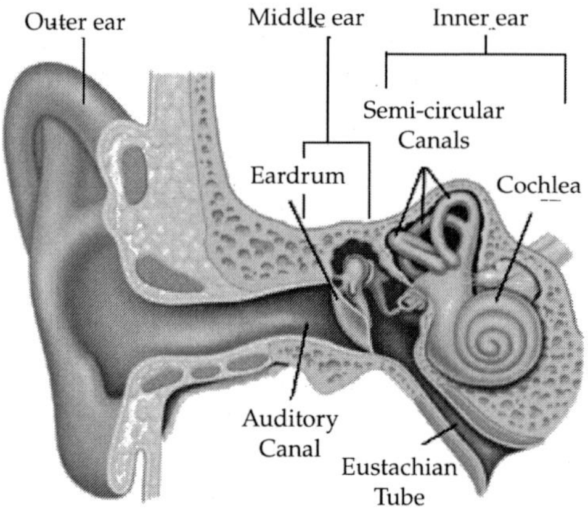

Ear

The ear is the organ of hearing. The outer ear protrudes away from the head and is shaped like a cup to direct sounds toward the tympanic membrane, which transmits vibrations to the inner ear through a series of small bones in the middle ear called the *malleus*, *incus* and *stapes*. The inner ear, or cochlea, is a spiral-shaped chamber covered internally by nerve fibres that react to the vibrations and transmit impulses to the brain via the auditory nerve. The brain combines the input of our two ears to determine the direction and distance of sounds.

The inner ear has a vestibular system formed by three semi-circular canals that are approximately at right angles to each other, and are responsible for the sense of balance and spatial orientation. The inner ear has chambers filled with a viscous fluid and small particles (otoliths) containing calcium carbonate. The movement of these particles over small hair cells in the inner ear sends signals to the brain that are interpreted as motion and acceleration.

The human ear can perceive frequencies from sixteen cycles per second, which is a very deep bass, to 28,000 cycles per second, which is a very high pitch. Bats and dolphins can detect frequencies higher than 100,000 cycles per second. The human ear can detect pitch changes as small as 300th of 1 per cent of the original frequency in some frequency ranges. Some people have "perfect pitch", which is the ability to map a tone precisely on the musical scale without reference to an external standard. It is estimated that less than one in 10,000 people have perfect pitch, but speakers of tonal languages like Vietnamese and Mandarin show remarkably precise absolute pitch in reading out lists of words because pitch is an essential feature in conveying the meaning of words in tone languages. The Eguchi Method teaches perfect pitch to children starting before they are four years old. After age seven, the ability to recognize notes does not improve much.

The receptors for taste, called taste buds, are situated chiefly in the tongue, but they are also located in the roof of the mouth and near the pharynx. They are able to detect four basic tastes: salty, sweet, bitter and sour. The tongue also can detect a sensation called "umami" from taste receptors sensitive to amino-acids. Generally, the taste buds close to the tip of the tongue are sensitive to sweet tastes, whereas those in the back of the tongue are sensitive to bitter tastes. The taste buds on top and on the side of the tongue are sensitive to salty and sour tastes.

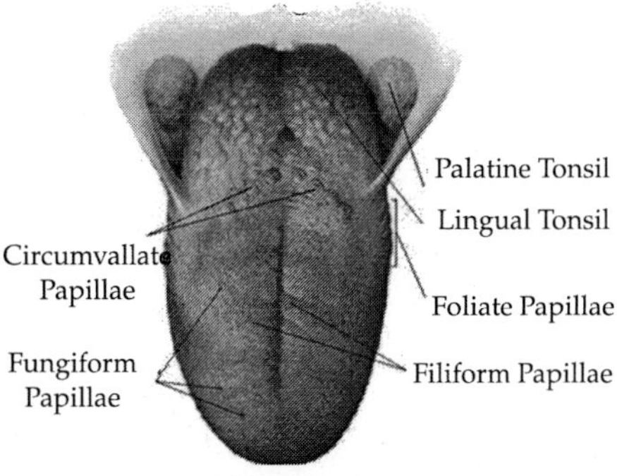

Tongue

At the base of each taste bud there is a nerve that sends the sensations to the brain. The sense of taste functions works in co-ordination with the sense of smell. The number of taste buds varies substantially from individual to individual, but greater numbers increase sensitivity. Women, in general, have a greater number of taste buds than men. As in the case of colour blindness, some people are insensitive to some tastes.

The nose is the organ responsible for the sense of smell. The cavity of the nose is lined with mucous membranes that have smell receptors connected to the olfactory nerve. The smells themselves consist of vapours of various substances.

The smell receptors interact with the molecules of these vapours and transmit the sensations to the brain. The nose also has a structure called the vomeronasal organ whose function has not been determined, but which is suspected of being sensitive to pheromones that influence the reproductive cycle. The smell receptors are sensitive to seven types of sensations that can be characterized as camphor, musk, flower, mint, ether, acrid or putrid. The sense of smell is sometimes temporarily lost when a person has a cold. Dogs have a sense of smell that is many times more sensitive than that of men.

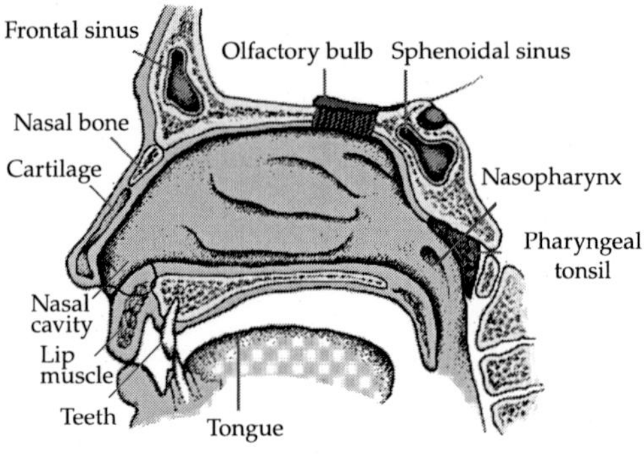

Nose

The sense of touch is distributed throughout the body. Nerve endings in the skin and other parts of the body transmit sensations to the brain. Some parts of the body have a larger number of nerve endings and, therefore, are more sensitive.

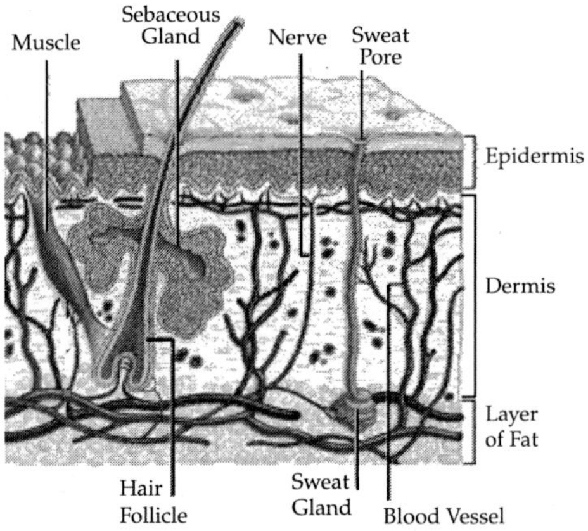

Skin

Four kinds of touch sensations can be identified: cold, heat, contact, and pain. Hairs on the skin magnify the sensitivity and act as an early warning system for the body. The fingertips and the sexual organs have the greatest concentration of nerve endings. The sexual organs have "erogenous zones" that when stimulated start a series of endocrine reactions and motor responses resulting in orgasm.

EXTRASENSORY PERCEPTIONS

Extrasensory Perception (ESP) is the knowledge of external objects or events without the aid of the senses. Since ancient times, people have wondered about various so-called psychic experiences that seem to defy scientific explanation. Often these phenomena have been associated with communication with the dead. Mediums, who purport to mediate between the living and the dead, were particularly popular in the nineteenth century. Often mediums deliver utterances while in a trance-like state and their followers believe that they can deliver messages from the deceased.

In 1882, a group of scholars in London founded the Society for Psychical Research to study such mysterious events. In the United States, philosopher and psychologist William James discovered a woman in Boston, Massachusetts, named Mrs Piper, who reportedly had the ability to disclose information about events of which she could not have had personal knowledge. James first began investigating Piper's trance phenomena in 1885, and he and others continued these investigations for thirty years. No adequate explanation was ever offered to explain Piper's seeming ability to communicate with the dead.

In 1930, Joseph Banks Rhine, a psychology professor at Duke University, founded a parapsychology laboratory at the school. The laboratory became a famous centre for investigating ESP. Rhine's investigations focused on what he called psi, or psychic phenomena. He believed that there might be natural, although unknown, causes for mysterious occurrences, and he attempted to establish their existence by use of experimental and mathematical techniques. These techniques included testing people who seemed to possess an unusual ability for ESP.

As part of these tests, Rhine developed a deck of twenty-five cards, each bearing one of five different symbols, and had his subjects attempt to guess the right symbol when the cards were concealed. Certain individuals guessed correctly more often than the law of averages would predict, and Rhine concluded those individuals possessed ESP. Rhine's investigations led him to believe that ESP underlies clairvoyance (the perception of external things without sensing them), telepathy (the perception of another person's thoughts) and precognition (the ability to predict events). However, later scientists criticized the methodology of Rhine's studies, noting some subjects could identify the symbols by physical marks on the cards.

More recently, computers and other instruments have been used in the study of ESP. However, most scientists do not believe that ESP exists. These scientists note that thousands of controlled studies have failed to show any evidence of psychical phenomena, and that no person has ever successfully demonstrated ESP to independent investigators. Despite these findings, surveys indicate that a substantial portion of the public believes in ESP.

In addition to sight, smell, taste, touch and hearing, humans also have awareness of balance (equilibrioception), pressure, temperature (thermoception), pain (nociception) and motion all of which may involve the co-ordinated use of multiple sensory organs. The sense of balance is maintained by a complex interaction of visual inputs, the proprioceptive sensors (which are affected by gravity and stretch sensors found in muscles, skin, and joints), the inner ear vestibular system, and the central nervous system. Disturbances occurring in any part of the balance system, or even within the brain's integration of inputs, can cause the feeling of dizziness or unsteadiness.

Kinesthesia is the precise awareness of muscle and joint movement that allows us to co-ordinate our muscles when we walk, talk and use our hands. It is the sense of kinesthesia that enables us to touch the tip of our nose with our eyes closed or to know which part of the body we should scratch when we itch.

Synesthesia: Some people experience a phenomenon called synesthesia in which one type of stimulation evokes the sensation of another. For example, the hearing of a sound may result in the sensation of the visualization of a colour, or a shape may be sensed as a smell. Synesthesia is hereditary and it is estimated that it occurs in one out of 1,000 individuals with variations of type and intensity. The most common forms of synesthesia link numbers or letters with colours.

Thinking: Basic Elements of Thought Proposition

Thinking is the highest mental activity present in man. All human achievements and progress are simply the products of thought. The evolutions of culture, art, literature, science and technology are the results of thinking.

Thought and action are inseparable — they are actually the two sides of the same coin. All our deliberate action starts from our deliberate thinking. For a man to do something, he should first see it in his *mind's eye* — he should imagine it, think about it first, before he can do it. All creations — whether artistic, literal or scientific — first occur in the creator's mind before it is actually given life in the real world.

THE CONCEPT OF THINKING

According to the classical view, thinking is a particular type of mental occurrence and the concept of thinking is essentially the concept of this mental occurrence.

In the *Concept of Mind* (CM) thinking is an activity that terminates in a thought, which is a state of being prepared for a performance. Thinking is characterized by intention–parasitism; acts of thinking, owing to their intention–parasitism, can be described in a tactical idiom, with reference to the final performance for which it was intended.

However, thinking cannot be described within this framework of intention–parasitism, in cases of *non-achieving thinking*, where acts of thinking do not quite terminate in thoughts. For example, "a poet, essayist or philosopher may be trying hard to find the word, phrase or argument that he needs, but the time when he is thinking what to say is the time when he still has nothing to say". We cannot decide how to portray such acts of thinking as parasitic on some actual goal, thereby failing to produce a meaningful narrative of thinking in such cases. We can only try to compensate indescribability by constructing narratives around results of thinking rather than thinking itself.

This, however, does not mean that the conception of thinking, as an activity conditioned just by a thinker's efforts, is a useful fiction. This conception of thinking, which originates in *CM* itself, stands in clear opposition with the "psychological" interpretation of mental concepts ordinarily ascribed to Ryle, for it does not explain thinking in terms of observable behaviour or behavioural dispositions. This is because it understands thinking as an autonomous, circumstance-independent sequence of activities and places it outside the framework of intention–parasitism. Thus, it severs the ties of thinking with the describable world and emphasizes its privacy.

CRITICAL THINKING

Critical thinking is defined as disciplined, self-directed thinking displaying a mastery of intellectual skills and abilities — thinking about your thinking while you're thinking to make your thinking better.

Critical thinking is the intellectually disciplined process of actively and skilfully conceptualizing, applying, analysing, synthesizing, and/or evaluating information gathered from, or generated by, observation, experience, reflection, reasoning, or communication, as a guide to belief and action. In its exemplary form, it is based on universal intellectual values that transcend subject matter divisions: clarity, accuracy, precision, consistency, relevance, sound evidence, good reasons, depth, breadth and fairness.

Critical thinking is that mode of thinking — about any subject, content or problem — in which the thinker improves the quality of his or her thinking by skilfully taking charge of the structures inherent in thinking and imposing intellectual standards upon them.

BASIC ELEMENT OF THOUGHT

Eight elements of thought identified by Richard Paul (1992: 5-24) are the basic building blocks of productive thinking. In literature interpretation and listening, they help one make sense of the reasoning of the author or speaker. In writing and speaking, they enable authors or speakers to strengthen their arguments.

However, between pure opinion and hard facts lie reasoned judgements in which beliefs are supported by reasons. Instruction in this area needs to be included in all forms of communication in the language arts. The eight elements of reasoning are as follows:

Purpose, Goal, or End View

We reason to achieve some objective, to satisfy a desire, to fulfil some need. For example, if the car does not start in the morning, the purpose of my reasoning is to figure out a way to get to work. One source of problems in reasoning is traceable to "defects" at the level of purpose or goal. If our goal itself is unrealistic, contradictory to other goals we have, confused or muddled in some way, then the reasoning we use to achieve it is problematic. If we are clear on the purpose for our writing and speaking, it will help focus the message in a coherent direction. The purpose in our reasoning might be to persuade others. When we read and listen, we should be able to determine the author's or speaker's purpose.

Question at Issue (*or Problem to Be Solved*)

When we attempt to reason something out, there is at least one question at issue or problem to be solved (if not, there is no reasoning required). If we are not clear about what the question or problem is, it is unlikely that we will find a reasonable answer, or one that will serve our purpose. As part of the reasoning process, we should be able to formulate the question to be answered or the issue to be addressed. For example, why won't the car start? or should libraries censor materials that contain objectionable language?

Points of View or Frame of Reference

As we take on an issue, we are influenced by our own point of view. For example, parents of young children and librarians might have different points of view on censorship issues. The price of a shirt may seem low to one person while it seems high to another because of a different frame of reference. Any defect in our point of view or frame of reference is a possible source of problems in our reasoning. Our point of view may be too narrow, may not be precise enough, may be unfairly biased and so forth. By considering multiple points of view, we may sharpen or broaden our thinking. In writing and speaking, we may strengthen our arguments by acknowledging other points of view. In listening and reading, we need to identify the perspective of the speaker or author and understand how it affects the message delivered.

Experiences, Data, Evidence

When we reason, we must be able to support our point of view with reasons or evidence. Evidence is important in order to distinguish opinions from reasons or to create a reasoned judgement. Evidence and data should support the author's or speaker's point of view and can strengthen an argument. An example is data from surveys or published studies. In reading and listening, we can evaluate the strength of an argument or the validity of a statement by examining the supporting data or evidence. Experiences can also contribute to the data of our reasoning. For example, previous experiences in trying to get a car to start may contribute to the reasoning process that is necessary to resolve the problem.

Concepts and Ideas

Reasoning requires the understanding and use of concepts and ideas (including definitional terms, principles, rules or theories). When we read and listen, we can ask ourselves, "What are the key ideas presented?" When we write and speak, we can examine and organize our thoughts around the substance of concepts and ideas. Some examples of concepts are freedom, friendship and responsibility.

Assumptions

We need to take some things for granted when we reason. We need to be aware of the assumptions we have made and the assumptions of others. If we make faulty assumptions, this can lead to defects in reasoning. As a writer or speaker we make assumptions about our audience and our message. For example, we might assume that others will share our point of view; or we might assume that the audience is familiar with the First Amendment when we refer to "First Amendment rights". As a reader or listener we should be able to identify the assumptions of the writer or speaker.

Inferences

Reasoning proceeds by steps called inferences. An inference is a small step of the mind, in which a person concludes that something is so because of something else being so or seeming to be so. The tentative conclusions (inferences) we make depend on what we assume as we attempt to make sense of what is going on around us. For example, we see dark clouds and infer that it is going to rain; or we know the movie starts at 7:00; it is now 6:45; it takes 30 minutes to get to the theatre; so we cannot get there on time. Many of our inferences are justified and reasonable, but many are not. We need to distinguish between the raw data of our experiences and our interpretations of those experiences (inferences). Also, the inferences we make are heavily influenced by our point of view and our assumptions.

Implications and Consequences

When we reason in a certain direction, we need to look at the consequences of that direction. When we argue and support a certain point of view, solid reasoning requires that we consider what the implications are of following that path; what are the consequences of taking the course that we support? When we read or listen to an argument, we need to ask ourselves what follows from that way of thinking. We can also consider consequences of actions that characters in stories take. For example, if I don't do my homework, I will have to stay after school to do it; if I water the lawn, it will not wither in the summer heat.

Learning: Meaning and Applications

Learning is the lifelong process of transforming information and experience into knowledge, skills, behaviours and attitudes. Learning is the process by which knowledge is acquired and modified. It is the necessity of life. The best thing about learning is that there is no age bar or time bar for learning. Today's learning has become easy, comfortable and flexible with the advancement of technologies.

Learning is often defined as a change in behaviour (Birkenholz 1999: 91), which is demonstrated by people implementing knowledge, skills or practices derived from education. Basically, from an educator's perspective, learning involves helping people along the learning process, and learning includes all of the things that we do to make it happen. As an end result, we know that learning occurs when people take newfound information and incorporate it into their life. For example, if we are working with an audience that lacks basic financial management skills for budgeting, one of our objectives is to see people gain knowledge in this area and to actually implement the new skills — hopefully, over a long period of time.

Changes in the knowledge state of a person or changes in the "knowledge" state of the environment are usually only deemed to be learning if human performance improves on some task. When we think about changes in the knowledge state of a person, three possibilities are there, which are as follows:

1. *Remind and Remediate*: The knowledge has existed in the person's brain before, but been forgotten or made inaccessible. In this case, the person must be reminded of what they once knew or be remediated (lots of practice) to allow the person to again perform a task competently.
2. *Receive and Reconstruct*: The knowledge has existed in someone else's head, but never in the particular person's head. In this case, the person must receive the information (training is doing this receiving as fast as possible) or reconstruct the information (education is learning to flexibly reconstruct knowledge either by following the ways others obtained the knowledge or obtaining the knowledge in novel ways).
3. *Research and Reflect*: The knowledge has never existed in any human's brain, and so the learner must discover it on his own. Often times this may require the learner to research questions and find their own answers. Often, the learner must "reflect"

in order to create the question that research will eventually answer. Asking the right questions then becomes the highest level of learning meta-skill to be developed.

Similarly, there are three possibilities for knowledge in the environment — it has existed in the learner's environment before, it has existed in someone else's environment before but not the learner's, or the knowledge has never existed in any environment before. Again, rapid change has an impact. Knowledge that led to superior performance in the past may actually lead to inferior performance in the future. We all know people who were successful in their day and age, but have developed beliefs and perspectives that are maladapted when the world changes too much. We can refer to the half-life of knowledge — knowledge is only valuable for particular limited periods of time, and then is useless or counterproductive.

As technological advances change us and our environment making the half-life of knowledge shorter and shorter, we can expect to see a shift in the meaning of learning. In the early stages of human history, learning allowed us to cope with a physically hostile environment. In this stage of human history, learning is allowing us to cope with a rapidly changing environment. Ultimately, we will either discover ways to make the environment seem more stable, or we will redefine the human condition to allow us to learn and evolve more rapidly than natural biological processes can sustain. In one scenario the rate of change is controlled allowing us to learn more like we do today, and in the other scenario the rate of change continues to accelerate requiring that we re-invent ourselves and thus the meaning of learning. Or we pursue these two possibilities in parallel, creating both a stable and satisfying path for people as we are physically today and a path with a new species able to learn in an environment that continues to change at an accelerating rate. It is likely that both paths will be explored in the next 100 years. The former path may focus on established values (probably not like the Amish exist, but allowing advances in only certain areas and not others — energy reduction, weight reduction, strength of materials). The latter path will place no barriers on advancement of knowledge, but will require a new species fit enough to live with hyper change.

Psychologists refer to learning as a relatively permanent change in behaviour as a result of experience. Learning is a fundamental process in all animals and the higher up the evolutionary scale the animal, the more important is the ability to learn. All animals need to adapt their behaviour in order to fit in with the environment and to adapt to changing circumstances in order to survive.

Much of our behaviour consists of learned responses to simple signals. Can all behaviour be analysed in the same way? Some psychologists believe that behaviour is the sum of many simple stimulus–response connections. However there are other psychologists who think that stimulus–response is too simplistic and that even simple responses to stimuli require the processing of a vast amount of information.

CLASSICAL CONDITIONING

One of the best-known aspects of behavioural learning theory is classical conditioning. Discovered by Russian physiologist Ivan Pavlov, classical conditioning is a learning process that occurs through associations between an environmental stimulus and a naturally occurring stimulus.

It is important to know that classical conditioning involves placing a neutral signal before a naturally occurring reflex. In Pavlov's classic experiment with dogs, the neutral signal was the sound of a tone and the naturally occurring reflex was salivating in response to food. By associating the neutral stimulus with the environmental stimulus (the presentation of food), the sound of the tone alone could produce the salivation response.

INSTRUMENTAL CONDITIONING

Instrumental conditioning, also known as operant conditioning, is the process of reinforcing a behaviour by consistently giving positive or negative reinforcement — the goal being to increase the probability that the rewarded behaviour will occur more frequently. For example, if a child is always given a chocolate-chip cookie after cleaning his room (desired behaviour), it is likely that he will clean his room more frequently. In this case, the parent is using instrumental conditioning to teach the child to clean his room.

Operant conditioning was coined by behaviourist B.F. Skinner, which is why you may occasionally hear it referred to as Skinnerian conditioning. As a behaviourist, Skinner believed that internal thoughts and motivations could not be used to explain behaviour. Instead, he suggested, we should look only at the external, observable causes of human behaviour. Skinner used the term *operant* to refer to any "active behaviour that operates upon the environment to generate consequences" (1953: 461). In other words, Skinner's theory explained how we acquire the range of learned behaviours we exhibit each and every- day.

Memory: Meaning, Definition, Types and Processes

Memory is a property of the human mind: the ability to retain information. Memory is much studied by cognitive psychology and neuroscience. There are multiple types of classifications for memory based on duration, nature and retrieval of perceived items.

"The ability, process, or act of remembering or recalling; especially the ability to reproduce what has been learned or explained" *(American Psychiatric Glossary*, p. 126). The question, "what is a memory?" has become increasingly controversial in the last decade. As Post Traumatic Stress Disorder (PTSD) and dissociative disorder clients report delayed and dissociated memories of childhood trauma, the accuracy or validity of these memories has been questioned. At the present time there is no reliable scientific method to assess the self-report of traumatic events. While the presence of corroborating evidence (or witnesses) may support a survivor's memories, it does not in itself determine.

In more physiological or neurological terms, memory is, at its simplest, a set of encoded neural connections in the brain. It is the re-creation or reconstruction of past experiences by the synchronous firing of neurons that were involved in the original experience. As we will see, though, because of the way in which memory is encoded, it is perhaps better thought of as a kind of collage or jigsaw puzzle, rather than in the traditional manner as a collection of recordings or pictures or video clips, stored as discrete wholes. Our memories are not stored in our brains like books on library shelves, but are actually on-the-fly reconstructions from elements scattered throughout various areas of our brains.

Memory is related to but distinct from learning, which is the process by which we acquire knowledge of the world and modify our subsequent behaviour. During learning, neurons that fire together to produce a particular experience are altered so that they have a tendency to fire together again. For example, we learn a new language by studying it, but we then speak it by using our memory to retrieve the words that we have learned. Thus, memory depends on learning because it lets us store and retrieve learned information. But learning also depends to some extent on memory, in that the knowledge stored in our memory provides the framework to which new knowledge is linked by association and inference. This ability of humans to call on past memories in order to imagine the future and to plan future courses of action is a hugely advantageous attribute in our survival and development as a species.

There are some popular definitions of memory. One of them is — the faculty of the mind by which it retains the knowledge of previous thoughts, impressions, or events. In other way we can say memory is — the reach and positiveness with which a person can remember; the strength and trustworthiness of one's power to reach and represent or to recall the past; as, his memory was never wrong. Another definition of memory is — the actual and distinct retention and recognition of past ideas in the mind; remembrance; as, in memory of youth; memories of foreign lands. One of the definitions describes that the time within which past events can be or are remembered; as, within the memory of man. Another author says that something, or an aggregate of things, is remembered; hence, character, conduct, etc., as preserved in remembrance, history or tradition; posthumous fame; as, the war became only a memory.

Memory actually takes many different forms. We know that when we store a memory, we are storing information. But, what that information is and how long we retain it determines what type of memory it is. The biggest categories of memory are Short-Term Memory (STM) (or working memory) and Long-Term Memory (LTM), based on the amount of time the memory is stored. Both can weaken due to age or a variety of other reasons and clinical conditions that affect memory.

STM, sometimes referred to as "primary" or "active" memory, is that part of memory, which stores a limited amount of information for a limited amount of time (roughly 30-45 seconds). This can be contrasted to LTM, in which a seemingly unlimited amount of information is stored indefinitely. It can be described as the capacity (or capacities) for holding in mind, in an active, highly available state, a small amount of information.

LTM is our brain's system for storing, managing and retrieving information. There are many different forms of LTM. Explicit memory or declarative memory, is a type of LTM which requires conscious thought; what most people have in mind when they think of memory. Implicit memory is the other major form of LTM that does not require conscious thought. It allows you to do things by rote. Autobiographical memory is memory system for recalling life experiences, which involves both the episodic memory and the semantic memory.

PROCESS AND STAGES OF MEMORY

Memory is the ability to encode, store and recall information. The memory process consists of many parts, with certain focus placed on the three processes that are involved in human memory — encoding, storage and recall (retrieval). Additionally, the process of memory consolidation (which can be considered to be either part of the encoding process or the storage process) is treated here as a separate process in its own right.

The first is Sensory Information Storage (SIS). This is when your brain snaps a mental picture of what your senses are taking in. "The functioning of SIS may be observed if you close your eyes, then open and close them again as rapidly as possible. As your eyes close, notice how the visual image is maintained for a fraction of a second before fading", says Richards Heuer Jr. (1999) in his *Psychology of Intelligence Analysis,* p. 18. This image dissolves quickly and is only meant to provide your brain with a chance to process what it has just seen.

From SIS, information could move to STM. STM allows a person to retain handfuls of knowledge. Five to nine pieces of information can be stored indefinitely if they always remain at the forefront of a person's mind. Once another thought enters, something must be released to allow room for the new information. It can either be transferred to LTM or forgotten. The limit is on quantity, not time, and information can be retrieved almost instantly.

The storage potential for LTM is limitless, but that has its drawbacks. Stored facts suffer during transfer. Knowledge entering SIS, then moving to STM and finally to LTM can lose clarity and sharpness along the way. It is also lodged deep in the brain and, when called upon, may take a while to be retrieved. It takes substantial effort to convert information from STM to LTM.

Repetition is a way to solidify something into LTM. "Information from STM is stored in LTM by rehearsal. The repeated exposure to a stimulus or the rehearsal of a piece of information transfers it into LTM," says Harish Kotbagi (1997: 72), of the Georgia Institute of Technology. Repetition priming is a "form of memory that is accompanied by reductions in neural activity when an experience is repeated". More often you recall a specific piece of information, the less brain activity it eventually takes.

Emotion: Meaning, Nature, Types and Emotional Intelligence

The word emotion includes a wide range of observable behaviours, expressed feelings and changes in the body state. This diversity in intended meanings of the word emotion makes it hard to study. For many of us emotions are very personal states, difficult to define or to identify except in the most obvious instances. Moreover, many aspects of emotion seem unconscious to us. Even simple emotional states appear to be much more complicated than states as hunger and thirst.

Emotions are reactions that engage the mind and the body. Emotions are the result of a logical appraisal of the probability that a situation will effect a positive or negative change to our physical or psychological well-being. There are consequently positive and negative emotions, depending upon the predicated change.

Emotions have physical and psychological effects on our bodily systems. In general, positive emotions stimulate thought, flexibility and creativity, offering optimism, risk-taking and confidence. Negative emotions promote more rigidity of thoughts, increase muscular tension, and can promote a pessimistic outlook. To clarify the concept of emotions, three definitions of various aspects of emotions can be distinguished:

- Emotion is a *feeling* that is private and subjective. Humans can report an extraordinary range of states, which they can feel or experience. Some reports are accompanied by obvious signs of enjoyment or distress, but often these reports have no overt indicators. In many cases, the emotions we note in ourselves seem to be blends of different states.

- Emotion is a state of *psychological arousal,* an expression or display of distinctive somatic and autonomic responses. This emphasis suggests that emotional states can be defined by particular constellations of bodily responses. Specifically, these responses involve autonomously innervated visceral organs, like the heart or stomach. This second aspect of emotion allows us to examine emotions in both animals and human beings.
- Emotions are *actions* commonly "deemed", such as defending or attacking in response to a threat. This aspect of emotion is especially relevant to Darwin's point of view of the functional roles of emotion. He said that emotions had an important survival role because they generated actions to dangerous situations.

Some psychologists have tried to subdivide emotions in categories. For example, Wilhelm Wundt, the great nineteenth-century psychologist, offered the view that emotions consist of three basic dimensions, each one of a pair of opposite states: pleasantness/unpleasantness, tension/release and excitement/relaxation. However, this list has become more complex over time.

Psychologists suggest that there are eight basic emotions grouped in four pairs of opposites:

1. joy/sadness
2. acceptance/disgust
3. anger/fear
4. surprise/anticipation.

In Robert Plutchik's view, all emotions are a combination of these basic emotions. This hypothesis can be summarized in a three-dimensional cone with a vertical dimension reflecting emotional intensity.

EMOTIONAL INTELLIGENCE

Emotional Intelligence (EI) is the ability to recognize your emotions, understand what they're telling you and realize how your emotions affect people around you. EI also involves your perception of others: when you understand how they feel, this allows you to manage relationships more effectively. It refers to the ability to perceive, control and evaluate emotions. Some researchers suggest that EI can be learned and strengthened, while others claim it is an inborn characteristic.

Since 1990, Peter Salovey and John D. Mayer have been the leading researchers on EI. In their influential article "Emotional Intelligence" (1990: 185-211), they defined EI as, "the subset of social intelligence that involves the ability to monitor one's own and others' feelings and emotions, to discriminate among them and to use this information to guide one's thinking and actions".

Daniel Goleman, an American psychologist, developed a framework of five elements that define EI:

1. *Self-Awareness* — People with high EI are usually very self-aware. They understand their emotions, and because of this, they don't let their feelings rule them. They're confident — because they trust their intuition and don't let their emotions get out of control.

   They're also willing to take an honest look at themselves. They know their strengths and weaknesses, and they work on these areas so they can perform better. Many people believe that this self-awareness is the most important part of EI.

2. *Self-Regulation* — This is the ability to control emotions and impulses. People who self-regulate typically don't allow themselves to become too angry or jealous, and they don't make impulsive, careless decisions. They think before they act. Characteristics of self-regulation are thoughtfulness, comfort with change, integrity and the ability to say no.

3. *Motivation* — People with a high degree of EI are usually motivated. They're willing to defer immediate results for long-term success. They're highly productive, love a challenge and are very effective in whatever they do.

4. *Empathy* — This is perhaps the second-most important element of EI. Empathy is the ability to identify with and understand the wants, needs and viewpoints of those around you. People with empathy are good at recognizing the feelings of others, even when those feelings may not be obvious. As a result, empathetic people are usually excellent at managing relationships, listening and relating to others. They avoid

stereotyping and judging too quickly, and they live their lives in a very open, honest way.

5. *Social Skills* — It is usually easy to talk to and like people with good social skills, another sign of high EI. Those with strong social skills are typically team players. Rather than focus on their own success first, they help others develop and shine. They can manage disputes, are excellent communicators, and are masters at building and maintaining relationships.

Salovey and Mayer proposed a model that identified four different factors of EI: the perception of emotion; the ability to reason using emotions; the ability to understand emotion; and the ability to manage emotions.

1. *Perceiving Emotions*: The first step in understanding emotions is to accurately perceive them. In many cases, this might involve understanding non-verbal signals such as body language and facial expressions.
2. *Reasoning with Emotions*: The next step involves using emotions to promote thinking and cognitive activity. Emotions help prioritize what we pay attention and react to; we respond emotionally to things that garner our attention.
3. *Understanding Emotions*: The emotions that we perceive can carry a wide variety of meanings. If someone is expressing angry emotions, the observer must interpret the cause of their anger and what it might mean. For example, if your boss is acting angry, it might mean that he is dissatisfied with your work; or it could be because he got a speeding ticket on his way to work that morning or that he's been fighting with his wife.
4. *Managing Emotions*: The ability to manage emotions effectively is a key part of EI. Regulating emotions, responding appropriately and responding to the emotions of others are all important aspects of emotional management.

According to Salovey and Mayer, the four branches of their model are, arranged from more basic psychological processes to higher, more psychologically integrated processes. For example, the lowest level branch concerns the (relatively) simple abilities of perceiving and expressing emotion. In contrast, the highest level branch concerns the conscious, reflective regulation of emotion.

The ability to manage people and relationships is very important to all leaders, so developing and using your EI can be a good way to show others the leader you.

How to improve EI? The good news is that EI can be taught and developed. Many books and tests are available to help you determine your current EI and to identify where you may need to do some work. There are several yogic techniques to develop EI. Some of the practical guidelines which help developing EI are given below:

- *Observe how you react to people*: Do you rush to judgement before you know all of the facts? Do you stereotype? Look honestly at how you think and interact with other people. Try to put yourself in their place, and be more open and accepting of their perspectives and needs.
- *Look at your work environment*: Do you seek attention for your accomplishments? Humility can be a wonderful quality, and it does not mean that you are shy or lack self-confidence. When you practise humility, you say that you know what you did, and you can be quietly confident about it. Give others a chance to shine — put the focus on them, and don't worry too much about getting praise for yourself.
- *Do a self-evaluation*: What are your weaknesses? Are you willing to accept that you are not perfect and that you could work on some areas to make yourself a better person? Have the courage to look at yourself honestly — it can change your life.
- *Examine how your actions will affect others — before you take those actions*: If your decision will affect others, put yourself in their place. How will they feel if you do this? Would you want that experience? If you must take the action, how can you help others deal with the effects?
- *Examine how you react to stressful situations*: Do you become upset every time there is a delay or something does not happen the way you want? Do you blame others or become angry at them, even when it is not their fault? The ability to stay calm and in control in difficult situations is highly valued — in the business

world and outside it. Keep your emotions under control when things go wrong.

- *Take responsibility for your actions*: If you hurt someone's feelings, apologize directly — do not ignore what you did or avoid the person. People are usually more willing to forgive and forget if you make an honest attempt to make things right.

Personality: Meaning, Definition and Dimensions

Personality is a set of qualities that make a person (or thing) distinct from another. An assumed role or manner of behaviour; qualities that make a person stand out from the crowd — the complex of all the attributes — behavioural, temperamental, emotional and mental — that characterize a unique individual.

CONCEPT OF PERSONALITY

Personality can be defined as a dynamic and organized set of characteristics possessed by a person that uniquely influences his or her cognitions, motivations and behaviours in different situations. The word "personality" originates from the Latin *persona,* which means mask. Significantly, in the theatre of the ancient Latin-speaking world, the mask was not used as a plot device to *disguise* the identity of a character, but rather was a convention employed to represent or *typify* that character.

Personality can be divided into three types: Type A, Type B and Type AB. Type A individuals can be described as impatient, time-conscious, controlling, concerned about their status, highly competitive, ambitious, business-like, aggressive, having difficulty relaxing; and are sometimes disliked by individuals with Type B personalities for the way that they are always rushing. They are often high-achieving workaholics who multi-task, drive themselves with deadlines and are unhappy about delays. Because of these characteristics, Type A individuals are often described as "stress junkies".

Type B individuals, in contrast, are described as patient, relaxed and easy-going, generally lacking an overriding sense of urgency. This can also be described as lazy and lacking ambition. People who live in their mother's basements are an example. Because of these characteristics, Type B individuals are often described by Type As as apathetic and disengaged. There is also a Type AB mixed profile for people who cannot be clearly categorized.

MEANING OF PERSONALITY

Personality is a patterned body of habits, traits, attitudes and ideas of an individual as these are organized externally into roles and statuses and as they relate internally to motivation, goals and various aspects of selfhood.

According to Robert Park and Ernest Burgess (1921: 11), "personality is the sum and organization of those traits which determine the role of the individual in the group".

According to Ralph Linton (1936: 201-03), "personality embraces the total organized aggregate of psychological processes and status pertaining to the individual". "Personality," says R.M. MacIver (1915: 48) "is all that an individual is and has experienced so far as this all can be comprehended as unity." According to Gary Lundberg (1999: 301), the term personality refers to the habits, attitudes and other social traits that are characteristic of a given individual's behaviour.

By personality William F. Ogburn (1964: 347) means the integration of the socio-psychological behaviour of the human being, represented by habits of action and feeling, attitudes and opinions.

K. Davis (1989:) regards personality a psychic phenomenon which is neither organic nor social but an emergent from a combination of the two. According to Yinger J. Milton (1965: 141), "personality is the totality of behaviour of an individual with a given tendency system interacting with a sequence of situations".

DEFINITIONS OF PERSONALITY

It can be said that there is one central definition of *personality* in use today (and historically) within our discipline. Although it is worded differently by various psychologists, its central idea remains: personality is a system of parts that is organized, developed and expressed in a person's actions. The system of parts includes such components as motives, emotions, mental models and the self. We have some more definitions of personality:

> Personality refers to an individual's characteristic patterns of thought, emotion, and behaviour, together with the

> psychological mechanisms — hidden or not — behind those patterns.
> — Funder 2004

> Personality is the set of psychological traits and mechanisms within the individual that are organized and relatively enduring and that influence his or her interactions with, and adaptations to, the intrapsychic, physical, and social environments.
> — Larsen and Buss 2005

> Personality psychology is the *scientific study of the whole person* . . . psychology is about many things:
>
> Perception and attention, cognition and memory, neurons and brain circuitry. . . . We try to understand the individual human being as a complex whole . . . [and] to construct a scientifically credible account of human individuality.
> — McAdams 2006

> Personality is the organized, developing system within the individual that represents the collective action of that individual's major psychological sub-systems.
> — John D. Mayer 2007: 1-4

> Personality refers to those characteristics of the person that account for consistent patterns of feelings, thinking, and behaving.
> — Pervin et al. 2005: 513

DIMENSIONS OF PERSONALITY

The composition of human personality is the subject of innumerable theories. Each focuses on one or several particular aspects or dimensions of personality, but none appears to consider it in its full scope, depth and integrity. Some theories focus more on differences in type, others on the relative development of specific characteristics and competencies and still others on the dynamics of interaction between several psychological constructs such as Freud's ego, super ego and identity.

A typological approach to categorize personalities fails to take into account wide variations in intensity that would adequately distinguish a Napoleon from a dominant local leader. Behavioural descriptions do not adequately distinguish between external expressions of personality and inner motivation. In an effort towards scientific objectivity and impartiality, most theories omit assigning values to differences in personal orientation to other people and the world around, yet the distinction between a good, kind, generous person who relates positively to everyone and one who is jealous, mean or evil-motive cannot be merely dismissed as a difference in type.

Personality researchers have proposed that there are five basic dimensions of personality.

Today, many contemporary personality psychologists believe that there are five basic dimensions of personality, often referred to as the "big five" personality traits. Previous trait theorist had suggested a various number of possible traits, including Gordon Allport's list of 4,000 personality traits, Raymond Cattell's sixteen personality factors and Hans Eysenck's three-factor theory.

However, many researchers felt that Cattell's theory was too complex and Eysenck's was too limited in scope. As a result, the five-factor theory emerged to describe the basic traits that serve as the building blocks of personality.

Today, many researchers believe that there are five core personality traits. Evidence of this theory has been growing over the past fifty years, beginning with the research of D.W. Fiske (1949) and later expanded upon by other researchers including Norman (1967), Smith (1967), Goldberg (1981), and McCrae and Costa (1987).

The "big five" are broad categories of personality traits. While there is a significant body of literature supporting this five-factor model of personality, researchers do not always agree on the exact labels for each dimension. However, these five categories are usually described as follows:

1. *Extraversion*: This trait includes characteristics such as excitability, sociability, talkativeness, assertiveness and high amounts of emotional expressiveness.
2. *Agreeableness*: This personality dimension includes attributes such as trust, altruism, kindness, affection and other prosocial behaviours.
3. *Conscientiousness*: Common features of this dimension include high levels of thoughtfulness, with good impulse control and goal-directed behaviours. Those high in conscientiousness tend to be organized and mindful of details.

4. *Neuroticism*: Individuals high in this trait tend to experience emotional instability, anxiety, moodiness, irritability and sadness.
5. *Openness*: This trait features characteristics such as imagination and insight, and those high in this trait also tend to have a broad range of interests.

It is important to note that each of the five personality factors represents a range between two extremes. For example, extraversion represents a continuum between extreme extroversion and extreme introversion. In the real world, most people lie somewhere in between the two polar ends of each dimension.

3

Yogic Concept and Psychology

Concept of Yogic Psychology

THE philosophy of yoga and the psychology of yoga are present not only as a background to the science of yoga, but also as the basis for the practice of the yogic processes. Its subject matter, principles and techniques are a matter of the ancient glory of the Indian society. Yoga is referred to in the *Ṛgveda* and particularly in the *Atharvaveda* where there is an elaborate discussion on the individual's psyche and well-being. However, the most systematic presentation of yoga was made by Patañjali in his *Yoga-Sūtras* which, although a matter of disagreement, may go back as far as twenty-two centuries ago.

The principles and methods of yoga described in the ancient Indian scriptures remained neglected for a long time because they were written in different Sanskrit *śloka*s, and also because they were considered to be religious, philosophical and mystic. However, from the beginning of the twentieth century, good translations and commentaries of the yogic literature were made available by Indian seers and scholars in different modern languages. The medical scientists and therapists of other fields, including psychology, began verifying yogic principles and using its techniques for promoting health and human adjustment. The practices of yoga, particularly *rāja-yoga* and *haṭha-yoga*, have withstood scientific tests and they have been found useful in curing many of the so-called incurable diseases.

However, the world of science has to acknowledge and appreciate that yoga is basically a science of mind. Even certain steps of *rāja-yoga* such as *āsana* and *prāṇāyāma* are not just physical and physiological exercises. The eight steps of *rāja-yoga* present a balanced combination of the physiological yoga of vitality with the psychic yoga of meditation, and the real experience starts from the practice of *pratyāhāra*. Yoga has been rightly defined by Swami Satyananda

Saraswati (1980: 36) as "a complete science of consciousness. It provides mastery over all stages of consciousness." So, most of the yogic *sādhanās* aim to tune and control the mind. Other yoga practices and steps are a preparation for the same.

Thus yoga has a close link with psychology. We know that earlier modern psychology was also defined as the study of the soul or mind which was later on spelled out in operational terms like conscious experience, behaviour and human adjustment. Yoga psychology presents a synthesis of the two disciplines of yoga and psychology. Precisely speaking, it deals with yogic concepts, principles and techniques of psychological relevance. They need re-examination in the light of available findings and models. It is amazing to note that many of the concepts which were brought to light in psychology in the twentieth century were well-conceived and explained in the ancient literature of yoga psychology. In certain cases modern psychology has yet to match the progress made in the field of yoga psychology.

Yoga psychology is understood as a study of the human mind through the perspective of yoga. While the separate discipline of yoga psychology was formulated only under a modern context, the concept of psychology within the practice of yoga has existed from the beginning of yoga philosophy. Even the word *yoga* itself contains the basic guidelines for the practice of psychology from the perspective of yoga; one of the common translations of yoga is union. This union refers to the unification of the mind, body and spirit. It can also be considered a union between the lower and the higher, omnipotent states of consciousness.

Yoga psychology was created out of the growing need to implement Eastern philosophies of human welfare and health care into a modern medical environment, one which demands systematic and methodological approaches to treatments and cures of disorders and dysfunctions occurring within the mind and body. Psychology is predominantly a practice designed to help treat the mind, as the word itself implies a study of the psyche or soul.

While yoga psychology maintains some of the beliefs and ideologies encompassing the Western philosophy of the human brain, mind and functions of thought, there are many components to yoga psychology which delineate the general trends of modern-day clinical psychology. Although some alternative therapies parallel the theory, yoga psychology strongly maintains the belief that the mind, body and soul are dependently interlinked and ultimately exist as an inseparable entity. In yoga psychology it is believed that treating the mind, body or spirit independently can lead to the health of the other systems as well. However improper treatment of any of the systems can lead to disorders in the other two. For instance, using medication to treat the chemical imbalances within the brain may restore normal chemical functions for that specific system but will ultimately retract the proper functions of another. It will also influence the body's natural production of the chemical, thereby making the patient dependent upon the medication. Although some may argue that there are many medications which are considered to be physiologically addictive, they may still possess strong psychological addictive qualities.

Although yoga psychology does not seek to eliminate the use of medication, practices like Āyurveda and Siddha medicine can be used in conjunction with a treatment, it does pursue an approach to mental, physical and spiritual health care that is self-sustaining and sympathetic to all the systems within the body. Provide proper treatment to one of the bodies (i.e. mental body, physical body, spiritual body, etc.) and the others will follow suit. Create imbalance within one of the systems, and the others are likely to fail as well. This is true because all functions are interdependent. A depressed mind leads to depressed organ functions, leading to common disorders like constipation, poor circulatory function, and improper distribution of chemicals like dopamine, cretonne and hormones. Likewise, yoga says that constipation in the stomach leads to constipation in the mind; and so both the body can influence the mind just as much as the mind can influence the body.

Perhaps one of the most interesting features of yoga psychology that has only recently come into the perspective of Western psychology is the plasticity of the mind. In Western psychology they have created the term neuroplasticity which refers to the flexibility of the brain to change its functions over time. For instance, a specific region of the brain may house a different function today than it did ten years ago, and is so "plastic" the auditory cortex can become the optical. In yoga psychology a belief has been maintained for thousands of years that we become what we think. We have the ability to not only increase our IQ or develop a sharp sense of hearing but we can actually raise our consciousness from a lower state of awareness, one dependent upon independence or ego, and into a state of omnipotent consciousness, free of all boundaries and limitations. While this concept reaches beyond the boundaries of neuroplasticity, it suggests opportunities of the human mind that Western psychology is yet to explore.

The application of yoga psychology is gradually working its way into the everyday science of human health care and medicine, and may one day reveal some of the hidden secrets of the human mind, body and spirit. Although limited research has been conducted on the practice of yoga psychology, there are studies being conducted in many fields that are gradually revealing the potential of yoga psychology, such as those being done on the practice of meditation, breathing techniques and modifications of thinking patterns.

In order to understand the scientific foundation of yoga psychology, it would be proper to discuss its relevance for modern men, women and society. I would like to discuss this under two broad headings.

YOGA PSYCHOLOGY AS A BASIC SCIENCE

Yoga psychology is both a positive and a normative science. As such it not only analyses human personality and its growth, but sets normative ideals and prescribes techniques to achieve such objectives. Expansion of consciousness and making oneself the master of his mind are the broad objectives of yoga psychology.

The topographical aspect of mind as described by Freud, towards the end of the nineteenth century, in terms of conscious, subconscious and unconscious levels, was well-conceived in yogic literature thousands of years ago. It also emphasized that the vast area of our mind was unknown and dormant, which was called the level of *nidrā* or *suṣupti* (deep sleep). Going a step ahead, yoga accepts the fourth level — *turīya*, i.e. transcended consciousness or the superconscious mind. When the mind reaches such a height of *sādhanā*, cognitions do not remain dependent upon the senses, the individuality is transcended, and the mind acquires equanimity. This is called awakening of the superconscious mind.

The psychodynamic aspect of the mind has been described in terms of the identity (id), ego and superego. Psychoanalysis emphasizes that in order to live a normal life, an optimum strength of ego is a must to counterbalance the forces of the id, ego and superego. It underlines that too strong an id makes a person impulsive and sociopathic, and that too strong a superego makes him mentally ill. But what happens when the ego becomes very strong and dominant? According to yoga psychology, in such a condition the individual becomes egoistic and develops *ahaṁkāra* (pride) which is the root cause of all psychosomatic problems.

This brings to the forefront the concept of the evolution of the mind as conceived in yoga psychology. Consciousness has a wider connotation in yoga. It may be sensorial, intellectual or psychic. Sensorial consciousness is based on sense experiences, whereas the intellectual consciousness is based on cues and their interpretation through the intellect. On the other hand, the psychic consciousness refers to the extrasensorial awareness and parapsychological experiences. Yoga presents vivid and sound meditation procedures for the attainment of this psychic consciousness or superconscious mind through the awakening of *kuṇḍalinī*. The awakening of *kuṇḍalinī* takes place through gradual activation of the seven *cakra*s (psychic centres). They are *mūlādhāra, svādhiṣṭhāna, maṇipūra, anāhata, viśuddhi, ājñā* and *sahasrāra*. The literature prescribes the conditions, precautions and methods of *sādhanā* for stimulating the *cakra*s and awakening the *kuṇḍalinī*. Awakening of the 90 per cent dormant mind and union of the *kuṇḍalinī śakti* awakened in *mūlādhāra* with the pure consciousness of *sahasrāra* is called self-realization. This evolution of mind through yogic *sādhanā* is a gradual process. It brings balance and harmony in the personality and makes the life blissful.

It is only recently that there has been a global interest in the quality of human life and psychological well-being. Psychological well-being has been conceived by the psychologists in terms of happiness and satisfaction or gratification subjectively experienced by the individuals (Okun and Stock 1984). This affective reaction of satisfaction need not be positively related to the objective conditions of life. One may be dissatisfied with life in spite of having plenty of material and family richness (Lawton 1983). The psychological or subjective well-being is more a question of our own attitude and approach to life situations and events. Freedman (1978: 23) has shown that cognitive processes such as aspiration, social comparison and adaptation level have much to do with it.

Long ago yoga psychology emphasized the role of positive cognition, thinking and approach for achieving pleasure and satisfaction in life. Yogic practices reduce negative thinking and negative emotion. *Bhakti-yoga* and *Īśvarapraṇidhāna* of *rāja-yoga* provide the useful techniques of dedication to God and offering prayers with a feeling to help build positive attitudes and self-confidence. The practices of *śiva bhāvanā* and *maitrī bhāvanā* as described in *Yoga-Vāsiṣṭha* are good techniques for combating stress, anxiety, apprehension and hostility. Their psychotherapeutic significance has been established by a number of studies conducted earlier in Kāśī Manovijñānaśālā at Varanasi. The modern cognitive approach to life was well understood in yoga psychology. In the second *śloka* of his *Yoga-Sūtras*, Patañjali defined yoga as control of the *cittavṛtti*s (modifications of mind). He mentioned the following five *vṛtti*s (cognitive modifications) of mind. They are:

(i) *Pramāṇa* — proof or valid cognition,

(ii) *Viparyaya* — illusion or invalid cognition,

(iii) *Vikalpa* — objectless verbal cognition,

(iv) *Nidrā* — sleep or absence of all distinct cognitions, and

(v) *Smṛti* — memory or recollection of past cognitions.

These *vṛtti*s, when related to narrow worldly gains and losses, become sources of affliction or pain and are called *kliṣṭa vṛtti*s. But they can be transformed into *akliṣṭa vṛtti*s by making them positively and spiritually oriented. Patañjali has mentioned two broad methods of controlling the *vṛtti*s. They are (i) *abhyāsa* (practice) of meditation and other yogic practices, and (ii) *vairāgya* (detachment).

The cognitive mental modifications of *kliṣṭa* nature lead to pain and misery. Yoga psychology has enumerated five such basic distresses known as *pañca kleśa*s. They are (i) *avidyā* (ignorance or nescience), (ii) *asmitā* (egoism), (iii) *rāga* (attachment), (iv) *dveṣa* (hatred), and (v) *abhiniveśa* (fear of death). Patañjali has given an elaborate description of these *kleśa*s and has underlined that *avidyā* or false notion lies at the root of all other distresses. *Avidyā* does not mean absence of knowledge, rather it means looking for wrong actions and ideas, which ultimately give pain.

These *kleśa*s give rise to various psychological and psychosomatic problems. Yoga psychology explains them and their management on the basis of the attachment–detachment model of mental health. *Āsakti* (attachment) and *vairāgya* (detachment) are the two extreme points on the same scale of a continuum with *anāsakti* (non-attachment) being in between the two. *Āsakti* means attachment with worldly affairs and things. Literally, it means narrowing the area of consciousness. This leads to *rāga, dveṣa* and *ahaṁkāra* which manifest as insecurity, possessiveness, aggression, anxiety, depression and other mental and psychosomatic problems. *Vairāgya* is the height of the *nivṛtti* way of life which is too difficult to be achieved by normal householders. It is the ideal mode of life set by the saints and *ṛṣi*s. Yoga psychology prescribes *anāsakti* as the middle path to enjoy lasting happiness and peace without being involved and disturbed by *āsakti*. An elaborate description of the *āsakti–anāsakti* model of mental health has been presented by Bhushan (1994).

As regards methods of study, looking within is the primary method of understanding yogic experiences. This is different from the ordinary method of introspection used in psychology. Visualization, awareness and witnessing the images in a neutral manner with *draṣṭa bhāva* are the keys of yogic meditation and *sādhanā*.

The principle of homeostasis or balance is central in yoga psychology. It holds that any sort of imbalance in the physical, psychological or prāṇic system creates problems and disorders and the cure lies in rebalancing it. Another scientifically sound concept is acceptance of individual differences. Yoga psychology presents a clear description of different types of human personality and prescribes different yogic practices for them. The most important one is based on the three *guṇa*s of *sattva, rajas* and *tamas*. These *guṇa*s are largely acquired and so through them a desired transformation in attitude and personality is possible by yogic practices.

YOGA PSYCHOLOGY AS AN APPLIED SCIENCE

The relevance of an academic discipline lies in its utility and application in finding solutions to the problems facing the individual and society. From this viewpoint, yoga psychology has special significance. Some of the issues and areas in which it has important applications are mentioned below.

Promoting Health

Yoga believes in total health. But it does hold that health has three integrated aspects, i.e. physical, psychological and spiritual. We cannot think of good health by taking care of one aspect and ignoring the other ones. The fact is that if we ignore the mental or the spiritual aspects, we cannot remain healthy physically. Each aspect of health influences the other. Total good health means physical fitness, mental ability and spiritual verve.

Yoga stands for both physical and mental well-being and higher spiritual attainments. Thus it presents a wider spectrum than the modern viewpoint of psychosomatics. Good illustrative books are now available which discuss in detail the possible effects of yogic *āsana*s, *prāṇāyāma*s, *pratyāhāra* and meditation techniques on the body, mind and expansion of consciousness. Tracing the link between yoga and oriental medicine has concluded that yoga is based on the holistic knowledge of different aspects of a person's being.

A good number of studies have established the beneficial effects of meditation and other yogic practices in managing anxiety (Jangid et al. 1988: 77-79; Sharma and Agnihotri 1982), depression and other types of neurotic disorders (Nagarathna and Nagendra 1980: 3). They have been found equally useful in treating stress-related psychosomatic disorders like diabetes (Divekar 1982), tension headache (Sethi et al. 1981), hypertension and schemic heart (Swami Karmananda Saraswati 1982; Ornish 1990: 15). Studies have been conducted to examine the effects of yogic practices on neural functioning, including the ANS and brain waves (Ramamurthi 1977: 16-17; Varma 1979). However, more well-designed experimental research is needed to examine the physiological basis of the different yogic techniques. Similarly, the psychotherapeutic use and rationale for the effects of specific *āsana*s, *prāṇāyāma*s and meditation techniques, like *antara-mauna, ajapa jāpa, cidākāśa dhāraṇā*, etc. need to be confirmed through planned experimental studies. There is also the need to review and integrate the findings of research conducted at a large number of centres in different places.

According to yogic theory, diseases develop because of imbalance in the psychosomatic and prāṇic systems. The yogic practices restore the balance and remove the toxins from the *nāḍīs* and the body systems. The same practices help build a defence against disease and promote healthy living. The practice of *haṭha-yoga* has special cleansing and balancing effects on body and mind.

Developing Positive Attitudes and Feelings

Everyone wants to be happy and to enjoy life, but because of our faulty approach and negative feelings we often carry fear, apprehension and suffer agony in life. Verma (1988) has proposed a dual-factor theory of mental health according to which the factors or conditions contributing to positive and negative mental health are different. As such, the absence of certain factors contributing to negative set and health does not lead to positive mental health. Yogic practices help one develop psychological well-being by providing the insight to perceive positive aspects in individuals and events, thereby developing positive effects, pleasure and satisfaction. Understanding and practising the principles of *karma- yoga* reduce the magnitude of expectation and consequential frustration.

Improving Concentration, Abilities and Skills

Most of our problems in life are on account of cortical excitations, and the flickering and fluctuating nature of the mind. Selected yogic practices enhance the mental alertness, creative ability and learning capacity of individuals (Swami Muktananda Saraswati 1982). This has received support from the recent findings of a research report undertaken on young scientists by Shelvamurthy (1996). The results indicate that, compared to the control group, the experimental group of young scientists who were given yoga practices performed better in concentration, memory, cognitive management of situations, stress management, coping with hot and cold conditions, etc. Such findings provide a basis for the introduction of yogic practices in different training programmes. The initiative taken by the central government and many state governments to introduce yogic training for school students is in the right direction.

Promoting a Congenial Organizational Climate and Work Proficiency

Recent experience of introducing yogic practices in management programmes shows that it may serve as a good relief in reducing organizational stress and in promoting a congenial work climate. The practice of *yoga-nidrā*, certain selected *āsanas*, *prāṇāyāmas* and meditations are useful to relax and quieten the mind (Bhole 1981; Datey 1978; Singh et al. 1978: 63-65). They can be conveniently introduced in an organizational set-up to promote alertness, congenial feelings, job satisfaction and work proficiency.

Combating Social Problems

Certain studies like that of Kaul (1993: 92) have shown that selected yogic practices are beneficial in managing drug addiction and alcoholism. Similarly, violence, group conflicts and prejudices prevail in society mostly on account of ego problems and emotional instability. As stated earlier, since the yogic practices are capable of reducing aggression and negative feelings, and are helpful in quietening the mind, they serve as important tools to combat many problems. The experience of conducting yoga programmes in jails provides convincing data on positive transformations in feelings, attitudes and expectations of the convicts in the jails and improvement in their interpersonal relationships. The principles of yoga psychology can, therefore, be used as corrective measures for promoting desirable social behaviour and minimizing many social problems based on distrust and hatred. The yogic literature says that a predominance of *tamas*, which often creates social problems, is minimized and transformed into *rajas* or *sattva* dominance by yogic practices. This theoretical assertion needs more experimental verification and proper application.

Promoting the Self

Yoga is not only a curative and preventive measure for diseases and social maladies, but also a promotive science of the human personality. The practice of meditational techniques brings a qualitative change in human personality and they are capable of taking the self to a higher level. Expansion of consciousness, development of extrasensorial capabilities and *samabhāva*, coupled with feelings of non-attachment are some of the characteristic features of a realized person. The self at this level of psychic development is called *sarveśvara*. This is a blissful life in which individuality is transcended and the mind acquires complete equanimity.

In short, yoga psychology has important applications in managing psychological, psychosomatic and social problems as well as in promoting and transcending the self. It provides theoretical models, and practical tools and techniques for their verification. However, many of the observational and theoretical assertions need experimental verification and re-interpretation in a changed context. Selection of yogic techniques for different purposes and individuals is a difficult task. It demands a long-term, detailed plan by devoted individuals and institutions. The co-operation of all those psychologists having an interest in the area is solicited.

Seven Psychic Centres in Human Body

Indian *yogī*s and mystics identified seven subtle psychic centres in our subtle body. What is this subtle body? An alternate human physiological system. It is called "subtle" because it exists on a different plane than gross matter, but it has certain correspondences with the anatomy of the material body. Different parts of the subtle body contain the microcosmic forms of the deities Śiva and Śakti, the bipolar forces believed to be the powers behind the cosmos. The subtle body is thus based on the principle of the homology of macrocosm and microcosm, of the Upaniṣads.

The Sanskrit texts describing the subtle body assume that there are different planes of reality, and thus that the subtle body actually exists, but given the network of symbols associated with it, one need not accept its literal reality for it to be religiously meaningful.

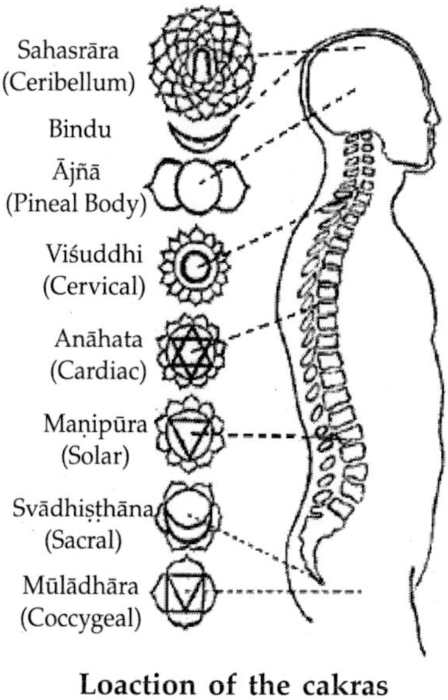

Loaction of the cakras

The subtle body is visualized as a set of seven psychic centres (*cakra*s), running roughly along the course of the spine: the *mūlādhāra cakra* at the base of the spine, the *svādhiṣṭhāna cakra* in the genital region, the *maṇipūra cakra* in the navel region, the *anāhata cakra* in the heart region, the *viśuddhi cakra* in the throat region, and the *ājñā cakra* in the forehead between the eyebrows. Associated with each of these *cakra*s is an elaborate symbolic system: all six *cakra*s can be seen as symbols for a human physiological capacity; the first five *cakra*s are associated with one of the subtle elements (and the sixth with thought), and the lotus petals on each *cakra* each contain a letter of the Sanskrit alphabet, thus encompassing all sacred sounds. Some models of the subtle body are even more developed, with each *cakra* associated with a certain colour and a certain presiding deity.

Cakra has always been a quite interesting topic for scientists, naturopaths and *yogīs*. The existence of *cakra* system in human body is also being recognized in the medical world as the new medical healing techniques like "radical healing" are coming up which involves the eradication of the disease with the help of aligning your *cakras*. According to ancient scriptures there are many energy centres in a human body out of which seven are main which are located in the spinal cord. Amazing powers devolve on a human on activation of the *kuṇḍalinī* and each *cakra* is related to the following attainments.

The first one is ***mūlādhāra*** situated in the basal region of the vertebral column at the mid-spot between anus and penis, this *cakra* forms our foundation. It represents the element earth, and is therefore related to our survival instincts, and to our sense of grounding and connection to our bodies and the physical plane. Ideally, this *cakra* brings us health, prosperity, security and dynamic presence.

In meditation, this *cakra* is visualized as a red lotus possessing four petals. This is the resting place of the *kuṇḍalinī śakti*, which lies here as a snake having three-and-half coil. This *cakra* is the symbol of earth element. Activation of this results in riddance from tensions, true happiness, beauty, perfect health and physical strength, magnetic personality.

The second *cakra* is ***svādhiṣṭhāna***. This *cakra* is located in the vertebral column just opposite to the pineal region. It is related to the water element, and to emotions and sexuality. It connects us to others through feeling, desire, sensation and movement. Ideally, this *cakra* brings us fluidity and grace, depth of feeling, sexual fulfilment and the ability to accept change.

In meditation, this *cakra* is visualized as a vermilion-coloured lotus having six petals. This semi-lunar *cakra* is the symbol of water element. Activation of this results in freedom from stomach ailments, increase in sex power, and cure of sexual debility, increase in courage and fearlessness and magnetism.

The third *cakra* is ***maṇipūra*** and the relative position of this *cakra* inside the vertebral column is just opposite to the navel region. This *cakra* is known as the power *cakra*, located in the solar plexus. It rules our personal power, will and autonomy, as well as our metabolism. When healthy, this *cakra* brings us energy, effectiveness, spontaneity and non-dominating power. Inside the vertebral column, this *cakra* is situated just opposite to the naval region. This ten-petalled lotus is of blue colour. The *yantra* of this *cakra* is triangular in shape and it represents the fire element.

Activation of this results in perfect digestion, riddance from ailments like kidney stones, diabetes and liver problems. Successes in amazing *sādhanā*s like flying in the air, walking on water, telepathic contact with animals and plants and perfection in *prāṇāyāma* are some ostensible effects, and the highest achievement is success in meditation.

The fourth *cakra* is ***anāhata*** and it is the middle one among seven. The relative position of this *cakra* inside the vertebral column is just opposite to the cardiac region. It is related to love and is the integrator of opposites in the psyche: mind and body, male and female, persona and shadow, ego and unity. A healthy fourth *cakra* allows us to love deeply, feel compassion, have a deep sense of peace and centredness. This red-coloured lotus possesses twelve petals and it represents the air element. Activation of this *cakra* illuminates the entire body and the entire vertebral column starts vibrating.

Activation of this results in peace of mind, boundless divine joy, total freedom from tensions, power to look into future, power of hypnosis, entering into *samādhi* (divine trance), riddance from problems related to heart, increase in soft emotions like love, affection and kindness.

The fifth *cakra* is ***viśuddhi***, inside the vertebral column this *cakra* is located opposite the throat region. This is the *cakra* located in the throat and is thus related to communication and creativity. Here we experience the world symbolically through vibration, such as the vibration of sound representing language. This lotus of smoky colour possesses sixteen petals and it represents the sky element.

Activation of this results in riddance from all ailments related to throat, thyroid, etc. increase in knowledge, gain of power of eloquence, deeper *samādhi*, perfection in the art of hypnotism, gain of power to die when one wills, total material success like comforts, wealth and fame.

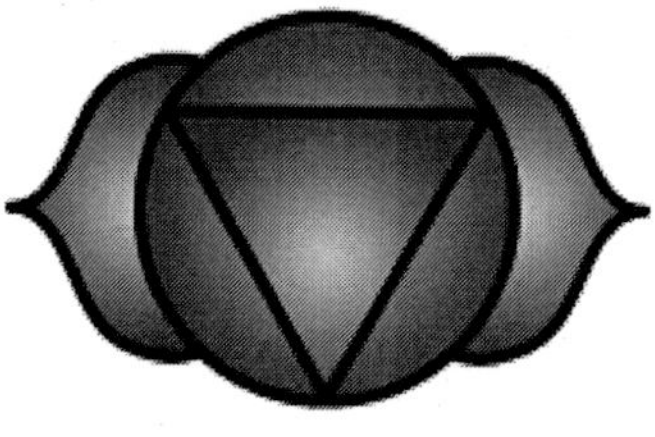

The sixth *cakra* is ***ājñā***. In *brahma-nāḍī* (enclosed by vertebral column) this *cakra* is located just opposite the mid-spot between the two eyebrows. This *cakra* is known as the brow *cakra* or third eye centre. It is related to the act of seeing, both physically and intuitively. As such it opens our psychic faculties and our understanding of archetypal levels. When healthy it allows us to see clearly, in effect, letting us "see the big picture". This white lotus has only two petals. Also called the Third Eye its activation brings wondrous powers like clairvoyance, telepathy, power of giving curses or blessings, instant fulfilment of anything one wishes, and gain of knowledge related to all subjects and sciences, power to control thoughts of others and interfere even in nature.

The seventh and topmost *cakra* is ***sahasrāra*** which is also termed as *daśama dvāra* of *brahmarandhra*. This is the crown *cakra* that relates to consciousness as pure awareness. It is our connection to the greater world beyond, to a timeless, spaceless place of all-knowing. When developed, this *cakra* brings us knowledge, wisdom, understanding, spiritual connection and bliss. Beyond the six *cakra*s, at the upper termination of the spinal cord, is the thousand-petalled lotus; the abode of Lord Śiva (Supreme Being). When the *kuṇḍalinī śakti* unites itself with the Supreme Being, the aspirant gets engrossed in deep meditation during which he perceives infinite bliss.

This is a subtle centre in the brain. On activation of *sahasrāra* a very fine, elixir-like secretion is produced from it which permeates the whole body thus making the human forever free of all ailments. This *cakra* is situated two inches deep inside both the temporal region and three inches deep from the mid-spot between the eyebrows that is in the middle portion of cerebral hemispheres. From the throat, it is located three inches above the palate and inside the brain it is located in a small hole above the *mahā vīvara,* foramen of cerebrum.

Awakening of *sahasrāra* renders the aspirant liberated from corporeal bondages and attachments. He is endowed with all kinds of divine attainments including *aṣṭa siddhi* and *nava nidhi*. He becomes an omniscient *yogī*. Being emancipated from the cycles of birth and death, he certainly achieves the final beatitude. One is fully enlightened and can then envision any event going on anywhere in the universe without entering into *samādhi*. All natural elements come under one's control.

Five Sheaths of Human Body

The yogic body goes beyond the physical and extends into more subtle layers of energy. Yoga says that each person has five distinct energy bodies (*koṣa*s), vibrating at different speeds. These interacting and overlapping layers of energy form the complete spiritual, mental and physical nature of the human personality.

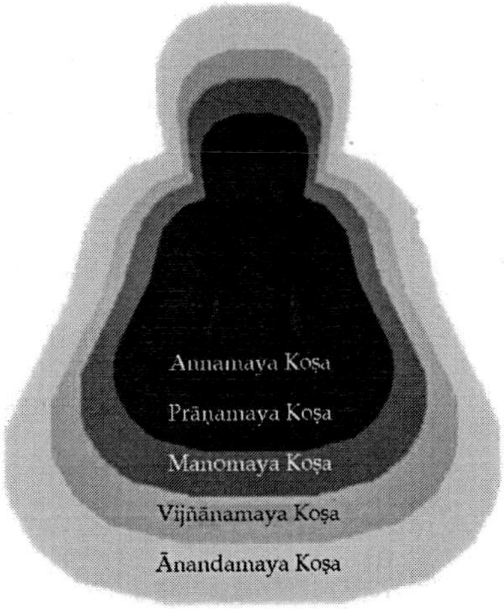

Koṣa is a Sanskrit word meaning sheath, moving from the gross physical body to the subtle spiritual body. Each *koṣa* signifies a more refined dimension of consciousness. The *koṣa*s are known as *annamaya, prāṇamaya, manomaya, vijñānamaya*

and *ānandamaya*. *Maya* means "composed of", so these sheaths are composed of food, energy, intellect, intuition and bliss.

The first two sheaths equate to the physical body. *Annamaya koṣa* is the actual physical body, that part dependent on *anna* (grain or gross food) for nourishment. *Prāṇamaya koṣa* is composed of *prāṇa* (the vital life energy) which organizes the body parts and provides movement for mental and physical expression.

What we can loosely term "the mind" exists in two parts. *Manomaya koṣa* is the dimension of the lower mind, incorporating intellect, reason, concept and memory. *Vijñānamaya koṣa* is a more subtle area of higher knowledge and intuitive awareness. The most subtle body is *ānandamaya koṣa*. It is essentially a body of pure light in the realm of spiritual bliss, beyond the reach of language.

A deeper understanding of the *koṣa*s of interacting consciousness reveals the interconnecting worlds in which body, mind and spirit exist. It reveals that the constant interplay of manifest and unmanifest consciousness is fuelled by very subtle, but potent forms of energy. This life process involves natural stress and fluctuation.

Purification of these energy bodies is the means of experiencing them. This is best approached through an understanding of the energy networks which bind and connect them. We can then utilize yoga in its purest sense, and go deeper into the regions of harmony and balance.

Annamaya koṣa is the material part of creation, regardless of whether it is a stone, a plant or a human being, which all exist in different degrees of consciousness. This *koṣa* is considered to be the gross manifestation of energy as matter in different strengths and quantities.

Prāṇa permeates the entire cosmos as life force or energy impulse. *Mahā prāṇa* is the initial impulse linking matter and consciousness. In general terms it is said that it is the pulsation of the atom within the planetary body. It forms the original wave of energy seen as light rays from stars or pulsars.

The impulses in our own bodies which travel from the body to the brain, and from the brain to the body are of physical *prāṇa*. The same *prāṇa* co-ordinates the activities of body, mind, rationality, emotions and other aspects of our personality. The five major *prāṇa*s

— *prāṇa, apāna, samāna, udāna* and *vyāna* — circulate within the body and perform different energy functions.

Manomaya koṣa is the energy field where the gross expression of mind occurs. When we relate mentally or emotionally with the world, then we are expressing *manomaya*. Our feelings of love, hatred, depression, joy, jealousy or compassion are played out on this level. Ego and its natural characteristics and needs are manifested in the domain of *manomaya*. This area of the mind is said to function through modifications or *vṛtti*s: correct cognition, incorrect cognition, fantasy and memory.

Vijñānamaya koṣa is the sheath where subtle intelligence evolves, where the four aspects of mind originate in their pure form, born of *mahat* (supreme intelligence). Deep *karma*s and *saṁskāra*s are stored at this level and form the reservoir of encoded experiences or memories which filter through to *manomaya koṣa* and manifest as our conditioned personality.

The concept of soul becomes a living experience in *ānandamaya koṣa* which is the sheath or body of bliss and happiness of attitude. All the impurities and dross evaporate, and effulgence of soul is experienced. At that point a human being experiences true divinity, the realization of Self or God.

The *koṣa*s symbolize an aspect of yoga psychology which tends to start where contemporary Western psychology ends. These energy sheaths portray our personality as permeating different fields of energy and consciousness. Yoga says we evolve through the *koṣa*s as our awareness deepens and expands, and that is a matter of *karma* and free will.

Some people remain in *annamaya* and *manomaya koṣa*s all their lives. They can literally subsist at a survival level without ever realizing more subtle intelligence. Very few people are aware of *prāṇamaya koṣa* which forms the intricate energy systems weaving the consciousness into personality. The blockages occurring at this level prevent people from knowing this part of themselves and condition them to grosser experiences of life. Difficulties with past life *karma* at *vijñānamaya koṣa* usually inhibit people from knowing the bliss or *ānanda* of soul.

According to spiritual seers these five bodily sheaths have extraordinary capacity. Just as each sperm can potentially give birth to a child, so too every sheath has the capacity to manifest a divine being.

Concept of Citta and Its Modifications

Citta is derived from the Sanskrit root *cit*, which means to see, to be conscious of, or to be aware. *Citta* is the Subconscious mind. It is the mind-stuff. It is the storehouse of memory. *Saṁskāras* (impressions of actions) are embedded here. It is one of the four parts of *antaḥkaraṇa*. Hence *citta* means individual consciousness, which includes the conscious, subconscious and unconscious states of mind. The totality of these three states of individual mind is symbolized by the expression *citta*.

Citta has been differently accepted in Vedānta, but here *citta* represents the whole of the individual consciousness, which is comprised of three stages: the sense or objective consciousness, the subjective or astral consciousness, and the unconsciousness or mental state of dormant potentiality. The verb *citta* means to perceive, to know or understand. *Citta* as noun means thought, vision, etc.

The process of modification which the objects undergo between the region of the mind and the *buddhi* or *mahat* (intellect) is called *vṛtti*. The psychic medium termed *vṛtti* always operates between the knower and the known. The *puruṣa* (the spirit) is subjected to enjoyment and sufferings in the material world due to these *citta-vṛttis* (functions of the mind). As a result the individual ego becomes restless and it is mainly due to five kinds of afflictions such as *avidyā, asmitā, rāga, dveṣa* and *abhiniveśa.*

In *Pātañjala Yoga-Sūtras* (1.2) yoga is defined as the *citta-vṛtti nirodha* which means yoga is the cessation of all the fluctuations of the mind. This restraint over the mind is attained through various steps of the yoga discipline.

Māṇḍūkyopaniṣad conveys the four stages of consciousness, i.e. *jāgrati* (awakened), *suṣupti* (sleep), *svapna* (dream) and *turīya* (bliss); the state of dream is the subtle world of *Parmātman* which is in between awaken and sleep states of consciousness.

जागरितस्थानो बहि:प्रज्ञः सप्ताङ्ग एकोनविंशतिमुखः स्थूलभुग्वैमनरः प्रथमः पादः।।

jāgaritasthāno bahiḥprajñaḥ saptāṅga ekonaviṁśatimukhaḥ ।
sthūlabhugvaiśvānaraḥ prathamaḥ pādaḥ ।।
— *Māṇḍūkyopaniṣad* 3

The first aspect is the waking state, the awareness of external things, the terrain of *vaiśvānara*. Seven limbs and nineteen mouths are possessed by him, and his enjoyment lies in the visible objects of the world.

स्वप्नस्थानोऽन्तःप्रज्ञः सप्ताङ्ग एकोनविंशतिमुखः प्रविकि भुक् तैजसो
द्वितीयः पादः।।

svapnasthāno 'ntaḥprajñaḥ saptāṅga ekonaviṁśatimukhaḥ ।
praviviktabhuk taijaso dvitīyaḥ pādaḥ ।।
— *Māṇḍūkyopaniṣad* 4

The dreaming state is the second aspect, over which *tejas* rules. Seven limbs and nineteen mouths belong to him, and the objects he enjoys are invisible.

यत्र सुप्तो न कंचन कामं कामयते न कंचन स्वप्नं पश्यति तत्सुषुप्तम्।
सुषुप्तस्थान एकीभूतः प्रज्ञानघन एवानन्दमयो ह्यानन्दभुक् चेतोमुखः
प्राज्ञस्तृतीयः पादः।।

yatra supto na kañcana kāmaṁ kāmayate na kañcana svapnaṁ
paśyati tatsuṣuptam ।
suṣuptasthāna ekībhūtaḥ prajñānaghana evānandamayo
hyānandabhuk cetomukhaḥ prājñastṛtīyaḥ pādaḥ ।।
— *Māṇḍūkyopaniṣad* 5

The third aspect is deep dreamless sleep, lying beyond desire. Prajñā is the Lord of this territory; he abides in deep sleep in which all things have vanished, and he enjoys bliss. *Prajñā* lies at the gateway to the dreaming and waking states.

नान्तःप्रज्ञं न बहिःप्रज्ञं नोभयतःप्रज्ञं न प्रज्ञानघनं न प्रज्ञं नाप्रज्ञम्।
अदृष्टमव्यवहार्यमग्राह्यमलक्षणमचिन्त्यमव्यपदेश्यमेकात्मप्रत्ययसारं
प्रपञ्चोपशमं शान्तं शिवमद्वैतं चतुर्थं मन्यन्ते स आत्मा स विज्ञेयः।।

nāntaḥprajñaṁ na bahiḥprajñaṁ nobhayataḥ prajñaṁ na
prajñānaghanaṁ na prajñaṁ nāprajñam ।।
adṛṣṭam avyavahāryam agrāhyam alakṣaṇam acintyam
avyapadeśyam ekātmapratyayasāraṁ prapañcopaśamaṁ śāntaṁ
śivam advaitaṁ caturthaṁ manyante sa ātmā sa vijñeyaḥ ।।
— *Māṇḍūkyopaniṣad* 7

Turīya, is the fourth aspect, according to the wise, remains unaware of the external, intermediate and internal worlds. He lies beyond bliss consciousness and unconsciousness; it is indescribable. *Turīya* enjoys pure awareness and experiences peace, bliss and non-duality. He is none other than *ātman*. Realize Him.

In conclusion it can be stated that *citta* is the memory bank, which stores impressions and experiences, and while it can be very useful, *citta* can also cause difficulties if its functioning is not co-ordinated with the others.

A good way to cultivate the witnessing of *citta* is to simply be aware of the streams of thoughts, emotions, images and impressions that arise in front of *manas* (on which *manas* may or may not act). Notice how the stream of thoughts comes from somewhere and then recedes back into that same place. This place is *citta*.

Now the question arises: What is *vṛtti*? In yoga, the fluctuations of consciousness, the waves of mental activities, can be understood as *vṛtti*. There are five *vṛtti*s according to Patañjali, which are as follows:

प्रमाणविपर्ययविकल्पनिद्रास्मृतयः।

pramāṇa-viparyaya-vikalpa-nidrā-smṛtayaḥ ।
— *Pātañjala Yoga-Sūtras* 1.6

> *Pramāṇa* means right knowledge, *viparyaya* means wrong knowledge, *vikalpa* means options, *nidrā* means sleep and the *smṛti* means the memory, these are the five *vṛtti*s, which are the real fluctuations of *citta*.

If *citta* is not co-ordinated with the other functions of mind, the thousands, millions or countless impressions in this bed of the lake of mind start to stir and arise. It is as if these many latent impressions, coming to life are all competing for the attention of *manas* to carry out their wants in the external world. In the absence of a clear *buddhi*, the competing voices of *citta* often drive *manas* to take actions in the world that are really not so useful.

Citta-Vṛtti-Nirodha Through Yoga

It is often said that yoga is control of the mind, and people struggle to restrain their minds in the name of yoga, and find that it is a difficult task, if not an impossible one. The reason behind this difficulty is that the mind is inseparable from the aspirant. And it will not yield to any threat or admonition, if it cannot appreciate or understand the significance behind the teaching that it is worthwhile restraining oneself. The mind is not easily convinced that it is good to restrain itself. Why should the mind be controlled at all? Where comes the necessity and why should people struggle to restrain the functions of the mind? Why should yoga be equated with control of the mind? Why should yoga not be something else? Unless this point is made clear, the effort at mind-control will not be successful. Without clear thinking, any effort in any direction will be a failure in the end.

We have heard that yoga is union, but many a time, we do not know the objects which are to be united. Now we know what "union" actually means in the language of yoga proper. It is a complete transcendence of our finitude. A separatist tendency persists in us, and yoga is nothing but overcoming the barriers of this individuality by entering into the oceanic expanse of our true nature, which is also the nature of everybody. When the mind is restrained in this manner, *citta-vṛtti-nirodha* is effected. This false feeling that we are different from others, that things are constituted of isolated particularities, leaves us; and we get established in our essential nature, which is the community of existence in all things, and not an isolated individuality. This establishment of one's own self in one's own true nature, in universal character, is the aim of yoga.

योगश्चित्तवृत्तिनिरोधः

yogaś-cittavṛtti-nirodhaḥ
— *Pātañjala Yoga-Sūtras* 1.2

Yoga is the cessation of mental fragmentation. *Yoga*: Oneness. *Citta*: mind. *Vṛtti*: wave, the action of rolling, modification, way of being. *Nirodha*: cessation.

There are four words in this *sūtra*; the four words of this *sūtra* define the "yoga" in a practical way. But then one should know their meaning and mostly how they beckon us. *Vṛtti* means a whirlpool. It is a wave of thought that arises in the *antaḥkaraṇa*. *Vṛtti*s are modifications of the mind. They are the effect of *avidyā*. When *avidyā* is destroyed by *jñāna*, *vṛtti*s get absorbed in *Brahman* (*laya*), just as water thrown in a heated pan is absorbed in the pan.

Wherefrom does a *vṛtti* arise? From the *citta* (mind). Why does a *vṛtti* arise? It is *svabhāva* of *antaḥkaraṇa*. What is its function? It causes *āvaraṇa-bhaṅga* (removes the veil of *sthūla avidyā* that envelops the objects). It helps the evolution of a man till he attains perfection (*jīvana-mukti*). It is *vṛtti* that opens the *kuṇḍalinī* in a *jñānī* in the *ājñā cakra* and joins it in *sahasrāra*. This is one path.

The *citta* is the mindstuff. It is the mental substance. *Vṛtti* or thought-wave is a modification of that mental substance. It is a process. Just as waves and bubbles arise from the surface of the ocean, so also these *vṛtti*s arise from the surface of the mind-ocean. Just as rays emanate from the sun, so also these mental rays (modification of *vṛtti*s) emanate from the mind-sun. Just as the sun merges itself in the horizon at sunset by collecting all its rays, so also you will have to merge in that sun of suns, absolute consciousness, eternal peace by collecting all the dissipated mental rays and dissolving the mind itself.

The function of a *vṛtti* in the mind is to cause *āvaraṇa-bhaṅga* (removal of the veil of ignorance covering objects). *Sthūla avidyā* (gross ignorance) is enveloping all objects. When the veil is removed, perception of objects becomes possible. *Vṛtti* removes the *āvaraṇa* (layer) of ignorance. When you pass through a big crowd of people, you are able to notice a few persons. You do not see some persons, though they happen to come in front of you. Why? Because there was no complete *āvaraṇa-bhaṅga*. When this is done, the object shines before you.

If these five *vṛtti*s are suppressed, the suppression of desires and other functions will follow. We all are subject to these five turnings in our minds, and they are not necessarily bad. Correct knowledge can help us do the right thing at the right time. But we can also do the right thing for the wrong reason; even incorrect knowledge can be helpful at times. The truth is, these fluctuations can be good or bad. Even right knowledge can be used in a harmful way. We have often seen things done with the best of intentions turn out drastically wrong. It not that these *vṛtti*s are good or bad that makes them worthy of study, it is their effect upon the state of our mind that is of interest. These turnings of the mind obscure the view of our real self and need to be calmed. Like the surface of a mountain lake on a clear moonlit night (our mind) when still, reflects perfectly the full moon (reality).

But with even a small ripple, caused by a *vṛtti*, the moon's appearance is distorted.

This *sūtra* can be translated in two ways, depending on if we translate *citta-vṛtti* by "mental activity" or by "mental fragmentation". "Yoga is the cessation of mental activity" would refer to a temporary cessation, a peace depending on particular circumstances. That would be a mental truce, even if the joy felt in it is definitely different than the joy linked to the objects and circumstance of mundane existence. That is what certain popular meditation techniques propose and it is after all much better than the usual mental agitation of man, because in this truce, the source of mental activity can be perceived. But then it is perceived only in the absence of thought or perception. The one who doesn't go beyond that kind of meditation eventually finds himself again powerless when mental activity and "the world" come back. Far from being the antithesis of the word, *nirodha* is its essence, its ultimate accomplishment.

The surface level agitation never disturbs the abyssal tranquillity of being. Patañjali calls such a tranquillity *nirodha*. But one has to know what is the cessation, the gathering and the silence of the mind. It is not a cessation imposed by the individual will or for some of coercion: that new form of project would only reproduce the dualistic mental activity, by introducing a distance between what is here and now, and what the mind wishes. Such is not the true silence or meditation. How does the cessation dawn in us? We only need to apply the meaning of *legein*: to let be there, to welcome in peace. It is really to gather the presence as it is, to remain attentive to it; that is to guard it faithfully, to identify with it.

The memory is then completely empty of its previous impressions based on the notions of subject and object. There is no more question of a difference between mental activity and cessation, between subject and object, and between spiritual life and mundane life. Any mental activity is perceived as a modality of the same, of the one. This goes beyond a mere state of consciousness (such as the waking state, deep-sleep state and dream state), because it is reality itself, whereas these states are mere modulations, *vṛtti*s. The expression itself reveals it: a "state" of consciousness really means a particular state of consciousness, exactly like ice, liquid water and water vapour are particular states of one and the same reality: water. True cessation is neither sleep (Patañjali designates explicitly sleep as a form of consciousness) nor unconsciousness, nor insensitivity. The *Spandakārikā*, an important text of the Kashmirian Śaivism tradition, reveals the same reality:

> Although that (*spanda*) spreads itself into the distinct states of waking, sleeping and others, which are in reality not distinct from it, it never leaves its own nature of subject who perceives. Where there is neither pain, nor pleasure, nor perceptible thing, nor perceiving agent, nor insensitivity, there abides what exists in the supreme sense.

Between the two possible translations of this *sūtra* the whole spectrum of spiritual life is unfolded. Meditation gathers span, taking under its cape not only the cessation of mental activity, but also that very activity. One doesn't try to empty himself, or to stop thoughts, even subtly. One only recognizes the One, Pure Gaze, through all its modalities, including perception and the absence of perception. It is thus that slowly the dualistic mental impressions loose their grip over the meditator.

In all its sobriety, this *sūtra* calmly announces something immense, unheard of, something that the intellect cannot possibly measure. It is the One. It is the end of mental fragmentation, the perfect cessation: *nirodha*.

DESTRUCTION OF VR̥TTIS LEADS TO MENTAL STRENGTH

Mind gains great strength when the *vr̥tti*s are destroyed. It is not easy to destroy *vr̥tti*s (thought-waves) because they are innumerable. They should be taken up one by one and dealt with separately. Some *vr̥tti*s are very strong. They demand strong efforts for their destruction. Most of the *vr̥tti*s are very weak. Weak *vr̥tti*s melt away like rain clouds. Strong thoughts remain and frequently recur daily in the morning as soon as you rise from your bed.

When the mind runs from one object to another, that state in the interval wherein you become mindless for a very short time is *svarūpa sthiti*. That is *Brahman*. When the mind is controlled fully, *vr̥tti*s cease. When all the modifications subside, you enter into the silence then and then alone. Realize this, this very moment. Feel the divine glory and Brahmic splendour now by closing the eyes, by drawing the *indriya*s, by stilling the mind, by silencing the thoughts, by sharpening the intellect, by purifying the *citta*, by meditating on *oṁ*, by chanting *oṁ* with *bhāva* (feeling). Keep up the continuity of Brahmic consciousness throughout the day. Have an unceasing flow of ātmic consciousness. When all the *vr̥tti*s die, *saṁskāra*s and the frame of the mind remain. *Saṁskāra*s can only be dried up by *nirbīja-samādhi*.

Yogic Psychology and Concept of Bhagavad-Gītā

Gītā literally means the song of God, which explains and elaborate the supreme truth of the Śruti (scriptural teaching actually revealed by God to man, as the Vedas and Upaniṣads). It has been said by God to his disciples and sometimes by the sages, saints and *r̥ṣi*s. There are four major and twenty-five minor *Gītā*s. Thereafter one more valuable *Gītā* — *Yuga Gītā* is available, which can be called contemporary *Gītā*. Among them the *Bhagavad-Gītā* is the most classical and renowned.

It is regarded by many seers and thinkers as the popular — most inspiring and most influential classic of India. In reality, none has power to describe in words the glory of the *Gītā* for it is a book containing the highest esoteric doctrines. It is the essence of the Vedas. Its language is so sweet and simple that a man can easily understand it after a little practice; but the thoughts are so deep that none can arrive at the conclusion even after constant study throughout the lifetime.

The *Bhagavad-Gītā* was born on the sacred soil of Kurukṣetra to inspire Arjuna so that he may perform his duties well. The *Gītā* with its 700 verses distributed in eighteen chapters looks like a lovely necklace. This is actually the teaching of Lord Kr̥ṣṇa (the Yogeśvara — the master of yoga) to his disciple Arjuna. Maharṣi Vedavyāsa compiled this gospel in his text the *Mahābhārata*. Śrī Vedavyāsa after describing the *Gītā* in the *Mahābhārata* says in the end:

गीता सुगीता कर्तव्या किमन्यैः शास्त्रविस्तरैः।
या स्वयं पद्मनाभस्य मुखपद्माद्विनिःसृता।।4।।

gītā sugītā kartavyā kimanyaiḥ śāstra-vistaraiḥ ।
yā svayaṁ padmanābhasya mukhapadmād-viniḥsr̥tā ।।4।।

The *Gītā* should be carefully studied. It emanated from the lotus-like lips of Lord Viṣṇu Himself, from whose navel sprung the lotus. What is the use of studying the other elaborate scriptures?

Some of the seers say that the *Gītā* is a text of philosophy whereas some say that it is a classical text of psychology. If psychology is a value-free objective study of mind then the *Bhagavad-Gītā* may not be qualified as a psychological treatise. The *Bhagavad-Gītā* studies mind in the context of the immutable consciousness/*ātman-Brahman* and the objective interpersonal world.

One is an ontological assumption and the other an experiential fact. The *Bhagavad-Gītā*'s interest in the mind, the mediating entity, is because it is the instrument of transcendence/self-knowledge. Mind with senses is the instrument of knowing the world, and when detached and reflective, it becomes capable of knowing the self/truth/God.

Psychology started with the study of neurosis, the various disfunctions of the mind. Discovery of the unconscious was a major turning point. The objective was to understand the hidden inner drives and organize them for a well-adjusted life. The stimulus–response model, the will to power model, sexual suppression model, drive to transcendence model, the rational choice maker model — all these ideas contributed to the understanding of mind and human behaviour. We find all these ideas explored in the *Bhagavad-Gītā* in understanding human mind and human motives and action.

Swami Bodhananda (1939: 16) states that the *Bhagavad-Gītā* begins with a description of the breakdown of a healthy, competent human being in a very stressful and conflicting situation. Stress was due to the stake involved and the immediacy of the crisis, and conflict because of the lack of acceptable choices. So the *Bhagavad-Gītā*'s focus is a healthy mind in a temporary crisis, which if not solved may deteriorate into mental, physical and social illness. Arjuna's problem is not due to sexual suppressions, past traumas, hormonal imbalance or due to brain damage. It is a thinking man's problem — *dharma sammūḍha cetā*.

The *Bhagavad-Gītā* begins with the exposition of the immortality of the Self and an exhortation not to grieve. Kṛṣṇa also appeals to Arjuna's pride: "give up this unbecoming, heaven denying, inglorious weakness"; reminds Arjuna of his vocation/duty: "get up and fight this righteous battle"; tickles Arjuna's ambition: "win the battle, gain glory and enjoy the kingdom". Kṛṣṇa also tries a pessimistic and materialistic piece of advice: "life is short and uncertain, so as well enjoy it". But the main line that Kṛṣṇa follows is that of the transcendental. We all are the immortal Self. The purpose of life is to discover that and abide in that. That is bliss. A pure mind is the instrument of knowing the self.

Purity of mind is gained by practising the twenty (*BG*, ch. 13)/ twenty-seven (*BG*, ch. 16) values while engaged in the worldly activities, i.e. the practice of *karma-yoga*. For the self-abiding work becomes a means of serving the world — *lokasaṁgraha*. The *Bhagavad-Gītā* gives a picture of the enlightened person — *sthitaprajña* — which is the ultimate possibility of human life — a mind abiding happily in the happy self while engaged in the world with altruistic intentions, calm and free from emotional fluctuations. Self-ignorance projects desire to possess and indulge leading to frustrations which leads to further desire-prompted activities and the cycle repeats endlessly. "Get off this cycle — *niṣtraiguṇyo bhava*", is the clarion call of the *Bhagavad-Gītā*.

The *Bhagavad-Gītā* is more prescriptive than descriptive, normative than narrative. Its focus never deviates from the goal while dealing with the various means to reach the goal. *Kāma, krodha, lobha, moha, ahaṁkāra, rāga, dveṣa, phalecchā* — all broods of ignorance are the root causes of human misery. These are mental impurities.

These impurities can be removed by practising all the values like *sthitaprajña bhava* and *niṣtraiguṇyo bhava* while engaged in the worldly duties. According to the *Bhagavad-Gītā*, mind is a combination of *manas, buddhi* and *ahaṁkāra*. The faculties of five sense-organs and five motor organs are also added to the mind. The activity of the mind is determined by *prakṛti/svabhāva*. This value can be equated with the unconscious of modern psychology. *'Prakṛti tvam niyogaśyati' prakṛti* will impel you, *svabhāvastu pravartate* it is aquired nature that propels, *sadṛśam ceṣṭate svasya prakṛte jñānavanāpi* — even a wise man functions according to his nature. *Prakṛti* is a carry forward from the previous life.

The *Bhagavad-Gītā* advocates a vocation in tune with ones *prakṛti*. It is called *svadharma*. *Prakṛti* is a dynamic of three *guṇas* — *sattva, rajas* and *tamas* (SRT). The *prakṛti* of an individual is determined by the predominant *guṇa* in his mental make-up.

Accordingly he is inclined to different pursuits/vocations. His ego, knowledge, work, inclinations, goals, happiness experience all are determined by this *guṇa* mix. In the area of mind and work the *Bhagavad-Gītā* is deterministic. There is no way a tāmasic mind can become rājasic and then sāttvic as far as the choice of vocation is concerned. That is why different disciplines are prescribed for brāhmaṇa, kṣatriya, vaiśya and śūdra:

ब्राह्मणक्षत्रियविशां शूद्राणां च परन्तप।
कर्माणि प्रविभक्तानि स्वभावप्रभवैर्गुणै:।।

brāhmaṇa-kṣatriya-viśāṁ śūdrānāṁ ca parantapa ।
karmāṇi pravibhaktāni svabhāva prabhavair guṇaiḥ ।।
— *Gītā* 18.41

Ones vocation is pre-determined, depending on the *prakṛti* which is a carry forward from the past. But this has nothing to do with ones birth in a particular social strata, but purely by inborn *guṇa* and the consequent *karma*. How to determine one's *guṇa/prakṛti/svabhāva*? The *Gītā* is silent here. In the *Mahābhārata* there are stories where *prakṛti* is determined by the fact of birth in the particular social group. But it has no *Bhagavad-Gītā* sanction. The *Bhagavad-Gītā* does not seem to recommend market competition either. May be the individual is the best authority to determine his *guṇa/prakṛti*. By this deterministic approach *Bhagavad-Gītā* skirts the issue of competition, evolution, material progress, conflicts, neurosis, violence, dialogue and decision-making. So what to do is question that is determined for us by our *prakṛti* — *sahajam karma kaunteya sadosamapi ne tyajet*. Peace is attained by accepting ones *prakṛti*, and choosing ones vocation accordingly.

Man–woman relationship also is subject to this law of *prakṛti*. Woman has a defined place and she has to accept that. "What is my *dharma*" this agonizing question is finally answered by submitting to ones pre-determined place and vocation. By putting individuals into these pre-determined procrustian boxes the *Bhagavad-Gītā* ensures social harmony, mental peace and detached reflectivity. All this mutilation of human psyche is done with the objective of obtaining transcendence. Do your work as an offering to Me (*bhakti-yoga*); detach from the fruits of work (*karma-yoga*); meditate on the immortal self (*jñāna-yoga*), became the clarion call of the *Bhagavad-Gītā*.

It is not the change of vocation or climbing the social or evolutionary ladder that is advocated. It is the alignment with ones *prakṛti*, avoiding inner conflicts of misalignment and transcending the entire infrastructure of *prakṛti*, including the mind. In this process, *buddhi* plays an important role:

> एवं बुद्धेः परंबुद्ध्वा संस्तभ्यात्मानमात्मना।
> जहि शत्रुं महाबाहो कामरूपं दुरासदम्।।
>
> *evaṁ buddheḥ paraṁ-buddhvā saṁstabhyātmānam-ātmanā* ।
> *jahi śatruṁ mahābāho kāmarūpaṁ durāsadam* ।।
>
> — *Gītā* 3.43

Buddhi is the faculty for understanding. *Buddhi* understands by study. *Manas* is purified by the practice of values. The *Bhagavad-Gītā* also advocates detachment — from sense objects by knowing them to be impermanent.

The *Bhagavad-Gītā* is for the healthy to become healthier, not for ones like Duryodhana who is a maniac nor for Karṇa who suffers from *severe complexes*, but for the likes of Arjuna, Dharmaputra and Bhīṣma. The *Bhagavad-Gītā* approach is preventive than curative, its goal is not to fix a broken mind but to inspire a stalled mind to come out of boxes. This approach is very relevant today as more people are suffering not from any diagnosable problems, but from existential crisis of purposelessness, boredom and lack of wholesome interests.

Śrī Kṛṣṇa said:

> Look here, O Arjuna! whatever your personal sentiments may be, you are a prince of the kṣatriya (son of a king) race, of the warrior clan, whose *dharma* (duty) is to defend the country and look after the welfare of the subjects and maintain law and order and *dharma*. Here is absolute chaos. At the helm of affairs there is a complete absence of *dharma*. So this is a *dharma-yuddha* (a righteous war). So, as a kṣatriya, as a prince, it is your duty to fight and moreover, on this first day of the war, you have taken over the task of leading your army as the commander-in-chief. So you must fight. It is your *dharma*.

So, Arjuna had this duty to do; it was facing him as his immediate duty also. Moreover, he had assumed his duty, agreed to perform it, and come right upon the battlefield, with the opposing army facing him there. In that particular context of his position as commander-in-chief of one of the two armies on the battlefield, as prince of the Pāṇḍava race, this man's 100 per cent duty was to fulfil his particular role, to fulfil the *kartavya karma* which was facing him. It was his *dharma* in that particular context to lead the army and try to see that the unrighteous Kauravas were overcome and defeated.

So, when Kṛṣṇa told Arjuna that he must fight, what He meant was that Arjuna must do his duty — the duty which then faced him. The general notion of people that the *Gītā* is a gospel of violence, a gospel of war, is a mistaken notion. It is a misconception. It betrays a complete failure to understand the central message of the *Gītā*. Because the *Gītā* happened to be delivered in a particular context, in the context of the battlefield, the dramatic effect of it was heightened. Arjuna was told that even in the midst of the war, he was to be completely detached. He was to be established in God. He was to be rooted in God-remembrance. The Lord gave him this *sandeśa*: *mamanusmara yudhyaca* (Remember Me constantly and fulfil your duty). When the Gītācārya, Lord Kṛṣṇa, addressed these words to Arjuna by the word *yudhyaca* He meant only, "Do your duty". And it just so happened that at that particular hour Arjuna's duty was to fight as a warrior in a righteous war. Be it noted that Kṛṣṇa's emphasis was not so much on the word *yudhyaca* as upon the word *mamanusmara*. If the *Gītā* had been preached to a brāhmaṇa in a forest hermitage, this word *yuddha* would never have got into the *Gītā*. It would have taken a different terminology altogether. What the Lord meant to say was that even in the midst of the most intense and dynamically active field of human life, one should be in a state of yoga inside — *yogastha kuru karmāṇi.* The entire emphasis in the *Gītā* is:

> Wherever you may be, and whatever you may be doing you must be in a state of yoga. You must be closely linked up with the Universal Soul. You must be closely linked up with the Divine, and thus linked up, you must perform your activities.

So, it means that when this message, this teaching, this yoga, that you must be linked up with the Divine and perform activities, that you must be grounded in God-remembrance and God-thought even while performing your activities, could be prescribed even in the tense circumstances of a battlefield, then it goes without saying that it applies to all other fields of human activity. The most difficult field of human activity is naturally the field of battle, where the people clash and kill under the most violent, most dynamic and most complicated circumstances. And if yoga can be practised there, then no one can give an excuse that he cannot practise yoga because he is a businessman or he is a somebody else. If Lord Kṛṣṇa had given His message in some other context, then the soldier of the battlefield might have protested that the *upadeśa* (teaching) could apply to anyone else, but not to him because he was in a very, very complicated and difficult field, namely, the life-and-death battlefield. Evidently, the Lord deliberately chose the most difficult, the most complicated, the most active and most violent, and the most externalized field of activity that is ever possible for a human being to practise the Gītā Yoga of inward living. If the Gītā Yoga is possible in the midst of the clash and clang of weapons in a field of battle, then it is possible anywhere and everywhere. Then, no one can ever come forward and say, "No, it is not possible in my particular context, in my particular circumstance". So, once and for all, the possibility of anyone putting forward an excuse for not practising the Gītā Yoga was effectively removed by the Lord when He chose the battlefield to give His *upadeśa* to Arjuna.

It is in the above context that we must understand *pratyāhāra* also. You must learn to be detached in the midst of activities. You must learn to be grounded in the inner background in the midst of outward activity or outer dynamism. And this process of *pratyāhāra* is an indispensable necessity if you want to practise yoga in daily life. If you want to practise *dhāraṇā, dhyāna* and *samādhi* in the context of a normal life lived in the world, the support of the process of *pratyāhāra* in the midst of your normal activity becomes most significant and most important. Nay, it is indispensable. So, *pratyāhāra* as a process has a greater importance to the *yogī* in the normal context of worldly life than *pratyāhāra* as a practice at a particular time just before meditation.

However this scripture is the best teaching of yogic psychology. Yoga has been defined in the *Gītā* in various ways:

योगस्थः कुरु कर्माणि संङ्गं त्यक्त्वा धनञ्जय।
सिद्ध्यसिद्ध्योः समो भूत्वा समत्वं योग उच्यते।।२.४८।।

yogasthaḥ kuru karmāṇi saṅgaṁ tyaktvā dhanañjaya ।
siddhy-asiddhyoḥ samo bhūtvā samatvaṁ yoga ucyate ।।2.48।।

O Arjuna! perform your duties well, established in the yogic way of life, without any attachment. Treat success and failure alike, such equanimity is called yoga.

बुद्धियुक्तो जहातीह उभे सुकृतदुष्कृते।
तस्माद्योगाय युज्यस्व योगः कर्मसु कौशलम्।।२.५०।।

buddhi-yukto jahātīha ubhe sukr̥ta-duṣkr̥te |
tasmād yogāya yujyasva yogaḥ karmasu kauśalam ||2.50||

Endued with this evenness of mind, one frees oneself in this life, alike from vice and virtue; devote yourself therefore, to this yoga. Yoga is the very dexterity of work. It is skill and effectiveness in action.

तं विद्याद् दुःखसंयोगवियोगं योगसञ्ज्ञितम्।।

taṁ vidyād duḥkha-saṁyoga-viyogaṁ yoga-sañjñitam ||
— 6.23

That state which is free from the contact of sorrow, is called yoga.

After a careful reading of the *Gītā* we find that all the chapters of the *Gītā* reflect yoga in some form or the other as shown in Table 3.1:

Table 3.1: Importance of Yoga in the Gītā

Chapter	Form of Yoga
1	yoga of dejection
2	Sāṁkhya-Yoga (the yoga of knowledge)
3	Karma-Yoga (the yoga of action)
4	yoga of knowledge as well as the disciplines of action and knowledge
5	yoga of action and knowledge
6	yoga of meditation
7	yoga of knowledge (knowledge of *nirguṇa Brahman*)
8	yoga of the indestructible *Brahman*
9	yoga of the sovereign science and the sovereign secrets
10	yoga of divine glories
11	yoga of the vision of the universe
12	yoga of devotion
13	yoga of discrimination between the field and the knower of the field
14	yoga of classification of the three *guṇas*
15	yoga of the supreme person

16	yoga of discrimination between the divine and the demonical properties
17	yoga of classification of the threefold faith
18	yoga of liberation through the path of knowledge and self-surrender

All the psychological and psycho-somatic problems are more or less due to sedentary lifestyle and stress. To combat this problem the *Bhagavad-Gītā* discusses *karma-yoga* (the yoga of action) as: Good deeds should be performed and never spoken about. In the same manner all duties should be performed with the sense that they are offerings to God. Man should realize that he is only an instrument of God. This is what the *Bhagavad-Gītā* refers to as *niṣkāma karma* (duty without attachment). This is also known as *karma-saṁnyāsa* or *karma-yoga*.

> कर्मण्येवाधिकारस्ते मा फलेषु कदाचन।
> मा कर्मफलहेतुर्भूर्मा ते सङ्गोऽस्त्वकर्मणि।।२.४७।।
>
> *karmaṇy evādhikāras te mā phaleṣu kadācana*।
> *mā karma-phala-hetur bhūr mā te saṅgo 'stv akarmaṇi*।।2.27।।
>
> Your right is to work only, but never to the fruit thereof. Be not instrumental in making your actions bear fruit, nor let your attachment be to in action.

Lord Kṛṣṇa says: O Arjuna! perform your duties established in yoga, renouncing attachment and even tempered in success and failure, evenness of temper is called yoga. Here is how beautifully the comprehensive essence of the yoga of action has been presented by the ninth verse of the third chapter.

> यज्ञार्थात्कर्मणोऽन्यत्र लोकोऽयं कर्मबन्धनः।
> तदर्थं कर्म कौन्तेय मुक्त सङ्गः समाचर।।
>
> *yajñārthāt karmaṇo 'nyatra loko 'yaṁ karma-bandhanaḥ*।
> *tad arthaṁ karma kaunteya mukta-saṅgaḥ samācara*।।
>
> Man is bound by his own action except when it is performed for the sake of sacrifice. Therefore, Arjuna, do you efficiently perform your duty, free from attachment for the sake of sacrifice alone.

Verses 10 and 12 of the fifth chapter of the *Gītā* highlight the yoga of action thus:

ब्रह्मण्याधाय कर्माणि सङ्गं त्यक्त्वा करोति यः।
लिप्यते न स पापेन पद्मपत्रमिवाम्भसा।।१०।।

brahmaṇy ādhāya karmāṇi saṅgaṁ tyaktvā karoti yaḥ ।
lipyate na sa pāpena padma-patram ivāmbhasā ।।10।।

युक्तः कर्मफलं त्यक्त्वा शान्तिमाप्नोति नैष्ठिकीम्।
अयुक्तः कामकारेण फले सक्तो निबध्यते।।१२।।

yuktaḥ karma-phalaṁ tyaktvā śāntim āpnoti naiṣṭhikīm ।
ayuktaḥ kāma-kāreṇa phale sakto nibadhyate ।।12।।

He, who acts offering all actions to God and shaking off attachment, remains untouched by sin as the lotus leaf by water. Offering the fruit of actions to God the *karma-yogī* attains everlasting peace in the shape of God realization, whereas he who works with a selfish motive, being attached to the fruit of actions through desire, gets tied down.

In this worldly illusion people may fall into the deligma; to remove the darkness of mind the *Bhagavad-Gītā* also throws light on *jñāna-yoga*, the yoga of knowledge, which paves the way for our salvation. It is the knowledge, which makes us know what we are. The second verse of the seventh chapter gives us a clear picture of the yoga of knowledge:

ज्ञानं तेऽहं सविज्ञानमिदं वक्ष्याम्यशेषतः।
यज्ज्ञात्वा नेह भूयोऽन्यज्ज्ञातव्यमवशिष्यते।।

jñānaṁ te 'haṁ savijñānam idaṁ vakṣyāmy aśeṣataḥ ।
yaj jñātvā neha bhūyo 'nyaj-jñātavyamavaśiṣyate ।।

Lord Kṛṣṇa says to Arjuna "I shall unfold to you in its entirety this wisdom (knowledge of God in His absolute formless aspect) along with the knowledge of the qualified aspect of God. Having known the qualified aspect of God, nothing else remains yet to be known in this world".

Hence in verses 20 and 23 of the second chapter of the *Gītā*, Lord Kṛṣṇa highlights the immortality of the soul when he says that:

अजो नित्यः शाश्वतोऽयं पुराणो न हन्यते हन्यमाने शरीरे।।२०।।

ajo nityaḥ śāśvato 'yaṁ purāṇo na hanyate hanyamāne śarīre ।।20।।

नैनं छिन्दन्ति शस्त्राणि नैनं दहति पावकः।
न चैनं क्लेदयन्त्यापो न शोषयति मारुतः।।२३।।

nainaṁ chindanti śastrāṇi nainaṁ dahati pāvakaḥ ।
na cainaṁ kledayanty āpo na śoṣayati mārutaḥ ।।23।।

The soul is unborn, eternal, everlasting and ancient. Even though the body is slain, the soul is not. Lord Kṛṣṇa says, Arjuna! weapons cannot cut it nor can fire burn it; water cannot wet it nor can wind dry it.

Verse 38 of the fourth chapter of the *Gītā* gives us a good description of the importance of knowledge.

न हि ज्ञानेन सदृशं पवित्रमिह विद्यते।
तत्स्वयं योगसंसिद्धः कालेनात्मनि विन्दति।।

na hi jñānena sadṛśaṁ pavitram iha vidyate ।
tat svayaṁ yoga-saṁsiddhaḥ kālenātmani vindati ।।

On earth there is no purifier as great as knowledge; he who has attained purity of heart through a prolonged practice of *karma-yoga* automatically sees the light of Truth in the self in course of time.

Verse 8 of the sixth chapter of the *Gītā* says:

ज्ञानविज्ञानतृप्तात्मा कूटस्थो विजितेन्द्रियः।
युक्त इत्युच्यते योगी समलोष्टाश्मकाञ्चनः।।

jñāna-vijñāna-tṛptātmā kūṭastho vijitendriyaḥ ।
yukta ity ucyate yogī sama-loṣṭāśma-kāñcanaḥ ।।

The *yogī* where mind is stated with *jñāna* and *vijñāna*, who is unmoved under all circumstances, whose senses are completely mastered and to whom earth, stone and gold are all alike, is spoken of as a God realized Soul.

Verse 16 of the fifth chapter of the *Gītā* presents the true picture of *jñāna-yoga*.

ज्ञानेन तु तदज्ञानं येषां नाशितमात्मनः।
तेषामादित्यवज्ज्ञानं प्रकाशयति तत्परम्।।

jñānena tu tad ajñānaṁ yeṣāṁ nāśitam ātmanaḥ ।
teṣām ādityavaj jñānaṁ prakāśayati tat param ।।

In the case of those whose said ignorance has been set aside by true knowledge of God; that wisdom shining like the Sun reveals the supreme.

The *Bhagavad-Gītā* discusses how to control our emotions and for that Lord Kṛṣṇa discussed the *bhakti-yoga*. The *Gītā* says that when a devotee's love for God reaches its climax, his love for God is known as the yoga of devotion.

Lord Kṛṣṇa also teaches the technique of *dhyāna-yoga* (the meditation) to Arjuna in verse 35 of the sixth chapter.

असंशयं महाबाहो मनो दुर्निग्रहं चलम्।
अभ्यासेन तु कौन्तेय वैराग्येण च गृह्यते।।

asaṁśayaṁ mahābāho mano durnigrahaṁ calam ।
abhyāsena tu kaunteya vairāgyeṇa ca gṛhyate ।।

The mind is restless no doubt and difficult to curb O Arjuna! But it can be brought under control by repeated practice of meditation and by the exercise of dispassion O son of Kuntī!

After a careful reading of the *Gītā* we can conclude that there is a proper combination of the yoga of action, yoga of knowledge and the yoga of devotion. The three broad aspects of yoga figure in the *Gītā* too as we have in Patañjali's *Yoga-Sūtras*.

Highlighting the importance of yoga, Lord Kṛṣṇa reveals in forty-sixth verse of sixth chapter of *Gītā* as:

तपस्विभ्योऽधिको योगी ज्ञानिभ्योऽपि मतोऽधिकः।
कर्मिभ्यश्चाधिको योगी तस्माद्योगी भवार्जुन।।४६।।

tapasvibhyo 'dhiko yogī jñānibhyo 'pi mato 'dhikaḥ ।
karmibhyaś cādhiko yogī tasmād yogī bhavārjuna ।।46।।

The *yogī* is superior to the ascetics; he is regarded as superior even to those versed in sacred lore. The *yogī* is superior to those who perform action with interested motive. Therefore, O Arjuna! you should become a *yogī*.

Personality Types According to Yoga

The concept of evolution in human personality is inherent in the description of the three *guṇas* — *tamas*, *rajas* and *sattva*. They are present in every person and the dominance of one over the other determines his personality. A person dominated by *tamas* is lethargic, static, self-centred and dominated by impulses to fulfil his ends. A rājasic person is aware of the social and moral codes but is dominated by worldly aspirations (*īśānas*), and is active, effortful and result-oriented. He may have more material richness, but suffers from the pain of expectations and attachments to persons and things. Different to these is the sāttvic person who is directed by human values, a transcended consciousness, feelings of compassion and love for all, which provide him with inner delight and happiness. A few studies have shown how the concept of the *guṇas* goes beyond Maslow's need-hierarchy theory (Daftuar and Sharma 1997: 363) and that the dispositions of the *guṇas* have practical significance even in an organizational set-up (Kaur and Sinha 1992). The yogic practices aim at transforming the tāmasic and rājasic nature to generate one's sāttvic nature.

There are many ways and systems of characterizing personality types. Here we will look at three basic types of human personality. The first type governs his or her life and reactions mainly with reason. The second type does so mainly with emotion, and the third does so with the will. A personality is never completely one-sided; every person is a mixture of types, but one is always predominant. In some cases, the predominance is obvious; in others, the mixture is more complicated, and therefore the predominant type is more difficult to detect.

In the ideal personality, each of the three aspects has a rightful place. The harmonious person functions with each aspect in a perfect way, each rising to the fore as appropriate. More often, the three trends are often in imbalance or predominance. For instance, where reason should prevail, emotions do, or vice versa.

Let us begin with the personality governed predominantly by reason. Those who conduct their lives mainly by the reasoning process are apt to neglect the emotions. They can be afraid of emotions, and tend to suppress and control them. Unfortunately those who are afraid of emotion often do not trust their intuition as they distrust its supposed intangibility.

The emotion-type is equally one-sided. Predominantly emotional people often pride themselves that only they are capable of truly feeling. They in turn can secretly look down on people they label "intellectuals". The emotion-type tends to have clearer intuition and is sometimes less afraid of feeling and inner experience than the reason-type. However, the emotion-type, contrary to the reason-type who holds life's reins too tightly, often loses his or her grip on life's reins altogether. When in a negative state they are often so carried away by uncontrolled feelings that they lose control of themselves. Due to their overemphasis on the emotional side, they neglect the equally important reasoning functions of thinking, discriminating, selecting and weighing. Uncontrolled emotions bring havoc into the extreme emotion-person's life, as well as into his or her surroundings. This type must cultivate the faculty of selecting, deliberately thinking and planning. This selecting process is the beginning of wisdom.

The emotion-type also uses will, of course, for no one can exist without doing so. But the emotion-type uses will chaotically and impulsively, without planning or deliberation. Submerged in unchannelled instincts rather than constructive intuition. The reasoning type and emotional type can be seen as polarities of each other. Both are subconsciously afraid of their opposite extremes, and therefore they remain in their own extreme. They thus act from a wrong conclusion. Led by the wrong conclusion, they feel or unconsciously think that their own extreme is a better solution to life than the opposite types. The reason-type, afraid of losing control, cuts out not only a major part of life's necessary experience, but beauty and happiness as well. The emotion-type fears that curbing and disciplining his or her nature.

In the third category is the will-type who is altogether different. Will is supposed to be a servant, never a master. Ideally the will should serve equally the reasoning process and the emotional and intuitive faculties. The will-type makes a master of the servant. This brings the personality out of focus in a way that can become dangerous. Like the other two types, such persons may unconsciously look down on both of the others. The will-type thinks or feels something to the effect of, "The reason-type is just an intellectual who talks well and has wonderful theories, but it is all in the abstract. Nothing is accomplished by that. Nothing is achieved. I am the achiever." The emotion-type, who accomplishes even less, is even more despicable to the will-type.

The person of will, for whom the servant is the master, is out for achievement and tangible results. This focus tends to make such a person impatient and apt to forfeit the very result he or she seeks. Or unable to enjoy them once achieved. Will dominance cripples the reasoning process, which, joined with the emotional nature, leads to wisdom. Without such wisdom, people either cannot accomplish what they set out to accomplish or, if they succeed, cannot benefit from the accomplishment in the right way and thus will lose it again. The will-type tends to lose sight not only of caution but also of many aspects and considerations of life that are essential in order to gain truth for oneself, for others, as well as for any given situation. The person of will also neglect the emotional side, fearing emotion as much as the reason-type does, but with a different purpose, often subconscious. Emotions are acceptable to the will-type only so long as she or he remains master of them; otherwise, emotions might hinder this person's aim. The will-type, like the reason-type, also misses an integral part of the life experience, of giving one's self up to a feeling without knowing the outcome and the possible advantage of doing so. Coming to recognize if, when, and how, we are dominant in reason, emotion or will is the first step toward a more balanced approach to life. The process of self-discovery is to utilize our natural strengths, and free ourselves from subconsciously held patterns of limitation, supposed intangibility. The reason-type can have an aloofness and often secretly looks down on the emotion-type. The will, which is not necessarily self-will, is, in this type, used mainly to follow deductions made with the reasoning process and is used pre-meditatedly, often overcautiously while seldom paying attention to the emotions or intuitions. Such a person of reason is often an intellectual, perhaps a scientist. He or she is often an agnostic or even an atheist, who tends to be materialistic. Furthermore, the reason-type has great difficulty with intuitive judgement of others and of the self.

The will, which is a necessity in life for all, is used one-sidedly by both types. The reason-type uses will, whereas the emotion-type is carried away by emotions and uses will-power unconsciously and erratically. The harmonious personality finds the healthy middle way and uses the will rationally or emotionally, depending on the situation. The will should be a servant both to reason and emotion.

That the things that we need in this world are included in that which we are aspiring for, is also a conviction that has to be driven into our mind: "The thing that I want in this world is not removed from my realm of aspiration." We don't lose the world when we go to God. We lose nothing, practically. That which is our need or a requirement externally, so-called, is included in that which is totally pervasive. The external thing or the internal thing, both are included in the total. So when you seek the total, it is futile to go on thinking of another thing which is outside. That which is the total operational conviction in the mind includes that which you are considering as that which is external or internal. The thing that you need is neither inside nor outside. To repeat, it is everywhere; and, therefore, the greed for grabbing things — running after that which the senses actually want — we are told that generally these things have to be restricted. But there is no need for restraining anything. You are not putting a pressure on the sense-organs not to do what they want; you are only enlightening them to see that what they see is not in that place where they are looking at. It is a situation which is larger, where even the seeing of a thing is included in the larger situation of your being included in that situation. The obtaining of it, for the matter of that, also is a total situation. Whole thing is a total thing. No particularity is allowed here. This is an exercise which is deeply psychological, subliminal. The subconscious mind does not permit such things, really speaking.

The *prārabdha*, as it is called, the *karma* that has come with us when we take a physical birth, has various phases of operation. We have committed some errors in the previous birth. We have done great good deeds, and we have also done mixed deeds — partially virtuous, partially not. All these will constitute the mode of our operation in this life. Where it is a very good, virtuous, pure white act, there we will find an occasion to live a comfortable life, happy life and listen to messages of glory and high achievements. But, at the same time, there are impediments.

There are sāttvic (pure) *karmas*, which allow us to think, sit without purpose are rājasic *karmas*, and distracting actions are tāmasic *karmas*. We are many a time stupid and lethargic and unable to think. That is due to a tāmasic aspect of *prārabdha* working in us. At other times we are very much excited, want to run here and there, do this or that. That is the rājasic *karma* that is operating. Now you are here in a sāttvic mood. You are not disturbed. You are not sleeping. You are awake, in a sāttvic mood, and able to understand and absorb into your mind that which is actually beyond the ordinary capacity of the mind. You have to adopt such means of performance by which the rājasic and the tāmasic potentials of *prārabdha* are effectively mitigated.

It is said that the *prārabdha karma* cannot be destroyed. What you have done in the previous birth will have to be experienced in this birth, whether you want it or not. You cannot destroy the result of an action that you have performed earlier. *Na bhuktam kṣīyate karma kalpa koṭistairapi* (*Brahmavaivartta Purāṇa*, Prakṛti 37.16): Inexpereinced result of an action will last forever, until it is experienced. You will get what you have given.

But the sāttvic meditational effort has a very imposing effect on the other *karma*s — rājasic and tāmasic. They are put down for the time being. You have got so many desires in your mind, but you put down all of that just now when you are listening to me. That is how the sāttvic *karma* acts in subjugating the impulses of that which is contrary to the actual spiritual practice. You are not agitated here and you do not want to run away immediately. That is, you have subjugated even the rājasic *karma*. That is the power of *sattva*. You are poised. The state of being in poise for the time being puts down the effects of rājasic and tāmasic *karma*. Inwardly the other *karma*s also will be acting, little by little, causing some inconvenience physically, mentally, etc., but the power of this pressure exerted upon them by the *sattva* activity will make them harmless — like toothless snakes. The snake will be there, but it has no teeth; the teeth have gone. The teeth have been pulled out by the *sattva*. Though the distracting tāmasic *karma*s are still there as cobras moving about, they cannot harm, because you have pulled the teeth out.

Meditation should be a daily practice. If you miss a meal one day and take your meal next day, it will disturb your stomach and your appetite. Like the intake of medicine is continuous, and the intake of diet also is continuous, the intake of the exercise of meditation should be continuous — though it need not be for a long time. That you have no time to sit is an irrelevant matter. You can sit for five minutes at least. The quantity or the duration of sitting is not what is important. The quality of your thinking is important. One minute of intense thinking is superior to an hour of dull thinking.

As the *sattva* predominates, the capacity to think becomes more and more intense. The love for contact with Reality is such a flaming passion in the minds of spiritual seekers that it will burn up all obstacles if the practice continues everyday. The strength of the *sattva* forces will go on getting accentuated and increased more and more so that the potential of distraction and lethargic quality may substantially get mitigated. This is one thing that you have to keep in mind.

There are many other aspects of our life that you have to look into also — the food that you eat, what you drink, the company that you keep, the books that you read, and your general activity. They have to be streamlined in such a manner that they do not harm your basic purpose. It is up to each person to keep a diary of this kind.

Today evening, assess yourself: "What have I done since morning? What is the first thought that occurred in my mind when I woke up?" It is very important to make note of what is the first thought that arose in your mind when you woke up. Similar is the case with the thought with which you are going to sleep in the night. Keep a note of this. "Now I am going to sleep, but what I am thinking at this moment." That thought will influence the condition into which you are entering in sleep. And the thought of the early morning, which is the first thought that arises after you wake up, will influence the whole day. It is commonly said, in a humorous way: Start the day with God, end the day with God, and live with God.

A diary of self-check about one's own personality — which is hidden inside, mostly unknown to even one's own self — is to be ransacked in order that the submerged potentials of difficulty, lying in ambush to pounce upon you one day or the other, have to be taken note of. What we are thinking now is practically an operation of the conscious mind. What is inside in the subconscious mind is not coming up at this moment.

Yoga is not merely *citta-vr̥tti-nirodha* in the sense of a restraint of the conscious mind. The word *citta* that is used in yoga does not mean only conscious operations. It is the total psychical energy that is called *cit*. The entire psychic power in all its levels is *citta*. Restraint of a total operation of all the three layers of the psyche is what is referred to as *citta-vr̥tti-nirodha*. When you are thinking something and you stop thinking, it does not mean that *citta-vr̥tti-nirodha* has been attained, because you may be stopping the process of thinking a particular thing due to a pressure from another side which is also calling your attention.

The necessity to be subject to impulses which are beyond our control, that necessity is the thing that is handled in yoga. Are we free in ourselves, or are we forced to do things and think in a particular manner? A cow that is tied with a rope — a rope that is sufficiently long — may not know that it is tied like that. It will be moving freely and grazing in the field, and will never know that it has been limited to the distance of the rope with which it is tied. It will know that it has been limited only if it moves a little further, to the full length of the rope. Then it will see that it is conditioned. So we have a kind of freedom which is granted by the distance of the rope with which we have been tied to our personality, and we may not know that the rope is there behind us. What is the rope? It is the impulse to be present in one particular body only, and concern oneself with one particular object only, and the incapacity to think that we are ubiquitously connected with ubiquitous things in the world and that no operation is localized. That object of achievement which brings a right-about turn of our operation so that situations are perceived as total, that they arise from everywhere, everything is there in a particular situation — as it is wisely said, everything is everywhere at all times — is the fundamental psychological approach which should form the practice of yoga.

Personality Transformation Through Yoga

Personality development quintessentially means enhancing and grooming one's outer and inner self to bring about a positive change to his life. Personality development is an art to have a magnetic personality, which everyone wants to achieve.

प्रियं मा कृणु देवेषु प्रियं राजसु मा कृणु।
प्रियं सर्वस्य पश्यत उत शूद्र उतार्ये।

priyaṁ mā kr̥ṇu deveṣu priyaṁ rājasu mā kr̥ṇu ।
priyaṁ sarvasya paśyata uta śūdra utārye ।।
— *Atharvaveda* 19.62.1

O Lord! Make me dear to gods. Make me dear to kings. May I be dear to all the viewers, be they śūdra or vaiśya (the servitors or the professionals).

Attractive personality is formed by the judicious mixture of strength and emotions. The better the synthesis of these two elements, the more magnetic and charming the personality will be. Both the attributes are doubtlessly essential but their real significance and meaning lie in their proper synthesis. In isolation, either of the two loses its effectiveness. Strength alone without emotion and sensitivity does make a person capable and competent, but simultaneously makes him cruel hearted too. Consequently, people, even as they feel attracted to a powerful person, also remain inwardly scared of him.

The same is the case with emotions without strength. In this condition, the personality develops tender feelings but lacks in determination and competence. This type acquires "the poor fellow" image inviting from the people a patronizing attitude. Such a personality can be anything but attractive.

It is true that the thinking and behaviour of such a person touch the inner chords of those who come in contact, but for want of sufficient capability he is unable to provide them any succour. All the tender emotions in life cannot add up to power and strength, and such persons are generally forced to lead the life of an imaginative and emotional but weak person.

Therefore, if you are desirous of making yourself magnetic, combine your strengths with emotions and then see how soon you become the centre of everybody's attraction. People of every age, class and qualification will vie with one another to be near you. The world will hold you up as a role model; it will talk about you, dream about you and want to become like you. Whether you are a man or woman, farmer or officer, student or housewife, it does not matter. In every condition and every situation, the doors to personality furbishing are open to you. You have only to make a start.

The first step is to get ready to make the body and mind receptive and deserving. Remember, body becomes capable by self-control and mind by introspection and contemplation. A disciplined and regulated lifestyle and light physical exercises impart a certain beauteous luster to the body.

For proper expression of this beauty, the dress should be in tune with the place and occasion. In this connection, the important thing to always bear in mind is that the real source of the accentuated charm of the body is the subtle vital energy and this vitality comes only by *tapa* and continence. Purity and piety increase person's vital force whereas unrestrained sensual proclivities sap it. To maintain attractiveness for a long time, one has to retain vitality and vigour for long too.

To become capable and strong at mental plane, develop the habit of introspection because it helps promote one's abilities and hidden talents. Identify what is your special talent, your innate aptitude and set about to work on that. It could by anything — music, sports, management, housekeeping, or any other branch of knowledge and art. If you find yourself unable to identify it, consult your friends, or guardians. Do not lag behind at any level in the rigorous striving for talent nurturing.

Physical strength and mental prowess make one powerful. Now the turn is of the virtuous qualities that give expression to this power. So, try your utmost to inculcate the qualities of courage, bravery, patience and fortitude in you. Make yoga a practice, part of your life. As purification and *āsana* strengthen your body, practice of *prāṇāyāma* makes the individual prāṇically and mentally strong. Practice of meditation makes you emotionally mature and spiritually evolved.

These attributes will make you the sinecure of all eyes, not only at home and in the immediate locality but the society at large. Only the virtuous and the righteous radiate real magnetic, not the vicious and the wicked. Even the latter need a cloak of virtues to look attractive. It is another matter that after the spurious façade is gone, they are in for great ridicule and derision. The truly virtuous, on the other hand, retain their pull till the last breath.

Besides being strong and capable, one must be sensitive and emotional, because power without sensitivity makes a person arrogant. People will soon start running away from him. The three expressions of sensitivity presently relevant here are: (i) service to the needy, (ii) generosity, and (iii) tolerance. You will be able to develop your abilities through the instrumentality of all the three.

In this way, the *yoga-sādhanā* of combining strength and emotion will continue to add charm to your personality. But you will have to remain continually vigilant for its full and effective expression.

4

Yogic Psychotherapy and Techniques

Meaning and Definition of Psychotherapy

PSYCHOTHERAPY is a general term that is used to describe the process of treating psychological disorders and mental distress. During this process, a trained psychotherapist helps the client tackle a specific or general problem such as a particular mental illness or a source of life stress. Depending on the approach used by the therapist, a wide range of techniques and strategies can be used. However, almost all types of psychotherapy involve developing a therapeutic relationship, communicating and creating a dialogue and working to overcome problematic thoughts or behaviours.

According to *Medilexicon's Medical Dictionary*, psychotherapy is the,

> treatment of emotional, behavioural, personality, and psychiatric disorders based primarily on verbal or non-verbal communication and interventions with the patient, in contrast to treatments using chemical and physical measures.

Simply put, psychotherapy aims to alleviate psychological distress through talking, rather than drugs.

Psychotherapy can be understood as a unique relationship between the clinician and the patient within which there is communication which can relieve distress and set conditions for relearning and personal growth. For therapeutic change to occur the process must also include new personally meaningful and emotionally important experience in the therapy relationship itself. The patient has to re-experience emotions which he has been unable to cope with in the past. Coming to know his problems better, including knowledge of their origin, is secondary.

Psychotherapists usually receive remuneration in some form in return for their time and skills. This is one way in which the relationship can be distinguished from an altruistic offer of assistance. The therapist is simultaneously compassionate and dispassionate, in another words, the ability for attachment and detachment.

When therapist feels that he has lost the balance of attachment and detachment required for giving the patient understanding, respect and help it is sometimes necessary to discontinue seeing a patient or to suggest another therapist. The relationship in psychotherapy is not egalitarian and symmetrical as the ideal of friendship and love, rather it is a professional relationship. He may still believe that it is the therapist acts rather than his own that make the difference.

Many patients start with the assumption that if they only do what is expected as the therapist dictates, they will immediately feel better. And, indeed many do. Early in therapy there is often a great sense of relief and some functional improvement, and many clinic patients terminate therapy at this point.

Many psychotherapists have pointed to the great importance of the patient's faith and trust in the therapist as a major, if not primary, determinant of therapeutic change. This is viewed as a common denominator to all professional efforts to change behaviour, which indeed is shared with shamans and other folk healers. All good therapists practise the principal of flexibility, adjusting their methods to the needs of a particular patient rather than staying firmly with one or another therapeutic approach.

The goal of therapy has been put in of removing symptoms, restoring earlier level of functioning, freeing the person to be self-actualizing or making a fully functioning person, helping the patient find personal meaning and values, or reconstructing defences and character, releasing pent-up feelings, becoming aware of unconscious impulses and muscular relaxation. During the 1950s, Albert Ellis originated Rational Emotive Behaviour Therapy (REBT).

A few years later, psychiatrist Aaron T. Beck developed a form of psychotherapy known as cognitive therapy. Both of these included generally relative short, structured and present-focused therapy aimed at identifying and changing a person's beliefs, appraisals and reaction-patterns, by contrast with the more long-lasting insight-based approach of psycho-dynamic or humanistic therapies. Cognitive and behavioural therapy approaches were combined and grouped under the heading and umbrella-term Cognitive Behavioural Therapy (CBT) in the 1970s.

Many approaches within CBT were oriented towards active/ directive collaborative empiricism and mapping, assessing and modifying client's core beliefs and dysfunctional schemas. These approaches gained widespread acceptance as a primary treatment for numerous disorders. A "third wave" of cognitive and behavioural therapies developed, including Acceptance and Commitment Therapy and Dialectical Behaviour Therapy, which expanded the concepts to other disorders and/or added novel components and mindfulness exercises. Counselling methods developed, including solution-focused therapy and systemic coaching. Postmodern psychotherapies such as Narrative Therapy and Coherence Therapy did not impose definitions of mental health and illness, but rather saw the goal of therapy as something constructed by the client and therapist in a social context. Systems Therapy also developed, which focuses on family and group dynamics and transpersonal psychology, which focuses on the spiritual facet of human experience. Other important orientations developed in the last three decades include feminist therapy, brief therapy, somatic psychology, expressive therapy and applied positive psychology.

Major purposes of different therapeutic interventions are said to be: Strengthening the patient motivation to do the right things, reducing emotional pressure by facilitating the expression of feelings, releasing the potential for growth, changing habits, modifying the cognitive structure of the person, gaining self-knowledge, facilitating interpersonal relations and communication, gaining knowledge and facilitating decision-making, altering bodily states, altering state of consciousness and changing the social environment. In the early treatment of hysteria, cure was seen to occur when the patient dramatically recovers a repressed memory in a flood of emotion. Except perhaps in case of traumatic anxiety neurosis, such as might result from the stress of combat. Psychotherapy rarely involves such intense and curative cathartic experiences. Catharsis in such cases is often facilitated by hypnosis or drugs. Modification of the cognitive structure of the person is related to his idea about the nature of the world, others and himself. It is surely true that bringing hidden motives to conscious critical examination reduces their potential for compulsive maladaptive action.

However, as noted earlier, the process involved is not one of intellectual mastery but rather involves emotional learning. Some interpersonal theorists focus on the earliest primary relationship within the family of origin while others are more concerned with contemporary relations with spouse, lover, children, parents, boss and colleagues. Relaxation training as a device to reduce tension and anxiety is of major importance in some approaches to behaviour therapy as a first and necessary step to counter-conditioning. In a more extensive sense, some therapists have focused on the interdependence of bodily and mental processes.

Techniques have been developed for explicitly increasing body awareness. This may involve focusing attention on particular muscular or somatic sensations, or they may make use of exercises, some derived from Indian yoga or of massage or dance. They are all intended to increase the range of experience by bringing to conscious awareness and control sensory experiences which normally occur outside of awareness. The value of such motoric and somatic experiences has been conceptualized in a variety of ways but specially emphasized are the sense of self-mastery of body activity, and thoughts, feelings and actions as necessary facets of psychological health. In these approaches, we see a new meaning to the ancient Greek idea "clean mind in a clean body".

Another therapeutic purpose involves altering state of consciousness in order to extend self-awareness, control and creativity. Paralleling the exploration of hitherto unknown somatic experience is a concern with normally inaccessible psychological experiences of the sort which, for example, occur in dreams and other altered states of consciousness. Psychoanalysis and other dynamic therapies have always emphasized the importance of reducing the constrains on conscious thought, as in free association, in order to make accessible unconscious wishes and impulses.

The present concern is more in line with Jung's creative unconscious, which expresses the belief that therein lay not the destructive and primitives in man's nature but essentially his highest potential. Oriental philosophies have long emphasized the importance of inner experience in distinction to the Western concern with rational thought and conscious, goal-directed action. People are honoured who can shut themselves off from ordinary stimuli and meditate on internal experience. Thus isolation, meditation and other techniques are used to facilitate a reduction of attention to the external real world and a corresponding inward turning of attention toward a realm of experience which is viewed as equal real and perhaps more important, particularly in a time when "the world is too much with us". Profound and mystic experiences are reported which lead the person to emotional peace and heightened self-awareness. As with body awareness, different rationales are used to justify different methods of consciousness expansion. Compared to conventional psychotherapies, such approach minimizes the importance of conscious communication and discussion of experience in favour of extending the range of experience itself.

Rogerian client-centred therapy put primary emphasis on the potential for growth. The Rogerian therapy of the early 1950s, for example, laid more weight on examining the conscious content of the patient's beliefs and feelings, then it moved toward greater emphasis on the interpersonal process, and most recently to an interest in the non-verbal, bodily and altered states of consciousness processes.

Contemporary psychotherapy is dominated by three major orientations: the psychoanalytic, the behavioural, and the humanistic-existential. The numerous distinct forms of psychotherapy currently being practised can be viewed in terms of belonging to one or another of these major groups, though any cataloguing is arbitrary. Psychoanalytic therapies, behaviour therapies and the humanistic–existential approaches differ not only in their techniques but in their very concepts as to the nature of man, the development of personality and in their values as to desired state of mental health.

Psychoanalytic psychotherapy has many approaches like standard psychoanalysis, psychoanalytically-oriented psychotherapy, neo-Freudian psychoanalysis, ego psychology, analytical psychology of Jung, individual psychology of Alfred Adler, non-verbal intervention of Wilhelm Reich and so on. There are some other approaches in psychotherapy which are as a product of the combination of other main schools of psychotherapy like cognitive-behaviour therapy and rational-emotive-behaviour therapy, family therapy and group therapy.

Psychoanalysis was developed in the late 1800s by Sigmund Freud. His therapy explores the dynamic workings of a mind understood to consist of three parts: the hedonistic id, the rational ego and the moral superego. Because the majority of these dynamics are said to occur outside people's awareness, Freudian psychoanalysis seeks to probe the unconscious by way of various techniques, including dream interpretation and free association. Freud maintained that the condition of the unconscious mind is profoundly influenced by childhood experiences. So, in addition to dealing with the defence mechanisms employed by an overburdened ego, his therapy addresses fixations and other issues by probing deeply into clients' youth.

The emphasis on gaining insight has considerable importance in psychoanalysis. It means recapturing repressed memories and bringing them to the light of consciousness which is the essence of therapeutic cure. But it is by now widely recognized by psychoanalyst as well as therapist of other persuasions that insight in its narrow meaning is insufficient. Thus psychoanalysts often distinguish between emotional insight and intellectual insight because change depends on experiential and emotional learning.

Other psychodynamic theories and techniques have been developed and used by psychotherapists, psychologists, psychiatrists, personal growth facilitators, occupational therapists and social workers. Techniques for group therapy have also been developed. While behaviour is often a target of the work, many approaches value working with feelings and thoughts. This is especially true of the psychodynamic schools of psychotherapy, which today include Jungian therapy and psychodrama as well as the psychoanalytic schools. Other approaches focus on the link between the mind and body, and try to access deeper levels of the psyche through manipulation of the physical body. Examples are Rolfing, bio-energetic analysis and postural integration.

Nature and Basics of Yogic Psychotherapy

Yogic psychotherapy may be understood as combination of conventional psychotherapy and yogic approaches and its various techniques; in which therapist tries to apply yogic practices as a complement for the treatment of mental disorders. Yogic psychotherapy is a unique relationship between a yoga expert and a patient within which there is communication as well as yogic, physical, emotional and mental experiences; which can relieve distress and set conditions for relearning and personal growth.

Sheldon J. Korchin (2004: 33-34) states that, for therapeutic change to occur, the process must also include new personally meaningful and emotionally important experiencing in the therapy relationship itself. The patient has to re-experiencing emotions which he has been unable to cope with in the past. Coming to know his problems better, including knowledge of their origin, is secondary. Affecting rather than intellectual learning is central. With the help of sub-divisions of unicentral confederative model of consciousness especially magnetic and pond model we understood that passive yogic concentration can reduce the affect-laden of self-conscious and unconscious contents.

Yoga is more based on affective and emotional experience rather than intellectual learning because of inductive and intuitional nature of yogic techniques so with the help of yoga we gain more emotional experience and with the help of conventional psychotherapy we gain more intellectual experience. Minimum role of yoga in psychotherapy is acceleration of emotional experience so the combination of yoga and psychotherapy can lead to more successful treatment. The emphasis on gaining insight has considerable importance in psychoanalysis. It means recapturing repressed memories and bringing them to the light of consciousness which is the essence of therapeutic cure. But it is by now widely recognized by psychoanalysts as well as therapists of other persuasions that insight in its narrow meaning is insufficient. Thus psychoanalysts often distinguish between emotional insight and intellectual insight because change depends on experiential and emotional learning.

State of yogic passive concentration accelerates the presence of subliminal impressions according to the oceanic model of consciousness so it is parallel to the work of psychoanalyst in which he tries to recapture repressed memories and bring them into the light of self-conscious mind. But as we quoted above yoga is more based on emotional experience so it can complement the work of psychoanalyst to direct the patient towards emotional insight. A unique advantage of yoga for psychotherapist is that he has to gain experience through practice of yogic technique.

Yoga is the process of the observation of our whole existence so it is possible only under the condition in which we are detached from external as well as internal stimulants; in another word, yoga is a practice of detachment from external world and attachment to internal world for the increment of the awareness about thoughts and emotions so it can help the therapist to control his emotions to prevent interference of emotions with his professional relationship.

Only in such conditions psychotherapist is able to control extra attachment and inappropriate detachment so it leads therapeutic relationship continues in proper channel. The relationship in psychotherapy is not egalitarian and symmetrical as the ideal of friendship and love rather it is professional relationship. He may still believe that it is the therapist's acts rather than his own that make the difference.

Sheldon J. Korchin writes in his book *Modern Clinical Psychology* (pp. 33-34) that in medical research it is well known that response to a drug may depend on belief as to the drugs action, faith in the doctor and other psychological factors unrelated to the specific physiological action of the drug. Faith is important in different ways and at different times in psychotherapy.

A.S. Dalal (2001: 55) says that many people see yoga teachers and *gurus* as with more integrated personality and higher level of consciousness rather than other persuasions; so it increases the expectations of the people as well as faith on the ability of yoga practitioners to impress the people with their personality. It is clear that faith provides proper background and matrix for change so it makes ready the mental condition of the people for more inductive effects of yogic techniques. In addition faith is as an important part of yoga philosophy. If we consider inductive power of faith as well as importance of faith in yoga then we are able to realize that the yogic psychotherapist has a better chance for the use of the faith and its inductive power to cure the patients.

The goal of therapy has been many — removing symptoms, restoring earlier level of functioning, freeing the person to be self-actualizing or making a fully functioning person, helping the patient find personal meaning and values, or reconstructing defences and character, releasing pent-up feelings, and becoming aware of unconscious impulses and muscular relaxation.

Major purposes of different therapeutic interventions are said to be strengthening the patient motivation to do the right things, reducing emotional pressure by facilitating the expression of feelings, releasing the potential for growth, changing habits, modifying the cognitive structure of the person, gaining self-knowledge, facilitating interpersonal relations and communication, gaining knowledge and facilitating decision-making, altering bodily states, altering state of consciousness and changing the social environment.

Among the purposes of psychotherapy, altering bodily states and altering state of consciousness are the main domains of yoga. Gaining self-knowledge, reducing emotional pressure by facilitating the expression of feelings, releasing the potential for growth are also the common purposes of yoga philosophy. It seems if yoga combines with psychotherapy the new approach which is called yogic psychotherapy has more capacity to make the goals of therapy accessible.

In the early treatment of hysteria, cure was seen to occur when the patient dramatically recovers a repressed memory in a flood of emotion. Except perhaps in the case of traumatic anxiety neurosis, such as might result from the stress of combat. Psychotherapy rarely involves such intense and curative cathartic experiences. Catharsis in such cases is often facilitated by hypnosis or drugs.

According to *Psychology, Mental Health and Yoga* confrontment with repressed and pent-up memory, called *saṁskāra*s and *vāsanā* in yoga philosophy, is accelerated with the help of passive yogic concentration. According to oceanic and magnetic model of consciousness, presented earlier in the state of passive concentration, the affect-laden of subliminal impressions reduces which seems similar to catharsis in psychotherapy so can facilitate the treatment of hysteria as well as traumatic anxiety neurosis.

In *Modern Clinical Psychology*, the author explains that modification of the cognitive structure of the person is related to his idea about the nature of the world, others and himself. Concomitant use of yogic techniques and cognitive therapy can accelerate the process of the modification of the cognitive structure of the patient.

It is true that bringing hidden motives to conscious critical examination reduces their potential for compulsive maladaptive action. However as noted earlier the process involved is not one of intellectual masteries but rather involves emotional learning.

This statement is pointing out to the role of yogic concentrative methods and meditation, which is a part of yogic techniques for the transformation of consciousness. As mentioned above the realm which is not accessible by conventional approaches of psychology is accessible through meditation and yogic experiences.

Psychology, Mental Health and Yoga states that conventionally yoga is seen as a part of ancient Indian spiritual and mystical practices; but only recently by the scientific tendency towards yoga, it has arrived in the realm of therapeutic use. In Eastern philosophical and psychological world-view yoga is still an important part of the spiritual and mystical experience. Recently, therapeutic use of mystical experiences has made a new approach in psychotherapy which is called transpersonal psychotherapy. Importance of mystical experiences is in therapeutic use is the common area of yoga and transpersonal psychotherapy.

As emphasized here, bodily experiences and altered states of consciousness have become important parts of client-centred therapy.

YOGIC PSYCHOANALYSIS

Unconscious forces, contents, conflicts, motives, symbols and resistance are the specific domain of psychoanalysis. The process of the treatment of neurosis, anxiety and other mental disorders is done by bringing unaware and unknown aspects of unconscious mind into the light of self-conscious mind which is called insight. A psychoanalyst, with the help of free association, catharsis, transference, abreaction, dream and symbol interpretation, tries to diagnose a patient's main problems and root causes of mental disorders, and decreases the affect-laden of unconscious thoughts and conflicts. Whatever screening and censoring function of self-conscious mind reduces the process of encountering with unconscious contents or subliminal impressions in result with free association is accelerated, in addition for better fulfilment of free association and catharsis, physical and emotional relaxation is required. Now we easily understand yogic passive concentration and relaxation can be used in the process of free association for effective confronting with unconscious contents or subliminal impressions simultaneously emotional release can be done under the process of yogic passive concentration which reduces affect-laden of revealed unconscious thoughts and contents. It can lead to effective catharsis so if the combination of yogic techniques and psychoanalysis is applied, obviously it improves the quality of psychoanalysis and decreases the period of psychoanalysis. Self-awareness and self-knowledge are important tasks of a psychoanalyst because if the psychoanalyst deeply realizes himself his ability to understand the patient is increased so yogic passive concentration method is the best way for enhancing self-awareness and self-perception. By the help of pure observation of our whole existence and also principal of effortless effort psychoanalyst effectively realizes himself.

Yoga has the high potential of getting combined with different approaches of psychotherapy because they have many similarities in their goals and procedures. Somewhere with the help of yogic approach and techniques we can facilitate the procedure of psychoanalysis and make more successful psychoanalysis. There are different approaches in psychoanalysis like classical psychoanalysis, analytical psychology of Jung, neo-Freudian psychoanalysis, ego psychology, individual psychology of Adler, interpersonal psychology of Otto Rank, non-verbal intervention of Wilhelm Reich and psychoanalytical-oriented psychotherapy which is the combination of neo-Freudian and ego psychology.

Yoga has a common realm with most approaches of psychoanalysis. This common realm is included in subliminal impressions and unconscious forces, self-awareness and insight, free association and passive concentration, dream interpretation and symbols, catharsis and abreaction, and affective and emotional atmosphere.

With the help of geometrical interference of human consciousness we can well understand the importance of the confrontation with unconscious realm; and with the help of unicentral confederative model of consciousness, pond model, magnetic model and oceanic model of consciousness, we can explain the procedure of the reduction of affect-laden of thoughts.

As we know the process of concentration in yoga consists of passive and active concentration. In the process of passive concentration confrontation with subliminal impressions, which are called *saṁskāras* and *vāsanās*, occurs. In this process, it is emphasized to a person under concentration to practise effortless effort skill and pure observation so it helps to bring the unconscious and subconscious contents to the light of self-conscious mind. Spontaneous stream of thoughts, which moves in self-conscious mind, is determined and controlled by affect-laden thoughts; so under the effect of passive concentration, those thoughts which are more affect-laden appear earlier than those thoughts which have less affect-laden. In contrast, in yogic active concentration, we just focus our attention on the central object and prevent the appearance of subliminal impressions. Imagination, embodiment and visualization are used in yogic active concentration. With the help of yogic active concentration we increase the affect-laden of specific thought or central object; but in passive concentration we decrease the affect-laden of subliminal impressions without increment of central objects affect-laden.

YOGIC BEHAVIOUR THERAPY

Systematic desensitization and assertive technique are two basic techniques of behaviour therapy. The use of relaxation and imagination is the popular procedure of systematic desensitization and assertive therapy, so with the help of yogic relaxation methods like *āsana*, breathing exercise and *yoga-nidrā*, we can increase the depth of relaxation. On the other hand, for better imagination, we can use yogic active concentration. As we know in systematic desensitization, Jacobson progressive muscle relaxation technique is used, which is a superficial method compared to yogic deep relaxation. Yogic lifestyle itself is a positive conditioning in behaviour therapy in which we try to substitute useful change in our overall behaviour like physical postures, rhythmic breathing, effective interpersonal relationship, regular sleep and waking time and diet adaptation. Prescription of yogic lifestyle for patient under behaviour therapy should be applied after emission of negative behaviour. If we apply yogic techniques in systematic desensitization or assertive therapy it can also help the patient to attentively observe the appearance of tension and relaxation in the muscles, leading to increased body awareness.

According to Hans Strupp and J. Binder (1984: 43), imagination and embodiment, expansion of body, and sensual awareness are the common areas of yoga and behaviour therapy. As we discussed above systematic desensitization and assertive therapy are the main methods of behaviour therapy in which muscle relaxation, imagination and embodiment techniques are used. With the help of yogic techniques, a patient can experience deeper and more effective relaxation — physical as well as emotional and mental relaxation. So, if yoga is combined with behaviour therapy, it improves the efficacy of therapy.

YOGIC HUMANISTIC-EXISTENTIAL PSYCHOTHERAPY

Self-actualization of Abraham Maslow is the prominent aspect of humanistic psychology. According to humanistic school of psychology, human conscious motives, feelings, wishes and desires are the determinants of human behaviour. Environmental factors which are in the core attention of behavioural psychology and unconscious forces which are central attentiveness of psychoanalyst are trivial determinants of human behaviour so self-improvement and enhancement should be the optimum desire and motive of human if any obstacle or barrier appears. For self-actualization of human, it creates disturbance and disorder; so humanistic psychotherapy tries to find out the obstacles and removes hindrances and motivates one to go for self-actualization. Responsibility, volition and will-power are the important facts of existential psychology; which has its roots in the European existential philosophy. It is believed that existential psychology and psychotherapy are the results of Americanization of European existential philosophy. Due to the common areas of both psychotherapeutic schools which are self-conscious and phenomenal determinants in human behaviour, they have combined to build humanistic-existential psychotherapy. Between three main branches of humanistic-existential psychotherapy — gestalt therapy of Fritz Perls, logo therapy of Viktor Frankl and client-centred therapy of Carl Rogers — is the common field of yoga, because yoga is the process of the expansion of self-conscious mind. Yoga is also the process of integration of personality and different dimensions of human life as physical, emotional, mental, social and environmental. So, yogic view corresponds to the holistic concept of Goldstein. Humanistic-existential psychotherapy has common area with yoga in concepts like importance of present time, integration of personality, self-awareness and emotional saturated atmosphere. Yoga has the capacity to combine with different approaches of humanistic-existential therapy, as we discussed earlier, altered state of consciousness and bodily experiences have located at the centre of the attention of client-centred and other approaches of humanistic-existential psychotherapy.

Jerome Frank (1988: 1-2) states that logo therapy, which is more related to the existential quest of the human to find out the meaning and purpose of life, is related to the contemplative and deliberative aspects of yoga; if any obstruction occurs for this essential quest, spiritual dilemma appears, thus with the help of logo therapy patient is cured. As we know yoga is a broad area and it is a concept for contemplation as well as spirituality which can be applied to help the patient to overcome spiritual dilemmas, so the combination of yoga and humanistic-existential psychotherapy can be called yogic–humanistic-existential psychotherapy.

YOGIC COGNITIVE THERAPY

Cognitive therapy, introduced by Beck, is related to modification and reconstruction of errors in thoughts, perception, believes and schema of the patient. According to cognitive psychology, behaviour is first determined by cognitive processes of mental functioning. If any disturbance occurs in mental functioning, it affects the behaviour. So, for modification of the human abnormal behaviour, we have to modify the mental and cognitive process.

Perception, affection and thinking are the core concepts of cognitive therapy. After emission of faulty thoughts and thinking pattern of the patient, cognitive therapist can conjoin it with yogic passive concentration to make the positive attitude towards himself, others and environment because yogic passive concentration makes the patient's mind peaceful and calm, providing better mental condition to consolidate effective and positive attitude.

Going by Jerome Frank (1988: 1-2), yogic passive concentration can also reduce the extra and negative affect-laden of thoughts. With the help of unicentral confederative model of consciousness we can understand the procedure of the reduction of affect-laden of conscious as well as unconscious thoughts. So, yoga may help a cognitive therapist with the help of active and passive concentration, meditation and contemplation to better modification and reorganization of thoughts, believes and schemas of the patient. This combination of yoga and cognitive psychotherapy can be called yogic cognitive therapy.

YOGIC COGNITIVE BEHAVIOUR THERAPY

According to cognitive behaviour therapy, abnormal behaviour is due to disturbance of thought and thinking process as well as negative conditioning and learning. For the treatment of abnormal behaviour, we have to change the learning and cognitive processes simultaneously. As we discussed above, yoga is a common field in both approaches thus the combination of yoga with cognitive behaviour therapy can be called yogic cognitive behaviour therapy, especially *aṣṭāṅga-yoga* is relatively a perfect approach of yoga to adapt in cognitive behaviour therapy.

Prayer: As Faith Healing

The life of man is a life of wants and needs and therefore of desires, not only in his physical and vital, but in his mental and spiritual being. When he becomes conscious of greater power governing the world, he approaches it through prayer for the fulfilment of his needs, for help in his rough journey, and for protection and aid in his struggle.

The word *prārthanā* (prayer) is derived from two words *pra* and *artha* meaning pleading fervently. In other words, it is asking God for something with intense yearning. The word "pray" comes from the Latin word *precari,* which simply means to entreat or ask. Through a prayer a devotee expresses his helplessness and endows the doership of the task to God. Giving the doership to God means that we acknowledge that God is helping us and getting the task done. Prayer is an important tool of spiritual practice in the generic spiritual path of devotion.

Prayer includes respect, love, pleading and faith. Faith is the foundation of a religion. Psychologists analyse its nature. Mystics describe its effects. Theologians dispute its meaning. When we hear of miracles, we hear that they were wrought through faith. When we pray and do not get what we pray for, we are likely to be told that we do not have enough faith.

What is this faith that we are told is so important to us? Faith is not so much a matter of the mind as of the heart. Sometimes in seeking to understand God as a principle, we lose sight of God as a presence. Theologians and philosophers can know God as words to set down in books, but a child that cannot even utter the name of God may have a faith beyond that of learned priests. To have faith is not to theorize God, but to experience God.

Faith is the opposite of fear. Have you ever felt the icy feet, the racing heart, the unnerved hands of fear? The hands of faith are strong and sure. The feet of faith move steady to the will. The heart of faith beats quietly in tune with God. Faith is warmth, a feeling of well-being that envelops the body and overflows the mind. Faith brings an inward peace, a tranquil spirit.

Faith is the expectation of the unexpected. Faith is an open and courageous heart. The arms of faith are outstretched, not in supplication but in surrender to life's sovereign will, in submission to the ruling order of the universe, in receptivity to good.

Faith is the power to see in the disappointment of today the fulfilment of tomorrow, in the end of old hopes the beginning of new life. Faith is the inward power to see beyond the outward signs, the power to know that all is right when everything looks wrong. When our fondest dreams seem to go amiss and our dearest prayers seem to remain unanswered, faith is a vision of life that soars beyond the limitations of the self — these narrow senses, this imperfect reason, this drift of circumstance — and sees that our life is a part of something more than we have ever understood. In spite of all that may seem and all that may happen there is an ultimate fulfilment, that all is truly well, that all must be well. Life has an eternal meaning, we are one with the infinite, and whatever may befall us, in the all-infolding, all-unfolding everness of God, life will work out for good.

To have such faith is to have the serenity of the saint, the passion of the poet and the exaltation of the mystic. You can learn to have faith. Faith is not an abstraction; it is an attitude toward life, a feeling about life. It does not come out of signs of miracles or any outward happenings so much as out of inward growth.

Spirituality has many forms and can be practised in many ways. Prayer, for example, may be silent or spoken out loud and can be done alone in any setting or in groups, as in a church or in a temple. Regular attendance at a church, temple or mosque may involve prayer that focuses on one's self (called supplication) or on others (called intercessory prayer). In this type of setting, the entire congregation may be asked to pray for a sick person or the person's family.

Some religions set aside certain times of day and days of the week for prayer. Standard prayers written by religious leaders are often memorized and repeated in private sessions and in groups. Prayer is also practised individually and in informal groups, without a specific religion or denomination, and on no particular schedule. Prayers often ask a higher being for help, understanding, wisdom or strength in dealing with life's problems.

Spirituality can also be practised without a formal religion. Meditation, twelve-step work (as practised in Alcoholics Anonymous and similar groups), and seeking meaning in life all involve spirituality. Even simple practices such as silent observation, listening or gratitude can become part of an open-ended spirituality that can infuse everyday life. Some people express their spirituality by spending time with nature, doing creative work or serving others.

Many medical institutions and practitioners include spirituality and prayer as important components of healing. In addition, hospitals have chapels and contracts with ministers, rabbis, clerics, and voluntary organizations to serve their patients' spiritual needs.

Proponents of spirituality claim that prayer can decrease the negative effects of disease, speed recovery and increase the effectiveness of medical treatments. Faith and religious beliefs are also thought to improve coping and provide comfort during illness. Attendance at religious events and services is sometimes linked with improvement of various health conditions such as heart disease, hypertension, stroke, colitis, uterine and other cancers, and overall health status. Scientific evidence is mixed.

Some religious groups, such as Christian scientists, claim prayer can cure any disease. These groups often rely entirely on prayer in place of conventional medicine. This belief is based on a spiritual rather than a biological explanation of how disease develops. There have been some reported cases that prayer has led to tumour regression. Many people believe that the spiritual dimension is important when a person is coping with serious illness. The ability to find meaning in life can be helpful when dealing with cancer, even though it cannot cure the disease. Spirituality may also help us accept death, both our own and the deaths of those we love.

Because religion or spirituality is important to many people, mental health workers need to be aware of the issues surrounding each so that they will be able to help clients more effectively.

Prayer plays a large part in the lives of many religious people, and sometimes, clients desire prayer to be a part of their therapy. Instead of ignoring the topics of religion and prayer, mental health practitioners need to be aware of the ethical guidelines surrounding these issues. Also, they should be educated in when and how to incorporate spiritual treatment methods into therapy and then strive to remain updated on these topics.

Mantra Sādhanā: Behavioural Techniques to Control Mind

*Mantra*s have a great significance in the mental and spiritual evolution of harmony. These could also manifest tremendous results in the physical world; they could be powerful like a Patton tank or an atomic bomb. Our spiritually empowered, eminent ancestors — the *r̥ṣi*s — knew this fact and had therefore developed a whole gamut of *mantra*s for specific purposes and had also devised the methods of experimentation with the use of these subliminal tools.

*Mantra*s also have their own history of discovery and mastery of inner realms of consciousness by a long line of masters and seekers of spirit. *Mantra*s and *yantra*s have been in existence since pre-historic times. The Vedic scriptures describe that once the *deva*s (gods) and the *asura*s (demons) argued as to what was superior — *mantra* or *yantra*? The demons regarded *yantra*s as superior and mightier as material resources and capabilities were more important to them. The gods affirmed the prominence of *mantra*s; that is, spirituality was of greater significance to them. We all have seen and used several types of *yantra*s in this age of materialistic progress. Let us acquaint ourselves with some knowledge of *mantra*s here.

The effects of *mantra*s largely pertain to the mental, emotional and spiritual realms of life. *Mantra*s inspire positive and penetrating thoughts and enlighten the emotional and deeper levels of consciousness. *Mananāt-trayate iti mantraḥ* — by the *manana* (constant thinking or recollection) of which one is protected or is released from the round of births and deaths — is *mantra*. That is called *mantra* by the meditation (*manana*) on which the *jīva* (the individual soul) attains freedom from sin, enjoyment in heaven and final liberation, and by the aid of which it attains the four *puruṣārtha*s, i.e. *dharma*, *artha*, *kāma* and *mokṣa*. A *mantra* is so-called because it is achieved by the mental process. The root *man* in the word *mantra* comes from the first syllable of that word, meaning "to think", and *tra* from *trai* meaning "to protect" or "free" from the bondage of *saṁsāra* (the phenomenal world). By the combination of *man* and *tra* comes *mantra*.

The phonemes of the Vedic hymns and the seven fundamental nodes — *sā, re, gā, mā, pā, dhā, ni* — of the Indian classical music have originated (distinctly recognized by the *r̥ṣis*) from the vibrations of the sublime sound of *oṁ* in the Nature. The Vedic quote — *eko 'ham bahusyāmi* — implies that all the sounds, all the energies, all the motions and everything existing in the universe have originated from the vibrations of this single *anāhata nāda*. This is the source of the manifestation of the *Śabda-Brahman* and the *Nāda-Brahman*.

Mantras are in the form of praise and appeal to the deities, craving for help and mercy. Some *mantras* control and command the evil spirits. Rhythmical vibrations of sound give rise to forms. Recitation of the *mantras* gives rise to the formation of the particular figure of the deity.

There are several ways to practise *mantra-yoga*. Repeat the *mantra* verbally for some time, in a whisper for some time, and mentally for some time. The mind wants variety. It gets disgusted with any monotonous practice. The mental repetition is very powerful. It is termed *mānasika japa*. The verbal or loud repetition is called *vaikharī japa*. The loud *japa* shuts out all worldly sounds. There is no break of *japa* here. Repetition in a whisper or humming is termed *upāṁśu japa*. Even mechanical repetition of *japa* without any *bhāva* has a great purifying effect on the heart or the mind. The feeling will come later on when the process of mental purification goes on.

Many define *mantra* as an uplifting, energy-charged sublimated thought current. For example, *gāyatrī mantra* is the most sacred and sublime thought in the whole creation. In it, prayer has been made to the Divine symbolized as sun on behalf of whole of humanity for the gifts of righteousness and enlightened intelligence.

> *oṁ bhūrbhuvaḥ svaḥ tat-savitur-vareṇyam bhargo devasya dhimahi dhiyo yo naḥ pracodayāt*
>
> May the Almightly illuminate our intellect and inspire us towards the righteous path.

But the intellectual understanding of the meaning of *mantra*, although good, is not in itself sufficient to make it efficacious. It does not encompass all the variegated dimensions of a *mantra*.

A *mantra* may have a meaning or it may not have one. It may be a sublime thought or it may not be. Many times, the arrangement of its syllables is such as to give out a meaning, while at other times, this construction is so haphazard that no intelligible meaning can be made out of it. There are several other *mantra*s like:

ॐ नमो भगवते वासुदेवाय।
ॐ नमो नारायणाय।
हरि ॐ तत् सत्।

oṁ namo bhagavate vāsudevāya ।
oṁ namo nārāyaṇāya ।
hari oṁ tat sat ।

ॐ त्र्यम्बकम् यजामहे सुगन्धिम् पुष्टिवर्धनम्।
उर्वारुकमिव बन्धनान् मृत्योर्मुक्षीय मामृतात्।।

oṁ tryambakam yajāmahe sugandhim puṣṭivardhanam ।
urvārukamiva bandhanān mr̥tyor mukṣīya māmr̥tāt ।।

— *Yajurveda* I.60.3

and

ॐ नमः शिवाय

oṁ namaḥ śivāya

*Mantra*s are not some verbal structures to be enunciated rhythmically and repeatedly. Rather, these are subtle means of contemplating that can reorient the mental tendencies. Many people suffer from a variety of adversities, scarcities and worries because they do not have the aptitude to be initiated into proper *mantra*s (of same thinking, righteous attitude, etc.). *Mantra*s are defined as the tools for liberation from ignorance, illusion, infirmities and sorrows. These can transform the course of life and convert agonies into joys. Indeed, *mantra*s, as special carriers of the energy of cosmic sound, do have amazing potentials for effecting the physical world also (as some of you might have seen or read about *mantra*-based healing of physical and mental ailments, etc.). But the spiritual powers and benefits of the *mantra*s are far more intense and creative.

The methodology of a *mantra*'s functioning is novel. As the specific phase of its practice is completed, it connects the practitioner's inner consciousness with the specific cosmic energy current or cosmic energy.

But this is one aspect of its function. In its other aspect, it simultaneously makes the practitioner qualified and fit to receive this special power. By *mantra*-practice, certain secret recesses or zones of the practitioner's interior become activated, and he becomes capable of receiving, bearing and harnessing those subtle energies. Only then the *mantra* is said to have become *siddha* (accomplished or mastered). This *mantra siddhi* does not come by mere rote chanting or mechanical repetition. This explains why a good many persons even after years of practice of a *mantra* have to meet with disappointment. Either they get no result at all or only partial and negligible result. The fault lies not with the *mantra* but with the practitioner. It is important to bear in mind that any *mantra*-practice requires the practitioner to attune his life to the peculiar nature of the *mantra*.

Healing by *mantras* is an important aspect of the science of occultism. It can provide healing even in incurable-looking diseases, remedy at personality disorders and enable one to overcome the greatest of difficulties. The impossible becomes possible; the unachievable is made achievable. The true adepts in the theory and practice of this science are capable of yoking the powers of nature favourably and positively modifying the course of destiny.

Mantras are very special configurations of sounds or syllables. Accordingly, each *mantra* has specific patterns of enunciation or chanting. *Mantras* work on the *yantra* of our physical body and also on our energy-body, mind and the inner-self. In the *mantra-yoga* meditation one has to chant a word or a phrase until he/she transcends mind and emotions. In the process the superconscious is discovered and achieved. The rhythm and the meaning of *mantras* combine to conduct the mind safely back to the point of meditation — the higher consciousness or the specific spiritual focus. Different syllables, phrases and words possess their unique healing potential. Hence they are chanted at a specific time. As a tool to achieve stillness, the *mantra* is to be discarded at the moment stillness is achieved. Sometimes *mantras* are also applied to modify circumstances. In the chanting of the *mantras* it is of immense importance that they are pronounced properly or else all their intended effect would not come. For such purposes it is important that the proper pronunciation is imparted.

Spiritual Counselling: A Cognitive Therapy

Spiritual counselling is a process by which the counsellor and the client sit together and get the solution for the obstacle in the path of spirituality from the *guru* or spiritual leader. This process helps people to learn how to handle the challenges of daily life as well as in relationship with God; how to manage between worldly desire and inner peace. For example one can get relief from the continuous failure in life may be through an astrologer's advice. Jyotiṣa, Vāstu and other suggestions like *vrata*, *anuṣṭhāna*, *yajña* or other rituals sometimes help in achieving several desired results in life. Nowadays various centres of spiritual counselling can be found easily.

Through this process we begin to understand that God is real, we start to see that life can be different. We learn that we are not alone, because God is with us . . . but during times of stress or challenge we may forget this. The long years of habit can be difficult to undo on our own.

When the session is finished, you should both feel better because together you've raised both of your vibrations to be more connected with God. In other words, your session has called more of God's Light which helps everyone. Most of us are accustomed to thinking of ourselves as alone in the world. We are used to thinking that we need to figure things out on our own, and fight to survive.

Spiritual counselling recognizes that the split between psychotherapy and spirituality in the West is a cultural, not a natural, phenomenon. It takes as its roots transpersonal psychology, spiritual psychology, humanistic psychology, psycho-synthesis, and person-centred counselling.

Spiritual counselling helps us to meet life's challenges from a new consciousness of connection with God. It offers support to you as a whole person . . . your soul and spirit, your emotions, mind and body, and your practical life here on the earth.

Spiritual counselling takes the soul, rather than the mind, as its starting point of balance. It has an expanded view of life, recognizing that the world is a complex mystery and it takes into account belief systems, universal and personal energy systems, intuitive psychic realities, kārmic interplay, subconscious and superconscious states of awareness, metaphysical experiences, spiritual theology, spiritual presence and higher self–cosmic connections.

Faith is one of the important aspects in this process, and it should be in four dimensions: *Faith in Self* — that we have within us the wisdom to make the right choices. *Faith in potential* — that every situation has a potential for growth. *Faith in the journey* — that our lives have meaning. *Faith in Spirit* — that we are truly spiritual beings. The second thing is having awareness of a spiritual identity — we are all more than our personalities and our problems.

Spiritual counselling sees that life is innately personal and individuals want to build their own unique, flowing relationship with it, organically and without force. With the soul being the starting point individuals come from the heart, whilst not forgetting their head, and from this heart space they care for the sacred interdependence of all life. Compassion for self and others is a core concept for their personal and collective growth. As spiritual counselling is holistic, there is no separation, no duality between personal or collective responses and reaction, all is intrinsically linked. There is awareness that life experiences become the greatest tool, with the integration of personal pains and personal journey. The aim is for clients to express themselves and their world with intimate wisdom, spiritual awareness and personal authenticity; using integrity and wise use of their spiritual gifts, skills and knowledge.

Spiritual counsellors need a cross-cultural awareness and an understanding around spiritual emergency and other issues of spirituality. They recognize, and are committed to, a spiritual journey in their own lives, and the lives of others. By focusing on their core inner connection, creating an open heart connection and a mindfulness state, they create a holding and sacred space for the personal unfoldment of their clients.

In spiritual counselling the emphasis is on wholeness, dealing with the whole person, and assisting the client in inner balance and integration of all the dimensions of self. It is experiential and focuses on the clients individual experiences and reality, so the counsellor respecting them as unique assumes that the client's reality is different from his own. As each client is seen as an individual the sessions are non-prescriptive and individually tailored. The counsellor is thus active and creative, responding to the immediate issues brought by the client. The assumption is that human beings are innately motivated towards achieving their highest potential of awareness and fulfilment; the counsellor's role is to support this and trust the clients process.

The spiritual journey can be blissful and awakening, but also it can be arduous, frightening and lonely. Anyone can have a spiritual experience, or peak experience, but holistic self-realization is a different matter. Spiritual development best occurs at the point when the Ego identity is strong enough to take a little disorientation. Understanding and meaning of ones life depends on the presence of ego. If the ego is not strong and does not hold the person in a healthy reality; the spiritual opening then results in fragmentation and crises. This altered state of consciousness can be catastrophic to the ego if the individual contacts the lower level of consciousness rather than the higher level of consciousness. A healthy ego arises from the healing and integration of past traumas and of self-realization or self-awareness.

Yajña Therapy

Yajña therapy or yajñopathy is regarded as most promising in the cure of psychosomatic diseases and improvement of human psychology in general. How and why this happens and how to perform scientific experiments on *yajña* — study, analysis and implementation of these issues — would open up a new branch of research for modern scientists. The present volume would provide necessary inputs and guidelines in this regard in a simple, illustrative manner within the grasp of all readers including those without scientific educational background.

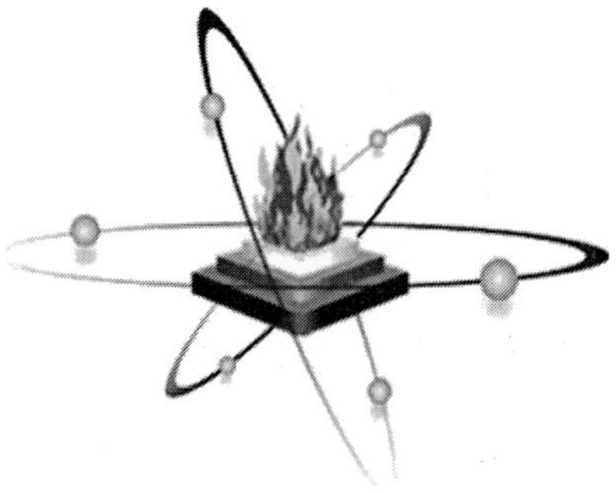

Yajña is a scientific method aimed at the finest utilization of the subtle properties of sacrificed matter with the help of the thermal energy of fire and the sonic vibrations of the *mantras*. In the process of *yajña*, herbal and medicinal plant sacrifices are made in the fire of specific type of wood in especially designed fire-pit or brick and clay structure called *yajña-kuṇḍa*. Slow combustion, sublimation, and most prominently, the transformation into vapour phase of the sacrificed herbal and medicinal plants and nutritious substances takes place in the *yajña*-fire.

Inhalation therapy and environmental purification are paramount applications of *yajña* apart from its enormous sublime impact and auspicious spiritual effects cited with reverence in the Śāstric literature.

All activities in the limitless expansion of the universe are said to have generated from a grand eternal *yajña*. *Atharvaveda* (9.15.14) describes *yajña* as:

श्र

ayaṁ yajño viśvasya bhuvanasya nābhirbrahmāyaṁ vācaḥ paramaṁ vyama ।

implying *yajña* as the fundamental process of manifestation of nature.

In physical terms, *yajña* (*homam*, *havana* or *agnihotra*) is a process of herbal sacrifices in holy fire aimed at the finest utilization of the subtle properties of sacrificed matter with the help of the thermal energy of fire and the sound energy of the *mantras*. Modern scientific research has also shown significant therapeutic applications of *yajña* and also affirmed its potential in purification of environment.

Literally speaking, *yajña* means selfless sacrifice for noble purposes. Sacrificing ego, selfishness, and material attachments, and adopting rational thinking, humane compassion and dedicated creativity for the welfare of all is indeed the best *yajña* which should be performed by all human beings. The philosophy of *yajña* teaches a way of living in the society in harmony, a living style to promote and protect higher humane values in the society, which is indeed the basis of the ideal human culture.

Yajña generates special energy fields and also increases the amount of negative ions and ozone in the surrounding atmosphere and thus activates the flow of vital energy in the *yājakas*. Understanding the interrelationship between the *yajñāgni* (fire and energy field of *yajña*) and the power of *prāṇa* — the subtle force of life — is fundamental to understand the principle of total natural cure by *yajña*. The Brahmvarchas Research Institute founded by Acharya Shriram Sharma has taken up pioneering research projects on scientific study and applications of *yajña*-based therapies — yajñopathy.

Acharya Shriram Sharma (2003: 27) writes that among the five basic elements (*pañca mahābhūta*), which constitute the human body, the *pṛthvī tattva* (substances and properties of earth) is most prominent. Absorption of different odours from the atmosphere affects the subtle properties of this element. Combustion of *havana sāmagrī* in *yajña* produces soothing odours, inhalation of which energizes the *pṛthvī tattva* in the bodies of the *sādhaka*s (*yājaka*s) who perform the *yajña*. The fumes and vapours of the herbs fumigated in *yajña* are absorbed by the skin-pores and the entire body. This removes the deficiencies of healthy products and natural substances of earth which are essential for the physical health of the body. Inhalation of the herbs and other nourishing substances of the *havana sāmagrī* which are sublimated and sublimed in *yajña*-fire takes them directly into the bloodstream and reaches every component, every corner of the body and thereby improves the body's resistance and vitality.

A large number of experiments are carried out on random samples of healthy and diseased persons. During such experiments, the subjects are asked to sit in the glass chamber and inhale the fumes of *yajña* for specific periods of time. A thorough analysis of their bodies and minds is made before and after performing this experiment.

Shelvamurthy (1996) has observed neurophysiological effects of the *mantra*s of a special kind of *agnihotra*, which is performed at the time of sunrise and sunset. In this experimental study eight healthy men were chosen as subjects. They reported on two consecutive days: First day was for control recording when rituals of *agnihotra* were performed but instead of the prescribed *mantra*s, some irrelevant syllables were uttered at specific time periods. Next day the *agnihotra* was performed with proper *mantra*s. Recording of physiological parameters — heartbeat rate, ECG lead-II, blood pressure, etc. — were made on both days. The results showed that while the mind (brain waves) remained unaltered during the first day *agnihotra*, significant changes occurred after the proper *agnihotra*; these included

— (a) GSR remained significantly higher during the proper *agnihotra*; (b) ECG showed DC shift in the base line; and (c) EEG showed alpha enhancement and delta suppression for more than 15 minutes.

An army officer of twenty-five years of age, who had been a poly-drug abuser in the past, was selected for the study by Lt. Col. G.R. Golecha, a senior advisor in the psychiatry division of the Indian army. The patient was at that time addicted to heroin for two years. He underwent some de-addiction courses twice in the past with no benefit and had become de-motivated and resistant to such methods. He was then introduced to *agnihotra*. The practice of *agnihotra* resulted in improving his motivation to abstain from smack and showed significant decrease in his urge for it within a few weeks.

R.R. Joshi (2006: 186) writes that the urine sugar level of some acute diabetic patients was found to be totally absent and the level of blood sugar was reduced to normal just after two to three weeks of daily *agnihotra*.

Yajñas Scientific Interpretation and *The New Age Force of Gayatri* reflect that in the recent years, the established healing therapies have begun to recognize the role of psychology in prevention and cure of diseases of different kinds. As the atmosphere, *prāṇa* and mind are interlinked; the individuals naturally experience relaxation, peace, quietening of the mind, loss of worries and stress in the *yajña* atmosphere. The increase in the level of *prāṇa* (vital energy) in the atmosphere when a *yajña* is performed — was also recorded with the help of Kirilian photographs of human hands before and after *yajña* in the experiments conducted by Matthias Ferbinger of Germany.

The atmosphere surrounding the place where a *yajña* (or *agnihotra*) is being performed and the ash produced in the *kuṇḍa* are suffused with energetic currents and soothing and uplifting ambience.

Further scientific research and large-scale experiments on the potentials of yajñopathy will help make it a distinct, alternative therapy of far-reaching benefits to humanity at large and open up newer directions for constructive integration of the modern and the ancient sciences.

Meditation: Mind Controlling Technique

Meditation classes are offered in schools, hospitals, law firms, government buildings, corporate offices and prisons. Specially marked meditation rooms can be found in airports, alongside the prayer chapels and Internet kiosks. *Time Magazine*, 4 August 2003, "Just Say Om", p. 48 states that in 2002, ten million American adults said that they practise some form of meditation regularly. The above report shows how sincerely the people are adopting the meditation. What is the reason behind it?

The mechanization of world, and the advancement of science and technology have provided us with enormous ranges of creature comforts. We have used it to move further towards the wrongly chosen valueless philosophy of loge and comfort-driven mode of living, generating restlessness, tensions, stress and a horde of new diseases and disorders. It is indeed a pity that man, the intelligent being, has chosen this dark path of self-inflicted pain and suffering for himself and of total annihilation of life. Man burns and ruins himself in the fire of unending cravings. His dire desire for fulfilment always remains unfulfilled. We want to be happy but often find that the circumstances of life pull us back into the mire of discontent, desperation and worries.

"Stress" has become a household word these days: even children are learning this name for the pervasive sense of pressure that shortens tempers, creates accidents, amplifies illnesses and obstructs creativity. Tension seems to be epidemic in our society. The only cure available is self-control: learning how to take responsibility for our physical, mental, emotional and spiritual reactions to life's changes. Change creates stress, and in our fast-changing world, we need effective tools to help us maintain a healthy balance.

All the worries and tensions are not capable of functioning on their own. They are guided and controlled by the mind. Maharṣi Patañjali has given the secret of controlling the mind in his *Yoga-Sūtras* — *yogaścittavr̥ttinirodhaḥ*. That is yoga is to control the wayward flow of tendencies of *citta* (mind). In other words, to become fully involved in the task at hand is yoga.

Practice of meditation is one of the important steps of eightfold path of yoga, guided by Patañjali. Even we find the mention of meditation in Vedic literatures, Upaniṣads, the *Gītā* and Purāṇas. Lord Kr̥ṣṇa says to Arjuna in thirty-fifth verse of the sixth chapter in the *Gītā*:

असंशयं महाबाहो मनो दुर्निग्रहं चलम्।
अभ्यासेन तु कौन्तेय वैराग्येण च गृह्यते।।

asaṁśayaṁ mahābāho mano durnigrahaṁ calam ।
abhyāsena tu kaunteya vairāgyeṇa ca gṛhyate ।।

The mind is restless no doubt and difficult to curb O Arjuna! But it can be brought under control by repeated practice of meditation and by the exercise of dispassion O son of Kuntī!

The word meditation is derived from two Latin words: *meditari* (to think, to dwell upon, and to exercise the mind) and *mederi* (to heal). Meditation usually refers to a state in which the body is consciously relaxed and the mind is allowed to become calm and focused.

Acharya Shriram Sharma (1976: 27) in a *sādhanā* camp unfolded the practical aspect of meditation. In his words, mental concentration on some gross objects, e.g. an idol, or a picture of a deity, is most convenient for majority of people; because, the human mind, in general, is not so developed that it could be focused for a stretch of without any visible or perceptible symbol. However with sincere practice, one begins to realize the presence of spirit in his inner self and learn to meditate upon it.

What is the real meaning of *dhyāna* (meditation)? It is a state of pure consciousness, which transcends the inner and outer senses. The climax of *dhyāna* is *samādhi*. In Indian tradition, it is used for inner soul growth. Western psychologists link it a special state of mind. The techniques and nature of meditation might vary but modern scientific researches validate and highlight its benefits. The practice of meditation helps in building up the coping ability. The practitioner of meditation slowly becomes aware of the inherent dormant potentialities and thus prevents himself from becoming a victim of distress.

K.N. Udupa (1977: 56) the author of *Stress and Its Management by Yoga*, suggests that stress-related disorders evolve gradually through four stages. In the first stage, psychological symptoms like anxiety and irritability arise due to over activation of the sympathetic nervous system. Research has shown that hormones and other biochemical compounds in the blood indicative of stress tend to decrease during meditation practice. These changes also stabilize over time, so that a person is actually less stressed biochemically during daily activity.

Judith Horstman (2005) states that meditation can help relieve many arthritis symptoms, such as pain, anxiety, stress and depression, as well as ease the fatigue and insomnia associated with fibromyalgia. It affects many body processes connected with well-being and relaxation. Recent studies suggest meditation may balance the immune system to help the body resist disease, and even heal. A 1998 University of Maryland study of twenty-eight women with fibromyalgia found that an eight-week programme of mindfulness meditation combined with the Chinese movement therapy *qi gong* and counselling in pain management techniques resulted in significant improvement in pain threshold, depression, coping and function.

Herbert Benson (1972) says that the practice of meditation changes the way our brain works, and find in his research study that thoughts can influence the brain and the body. When his research team used MRI imaging to study the brains of four people meditating, he says the team found increased activity in specific areas involved in attention and control of the autonomic nervous system.

Andrew Newberg (2001) has demonstrated a change in brain activity during meditation. Newberg infused a radioactive dye into the blood of eight experienced Tibetan Buddhist meditators to track the blood flow in the brain and light up the most active regions. Meditation allowed their brains to block information from the section of the brain that orients the body in space and time. Their bodies stopped responding to external stimuli and focused their energy inward. Newberg's experiment firmly established that the practice of meditation alters brain activity.

R.J. Davidson et al. (2003) in another study demonstrated positive effects on the immune system in participants achieving the shift in brain activity. Researchers at the University of Wisconsin gave flu shots to a group of newly-taught meditators and a control group of non-meditators and, then, measured the antibody levels in their blood. They also tracked brain activity to see how much the practitioner's mental activity shifted from the right hemisphere to the left. The meditators' blood contained more antibodies after flu shots. The participants whose brain activity shifted the most had even more antibodies.

The results suggest that people who take the time to cultivate their meditation technique will benefit from a healthier immune system. Meditation can also improve irritable bowel syndrome, ulcers and insomnia, among other stress-related conditions. Eighty per cent of the people who use meditation to relieve insomnia are successful. Meditation can help prevent or treat stress-related complaints such as anxiety, headaches, and bone, muscle and joint problems. Meditation also provides an inner sense of clarity and calm, and that, in it, may help to ward off certain illnesses.

What is the reason behind these changes? In the answer to this question Pranav Pandya in *Akhand Jyoti* (vol. 2 issue 5 (2004: 23)) says that meditation regulates and controls electrical and chemical activities in the brain, heart rhythm, blood pressure, skins capacity of resistance and many such functions inside the body. Meditation in real sense is an active hypometabolic condition.

Psychologists say that in a state of calm and quiet mind a great subtle energy field emerges from the deep recesses of the soul. It is very difficult for the ordinary people to get a feel of this energy field. A disciplined mind helps in physical, mental and spiritual well-being. There are several techniques of meditation among them *Savitā Dhyāna* (Meditation on Rising Sun) is highly effective and beneficial.

Prāṇāyāma: A Behavioural Technique to Control the Self

Prāṇāyāma is a traditional aspect of yoga. If we understand breath in terms of life force, there is a connection between controlling your breath and controlling your life force. The breath provides an easy access to gain an insight into the body and mind, and since it unites the two, breathing is essential to all yoga practices. According to *Haṭha-Yoga-Pradīpikā* (2.44):

> For he, who has gained control over his breath, shall also gain control over the activities of the mind. The reverse is also true. For he, whose mind is in control, also controls the breath. The mind masters the senses, and the breath masters the mind.

Through *prāṇāyāma* the mind can be brought under control. In many spiritual traditions, including Sufism, Buddhism and Yoga, it is known that by concentrating on the breath, one can still the mind, develop one-pointedness and gain entry into the deeper realms of the mind and consciousness.

With *prāṇāyāma* one achieves a higher energy level in his everyday life, and is granted the opportunity to reach a greater sense of self-insight and self-control. The word *prāṇāyāma* can be translated in several ways. Originally *prāṇa* refers to "the energy of life", but also covers concepts like the breath, wind, life, vitality, energy and strength. *Āyāma* can be translated as regulation, expansion or dimension. *Prāṇāyāma* is often directly translated as "breath control". This is not incorrect, but the essence of *prāṇāyāma* is the ability to take up and manage *prāṇa* mainly by using your breath.

Prāṇāyāma has an important role to play on the perceived mental health of the elderly. *Prāṇāyāma* has been found to help build that cheerful body–mind relationship, first by de-stressing the mind and then by freeing the body of its ailments. *Prāṇāyāma* works wonders for the human body, ridding it of all depressive energy and body tensions. Correct breathing can prevent most ailments. In this process we are transported to our very source — called the pure consciousness. Once one is in a state of pure consciousness, day-to-day worries and tensions disappear and the body begins to heal. When one is going through a stressful situation, the whole physiology; the brain and endocrine system, is influenced negatively. Breathing techniques *prāṇāyāma* establish a positive body–mind relationship. Removal of negative thoughts and tensions leads to a positive and healthy state of mind.

INCREASE IN CONCENTRATION, MEMORY AND IMAGINATIVE POWER

Once one starts concentrating on *prāṇāyāma*, the mind gets habituated to concentration and as a result the memory improves. According to Maharṣi Arvind, as quoted by K.V. Belsare (1989: 210):

> My experience is that with *prāṇāyāma* the brain gets enlightened. When I was in Baroda I used to practise *prāṇāyāma* daily for five to six hours, three hours in the morning and two in the evening. Then my mind used to function with great imaginative power and zeal. I used to write poetry then, on an average eight to ten lines per day, that is 200 lines per month. However after *prāṇāyāma* I could write 200 lines in just half an hour. Formerly my memory was weak; but after *prāṇāyāma* whenever I got the inspiration I would remember

the lines of the poem exactly and would write them down at my convenience.

WANDERING OF THE MIND DECREASES

Thinking and breathing are interrelated. If the mind does not wander from one topic to another, that is if it is steady then the respiratory rate is reduced. Contrary to this by practising *prāṇāyāma*, as the respiratory rate decreases so does the frequency of thoughts and that itself helps the mind to become steady.

ABILITY TO CONTROL THE MIND

With practice of *prāṇāyāma* one gets used to concentrating on breathing. In one technique of *prāṇāyāma*, one concentrates on maintaining a steady rhythm of breathing. Since one gets used to concentrating on breathing, when it becomes rapid one immediately becomes aware of it. This implies that indirectly one becomes aware that either thoughts have increased or emotions are being aroused. Then as one regulates the breathing so that it returns to normal, one can control thoughts and emotions. The biofeedback technique discovered after 1960 is based on the principle of "awareness of psychological changes due to alterations in body functions". In this technique sophisticated instruments were used to record blood pressure, body temperature, muscle tension, etc. On the other hand, our sages had discovered the simple cost-free technique of "concentrating on breathing", thousands of years ago.

Since during *prāṇāyāma* breathing is reduced, the oxygen supply to the brain is less. Less oxygen supply to the brain slows down its functions. Hence the waking state gradually starts decreasing and it facilitates entering a state of meditation. In one of the techniques of hypnosis, to reduce the oxygen supply to the brain, the carotid arteries are compressed for half to one minute. This reduces the oxygen supply to the brain and hence the wakefulness decreases and a hypnotic trance is induced. Since the above technique of hypnosis induction is dangerous, it is now obsolete.

GOING INTO MEDITATION

While practising *prāṇāyāma* the concentration is on breathing. This is akin to concentrating on a particular object during meditation. However when meditating on an object, the object of concentration, is usually fixed whereas in *prāṇāyāma* the mind concentrates on the rhythm of respiration. It is easier to concentrate on a moving than on a fixed object. Hence by concentrating on *prāṇāyāma* the chances of going into meditation are enhanced.

CURE OF MENTAL ILLNESSES

If particular types of *prāṇāyāma*s are performed then 3 per cent of patients suffering from minor mental illnesses are cured while another 5 per cent show improvement. Chanting the Lord's name proves more useful than *prāṇāyāma* in mental illnesses.

There are some specific techniques of *prāṇāyāma* mentioned in several texts, so all together have been mentioned below:

1. *Nāḍī Śodhana Prāṇāyāma means Nāḍī purifying Prāṇāyāma* — This particular *prāṇāyāma* should be taken as pre-*prāṇāyāma* practice. As according to its nature it purifies the all subtle energy channels called *nāḍīs*. This practice balancing the *iḍā* and *piṅgalā,* the mental force and vital force is one of the main objectives of *prāṇāyāma.* Left nostril (*iḍā*) and right nostril (*piṅgalā*) if balanced can awaken *suṣumṇā* (the psychic *nāḍī* or channel carrying *kuṇḍalinī*) *nāḍī.* Swami Swātmārāma recommends *nāḍī śodhana prāṇāyāma* (alternate nostril breathing with *kumbhaka* and *bandhas*) for purifying *iḍā* and *piṅgalā nāḍī*s.
2. *Sahita means "Combined"* — There are two types of *sahita prāṇāyāma*: first one is *sagarbha* (with seed) and second one is *nigarbha* (without seed). There are lots of benefits of this *prāṇāyāma* discussed in yogic texts. Practice of this *prāṇāyāma* leads to levitation; it cures diseases; it awakenes *śakti*; brings calmness, bliss of mind; exaltation of mental powers (e.g. clairvoyance).
3. *Sūrya-bhedana* (sun-piercing) to practise this *prāṇāyāma,* breath in through right nostril. Hold the breath inside and adopt *jālandhara bandha* so long as "the perspiration does not burst out from the tip of the nails and the roots of the hair" (according to Gheraṇḍa). Exhale through left nostril. This practice destroys decay and death; awakens *kuṇḍalinī śakti*; increases body fire (Gheraṇḍa); cleanses the brain, sinuses (Svātmārāma). This *prāṇāyāma* stimulates the sympathetic nervous system and left part of the brain. It eliminates wind

or gas-related trouble (*vāta doṣa*) balances mucus (*kapha doṣa*) and bile/acidity (*pitta doṣa*) as per Āyurveda.

4. *Ujjayī means "victorious"* — This is also called psychic breath. This type of *prāṇāyāma* is done with inhalation via nostrils then performing *bandha*s and exhaling through left. During inhalation and exhalation a typical sound (*ujjayī* sound) should be created by compressing epiglottis in the throat. *Ujjayī* sound can be combined with *so-haṁ* or *guru mantra* for better awareness of *mantra*. *Ujjayī prāṇāyāma* has therapy applications, especially useful in insomnia, tensions and heart diseases. This should not be practised in low blood pressure, as the practice of this *prāṇāyāma* puts pressure on carotid sinus which further reduces blood pressure. It destroys decay and death.
5. *Bhastrikā* (*Bellow's Breath*) — This literally means one has to operate lungs like the bellow, fast inhalation and fast exhalation, followed by inhaling through right nostril and performing *kumbhaka* with *bandha*s and exhaling through left nostril, this is *bhastrikā prāṇāyāma*. This is a vitalizing type of *prāṇāyāma*. This rhythmic inhalation and exhalation stimulates the circulation of cerebral fluid, creating compression and decompression in the brain. Rhythmic diaphragm movements stimulate heart and lung muscles improving blood circulation. Accelerated blood circulation and rate of gas exchange in each cell produces heat and washes out gases. This practice purifies energy channels (*nāḍī*s); the practitioner never suffer from any disease; it stimulates gastric fire; and later on the *kuṇḍalinī* rises quickly, it pierces the three "knots" (*granthi*) in *suṣumṇā* (i.e. Brahmā, Viṣṇu, Rudra), which allows the *prāṇa* to ascend *suṣumṇā* according to Svātmārāma.
6. *Bhrāmarī means Humming Bee Breath* — In this *prāṇāyāma* one has to make sound like humming bee while exhalation and inhalation as well. According to *Gheraṇḍa Saṁhitā* this should be done at the midnight. To practise it, close the ears with the hands. Listen to the sounds in the right ear. Listen for: crickets, lute, thunder, drum, beetle, bells, gongs, trumpets, etc. The last sound heard is the "unstruck" (*anāhata*) sound rising from the heart. In this sound is light, and in that light the "mind should be immersed". This *prāṇāyāma* increases psychic

sensitivity and awareness of subtle sound vibrations, this proves to be useful for *nāda* meditation. This is useful in removing stress and mental problems like anxiety, depression and anger etc. This practice gives success in *samādhi* and indescribable happiness.

7. *Sītkāri means "making the [sound] sīt"* — This is done by opening lips, keeping the upper and lower teeth touching each other, then inhaling through mouth with hissing sound, then performing *kumbhaka* with *bandhas* and then exhaling through nostrils. The air passing via tongue, cools the blood, lowering the temperature of the blood. This type of *prāṇāyāma* removes excess heat in the body. Also the diseases like acidity, hypertension, etc. This *prāṇāyāma* harmonizes the secretions of reproductive organs and all the endocrine system. Also it improves digestion, lowers high blood pressure, purifies the blood. According to Svātmārāma the practitioner becomes "next to the God of Love (Kāma) in beauty"; it removes heat, hunger, indolence, sleep and thirst.
8. *Śītalī means "cooling"* — To follow this practice imitation of the breathing of a serpent. Curl the tongue and protrude it through pursed lips (*kākī-mudrā*) then inhale through mouth with a hissing sound tongue is rolled and inhalation is done via mouth followed by *kumbhaka* with *bandhas* and then exhalation through nostrils. The effects of the *śītalī* are same as *sītkāri prāṇāyāma*. This is the "giver of bliss"; it makes free from indigestion, phlegm, and bilious disorders; purifies blood; cools system; quenches thirst, appeases hunger.
9. *Mūrchā means swooning breath or fainting* — This type of *prāṇāyāma* induces a state of "conscious unconsciousness" (in the words of Swami Satyananda of Bihar School of Yoga). One should inhale through both the nostrils, the *kumbhaka* with *bandhas*, but while exhaling the *jālandhara bandha* (chin lock) is kept intact and then exhalation is done with the *jālandhara bandha*. Excess pressure is exerted on carotid sinus during exhalation with *jālandhara bandha*, which further reduces blood pressure and one can experience a state of unconsciousness with practice. This *prāṇāyāma* involves high risks so should not be practised without the direct guidance of a *guru*.

10. *Plavinī is floating breath* — After inhalation the air is filled in to stomach and kept inside for some time. "When the belly is filled with air and the inside of the body is filled to its utmost 'floater' with air, the body floats on the deepest water, like the leaf of a lotus." Swami Svātmārāma mentions in the text of *Haṭha-Yoga-Pradīpikā* that one can float easily on water with this *prāṇāyāma*. This *prāṇāyāma* helps remove most of the ailments of stomach or digestive system.

11. *Prāṇākarṣana* — To practise this *prāṇāyāma*, adopt any comfortable meditative posture simply cross-legged, *padmāsana* or *siddhāsana* with spine erect. Relax the body and close the eyes. Observe the natural breath. Keep the hands on the laps in *vairāgya-mudrā* (both palm overlapping each other, left palm flat under the right palm). After the body mind relaxation, start deep breathing with outer and inner retention according to the capacity. Just visualize that during the inhalation the pure *prāṇa* with white colour coming inside the lungs, during the retention it got spreaded in all the organs up to the every cell. While exhalation just feel that all the wastes in the form of black-coloured air coming out from the body and during outer retentions just feel that it went away from the body and dissolved in the air. Keep on doing the same practice for as longer as possible, in this process the breathing pattern will be deeper and slower. As it may lead the aspirant at the state of *pratyāhāra* and *dhāraṇā*, one should not just suddenly stop the practice. For the ending slowly remove the visualization part and very slowly reduce the deep breathing. Slowly move the hands, rub the palm and sake the eyes. Gently open the eyes, practice of *prāṇākarṣana prāṇāyāma* ends.

Nāda Yoga: Music Therapy

As per the scriptural descriptions, often the vision of the syllables for subtle sounds (*nāda*) in the etheric ocean had been revealed to the *r̥ṣi*s through an afflatus or intuition in their inner selves or the *mantra*s were just "heard" by them in a state of trance. The phonemes of the Vedic hymns and the seven fundamental nodes — *sā, re, gā, mā, pā, dhā, ni* of the Indian classical music — have originated (distinctly recognized by the *r̥ṣi*s) from the vibrations of the sublime sound of *oṁ* in the nature. The Vedic quote — *eko 'ham bahusyāmi* implies that all the sounds, all the energies, all the motions and everything existing in the universe have originated from the vibrations of this single *anāhata nāda*. This is the source of the manifestation of the *Śabda-Brahman* and the *Nāda-Brahman*.

सर्वचिन्तां समुत्सृज्य सर्वचेष्टाविवर्जितः।
नादमेवानुसंदध्यान्नादे चित्तं विलीयते।।

sarvacintāṁ samutsr̥jya sarvaceṣṭāvivarjitaḥ ।
nādamevānusandadhyānnāde cittaṁ vilīyate ।।
— *Nādabindopaniṣad* 41

Practitioner should drop his thoughts and only concentrate on *nāda*, because through this practice the mind merges into *nāda*.

Scientists are taking the advantage of new technologies to see exactly what goes on inside the brains of *nāda-yoga* practitioners. The neuroscientists hypothesize that regular meditation actually alters the way the brain is wired, and that these changes could be at the heart of claims that meditation can improve health and well-being. But the rigours of the scientific method might never have been applied to studying the practice of meditation.

Modern psychology as well as yogic philosophy believe in three kinds of tension — muscular tensions, emotional tensions and mental tensions — which can be progressively released through the systematic and regular practice of yoga and meditation. Muscular tension is a result of nervous and endocrinal imbalances. It manifests in the form of stiffness and rigidity in the physical body. In the practice of meditation the body is progressively relaxed, which in turn releases the accumulated muscular tensions.

Psychologists tell that music works on a very subtle subconscious level. In particular they refer to the beat, or rhythm, of the music. They point to the fact that before birth we felt safe, warm and secure within the womb, and the most reassuring sound was that of the mother's heartbeat. The slow, rhythmic pulse of relaxing music may reflect the feelings first enjoyed when our lives were free of stress and anxiety. Thus we can withdraw for a while from the causes of our stress and anxiety to an imaginary place of refuge and safety.

Says Acharya Shriram Sharma (2001: 4), music provides the best way of expressing emotion. It is necessary that the words of a song also be the linguistic translation of the emotions. Even without the involvement of any vocal expression of language, the sounds (melody) of music can convey their emotions. The flow of music expresses itself even in the absence of an audience.

Listening to the music of nature — a babbling brook, birds singing or leaves whispering in the breeze — is a great way to induce a stress-relieving relaxed state. And instrumental music like flutes coupled with bass drums can work wonders.

Better health, improved relationships, enhanced moods and stress relief, these are only some of the benefits of music therapy. Just watch, you don't become addicted!

Several mindfulness researchers cite James Austin (1998: 78): as a reason for they became interested in the field. In it, Austin examines consciousness by intertwining his personal experiences with Zen meditation with explanations backed up by hard science. When he describes how meditation can "sculpt" the brain, he means it literally and figuratively.

Anil K. Rajvanshi (2002), states that music affects brain at different levels. Our moods change with different types of music. However, at a very deep level its effect is similar to that of deep meditation. Probably it is a reason why all great religions have stressed music as a means for praying and meditation.

Pranav Pandya (2005: 23) has an important finding. Those who find it difficult to concentrate upon the internal sounds of the body should take support of external sound of soothing music. After playing musical instruments like *sitār* or *ikatārā* or flute, or, after listening to their soft, soothing music with the help of a tape recorder for about 10 to 15 minutes in a quiet room, the *sādhaka* should close his ears and attempt mental perception of the echo of the same musical sound. He should repeat this cycle several times everyday for gradually longer durations (not more than an hour). He should keep the mind stress-free. Slowly and steadily, the mind would get trained to naturally "play or listen" this music internally without the help of any external devices.

According to Steven K.H. Aung and Mathew H.M. Lee (2004), there is no absolute answers, no final definitions of these hearing/

listening and silent sensations and encompassing psychological healing or pathogenic experience, because the answer depend on sensitivity of listening and performance, within the context of what they have learned to produce, reproduce and consume — and at a more academic level — the views and evaluations of professional music critics.

Jon Kabat-Zinn brought mindfulness into the mainstream by developing a standardized teaching method that has introduced multitudes of beginners to the practice of meditation. In 1979, he founded the Stress Reduction Clinic at the University of Massachusetts Memorial Medical Center in Worcester. He is professor emeritus of the university's medical school. Kabat-Zinn has written several books that show readers how to incorporate meditation into their daily lives.

Maharṣi Patañjali states that yoga is stopping the fluctuations of the mind (*yogaścittavr̥tti nirodhaḥ*). As the practitioner listens or sings the music the thoughtlessness of the mind brings relaxation to the brain and at this stage, the brain produces alpha waves.

When we hear soul-stirring music, we again get a feeling of well-being. Thus, the soul-stirring music and deep meditative thought have similar characteristics. This is the principle of equivalence. The brain therefore appreciates and absorbs the soul-stirring music by creating the same complex thought pattern as that during meditation.

Similar effects are also seen for different types of music, which produce anger, sadness and other human emotions. It is therefore quite possible that neurological studies on effects of music will serve as a model for studying how brain works in general and at different levels of thought complexity. As we evolve intellectually and spiritually, we become increasingly tuned to emotionally satisfying music, since the brain becomes supple and is able to focus on a single thought for a long time.

Trāṭaka: Concentration Technique

As man is a physical, mental and spiritual being, yoga helps to promote a balanced development of all the three stated above. Thus the practitioner should develop the spirit for a real health. The aspirant should go through a holistic practice of yoga. Which includes not only *āsana* or *prāṇāyāma*, but the cleansing (*ṣaṭ-karma*). *Āsana* and *prāṇāyāma* work on physical and mental level only. The cleansing removes the *mala* (the waste of body and mind); which is necessary for all.

Trāṭaka is one of the six cleansing processes of *haṭha-yoga*. It literally means gazing at a particular point. It works on the *ājñā cakra*. *Trāṭaka* is defined in Haṭha-yogic texts as:

निरीक्षेन्निश्चलदृशा सूक्ष्मलक्ष्यं समाहितः।
अश्रुसंपातपर्यन्तमाचार्यैस्त्राटकं स्मृतम्।।

nirīkṣen-niścaladṛśā sūkṣmalakṣyaṁ samāhitaḥ ।
aśrusaṁpāta-paryantam-ācāryais-trāṭakaṁ smṛtam ।।
— *Haṭha-Yoga-Pradīpikā* 2.31

Looking intently with an unwavering gaze at a small point until tears are shed is known as *trāṭaka* by the *ācāryas* (*gurus*).

Focusing the eyes or "gazing" at an object for a prolonged period without blinking. This creates tears to flow in many people, thus washing and cleansing the eyes from the inside out, without the need for eyecups or eye washes. The usual and sufficient procedure is to stare at a candle for 3 to 5 minutes without blinking.

Trāṭaka is most often preformed on a candle placed about 3 ft in front. Gaze steadily without blinking at the candle-flame without blinking or moving for 20 minutes (average). If the eyes feel strained visualize a light moving from the centre of the *ājñā cakra* above through your eyes to the candle. Relax the eyes and rest the mind.

One may mentally repeat if need be: "Just the flame. Just the candle. Just the breath. Just the light. Just this breath, relax, etc." Afterwards close the eyes and look for the subtle form of the candle inside (*antara*). This is said to help lead one to *antaraṅga trāṭaka*. Begin with external objects which will steady and strengthen the eyes while increasing the power of *dhāraṇā*. If an image appears to move, bring it back to the central space without moving the head or eye balls.

Other objects besides a candle can be used such as the *iṣṭa devī* (personal deity), a *yantra*, *oṁ* symbol, third eye (*ājñā cakra*), the sun, etc. Make sure that the object is sanguine. After *trāṭaka* bring cupped palms to the eyes and and apply a soft inward motion around the eye (cupping them but not creating any pressure on the balls of the eye).

Trāṭaka is also often performed on the setting sun or rising sun, on one's shadow at noon, on a black point, on the written symbol, *oṁ*, on other mystic diagrams or on other objects such as a candle, colour or for example *saṁyama* on a blue-coloured object to relax one in meditation or on any religious object, deity, picture, symbol, or artefact. *Trāṭaka* also aids the concentration. Breathe deeply and naturally and always stop before pain or strain while allowing the eyes to water and tear.

If at noon or when the sun is at a higher elevation, expose only the whites of the eyes to the sun. Move the whites in a circular movement keeping the pupils looking away by staring up to the third eye, low down, or extremely to one side or the other never looking directly into the sun (except sunset and sunrise). Another similar practice is to do eye circles looking into the sun, but with the eyelids closed. This latter exercise can be done for 10 minutes maintaining direct sunlight to shine on the closed eyelids while rotating the eyeballs.

Remember that unless you have gained expertise under tutelage of an experienced sun gazer, it is only safe to stare into the sun directly (eyelids open) only at sunrise and a few minutes before sunset when the sun is low on the horizon, for a minute or less. Normally one starts at 15 seconds and works up everyday 10 seconds in duration and only when the sun is very low in the horizon. Never look directly at the sun when it is above 25° above the horizon.

There are two general categories of *trāṭaka* — *bahiraṅga trāṭaka* (external) where one fixes his gaze on an external object and *antaraṅga trāṭaka* (internal) where the gaze is at the third eye (inward and upward) or the inner celestial spaces such as *cidākāśa* or *hṛdayākāśa*. Of these two, there exist an enormous amount of specific practices including but not limited to specific colours, diagrams and dynamic method.

When the eyes do not blink, the eyes tear, and are thus cleansed, washed and stimulated. They thus appear brighter and clear. *Trāṭaka* stimulates the activation of the *ājñā cakra*. *Trāṭaka* helps to focus and calm the nervous system and mind. It aids in concentration and will-power, thus expediting *dhāraṇā siddhi* (the entering into the more subtle awareness of *antaraṅga yoga*). *Trāṭaka* not only cleanses the eyes but rather removes the coverings of the third eye (gnosis). Always spend a minute or two cupping the eyes with the palms daily especially after *trāṭaka*.

मोचनं नेत्ररोगाणां तन्द्रादीनां कपाटकम्।
यत्नतस्त्राटकं गोप्यं यथा हाटकपेटकम्।।

mocanaṁ netrarogāṇāṁ tandrādīnāṁ kapāṭakam ।
yatnatastrāṭakaṁ gopyaṁ yathā hāṭakapeṭakam ।।
— *Haṭha-Yoga-Pradīpikā* 2.32

Trāṭaka eradicates all eye diseases, fatigue and sloth and closes the doorway creating these problems. It should be carefully kept secret like a golden casket.

Trāṭaka benefits not only the eyes but a whole range of physiological and mental functions. It is applicable in depression, insomnia, allergy, anxiety, postural problems, poor concentration and memory.

With regular practice of a balanced series of techniques, the energy of the body and mind can be liberated and the quality of consciousness can be expanded. This is not a subjective claim but is now being investigated by the scientists and being shown by an empirical fact. Experience the calming effect of *trāṭaka*, if only for 10 minutes each day, would create a period of physical relief that enhances immune function. Over time, the benefits of *trāṭaka* have a cumulative effect, improving the well-being of the practitioner.

Bandha and Mudrās: Prāṇa Controlling Technique

*Mudrā*s and *bandha*s act as safety valves in the human system. *Āsana*s act in a similar way. All three help to suspend the fluctuations of the mind, intellect and ego, so that attention is drawn in towards the Self. The union of the divine force with the divine Self is the essence of Part Three.

In order to follow the technique of *prāṇāyāma*, it is necessary to know something about *mudrā*s and *bandha*s. The Sanskrit word *mudrā* means a seal or a lock. It denotes positions which close the body apertures, and where the fingers are held together with special hand gestures.

Bandha means bondage, joining together, fettering or catching hold. It also refers to a posture in which certain organs or parts of the body are gripped, contracted and controlled. When electricity is generated, it is necessary to have transformers, conductors, fuses, switches and insulated wires to carry the power to its destination; otherwise the current would be lethal.

When *prāṇa* is made to flow in the *yogī*'s body by the practice of *prāṇāyāma*, it is equally necessary for him to employ *bandha*s to prevent the dissipation of energy and to carry it to the right places without damage. Without the *bandha*, the *prāṇāyāma* practice, and the flow of *prāṇa* can injure the nervous system.

JĀLANDHARA BANDHA

The first *bandha* the *sādhaka* should master is *jālandhara bandha, jāla* meaning a net, a web or a mesh. The solar plexus is situated at the centre. According to yoga, it is the seat of the digestive fire (*jaṭharāgni*), which burns food and creates heat. The lunar plexus is in the centre of the brain and creates coolness. By performing *jālandhara bandha,* due to the lock of the *nāḍī*s around the neck, the cool energy of the lunar plexus is not allowed to flow down or to be dissipated by the hot energy of the solar plexus.

In this way the elixir of life is stored. And life itself is prolonged. The *bandha* also presses the *iḍā* and *piṅgalā* channels and allows the *prāṇa* to pass through *suṣumṇā*. The *jālandhara bandha* clears the nasal passages and regulates the flow of blood and *prāṇa* (energy) to the heart, head and the endocrine glands in the neck (thyroid and parathyroid).

If *prāṇāyāma* is performed without *jālandhara bandha,* pressure is immediately felt in the heart, brain, eye-balls and in the inner ear. This may lead to dizziness. It relaxes the brain and also humbles the intellect (*manas*, *buddhi* and *ahaṁkāra*).

Those with stiff necks should keep the head as far down as possible without undue discomfort, or roll a piece of cloth and place it on the top of the collar-bones. Hold it by lifting the chest rather than by pressing down with the chin. This releases tension in the throat and breathing becomes comfortable.

UḌḌIYĀNA BANDHA

Which means flying up, is an abdominal grip. In it, the *prāṇa* (energy) is made to flow up from the lower abdomen up into the thorax, pulling the abdominal organs back and up towards the spinal column.

It is said that through *uḍḍiyāna bandha* the great bird *prāṇa* is forced to fly up through the *suṣumṇā nāḍī* (the main channel for the flow of nervous energy) which is situated inside the spinal column (*merudaṇḍa*).

It is the best of *bandhas*, and he who constantly practises it, as taught by his *guru*, becomes young again.

It is said to be the lion that kills the elephant, named death. It should be performed only during the interval between a complete exhalation and a fresh inhalation. It exercises the diaphragm and abdominal organs. The lift of the diaphragm gently massages the muscles of the heart, thereby toning them. It tones the abdominal organs, increases the gastric fire and eliminates toxins in the digestive tract. As such it is also called *śakti-cālana prāṇāyāma*.

MŪLA BANDHA

When the muscles of the perineum are contracted the whole pelvic floor is pulled up. In the text we are told to press the perineal/vaginal region (*yoni*) and contract the rectum. The word *tudam* indicates "rectum"; but it also means anus, bowels or lower intestine. However, it should be clearly understood that in *mūla bandha*, there should be absolutely no anal contraction.

Contraction of the anus is known as *aśvinī-mudrā*. *Aśvinī-mudrā* indicates the movement a horse makes with its rectum during evacuation of the bowels. In the *Gheraṇḍa Saṁhitā* it is said to contract and relax the anal aperture again and again.

When *mūla bandha* is initially practised, there is a tendency to control the two areas, i.e. the perineum and the anus. *Mūla bandha* takes place in the centre of the body, neither in the front nor back. Then *mūla bandha cakra* is directly contracted. In the beginning the student will find difficulty in asserting conscious control over the perineal area, as the brain is not tuned to such fine muscular manipulation in this area.

The practice of *mūla bandha* reactivates the areas in the brain controlling this region of the body, bringing the neuronal circuits responsible for its control into the sphere of consciousness. This growth process takes time, and in the meantime, while practising *mūla bandha*, it is important not to become frustrated if you cannot control the perineal body, or the cervix, without contracting the anus or genital organs also. In the initial stage this is to be expected. Controlled systematic contraction of the perineal body/cervix produces heat in the subtle body and this awakens the potential of *kuṇḍalinī*. Control will definitely come with time, practice and perseverance.

Saṅkīrtana: Catharsis Technique to Release Emotions

According to Swami Sivananda, *saṅkīrtana* is the easiest, surest, safest, quickest way to attain God consciousness. Those who do *saṅkīrtana* in the beginning for the sake of mental enjoyment will realize the purifying effects of *saṅkīrtana* after some time and then they will themselves do it with *bhāva* (intense feeling) and *śraddhā* (faith). There is a mysterious power in the name of the Lord. Man cannot live on bread alone, but he can live on the name of the Lord.

Saṅkīrtana actually is continuous repetition or chanting of any name of God or singing the glory of God. It is a deeply inspiring practice that opens the heart and reveals the experience of our own true nature. It calms the mind and helps us to release unwanted tensions allowing us to experience the freedom within. We chant in Sanskrit, a language revealed by sages in ancient times as the language of the heart. There is a deep wisdom within the vibration of each chant (*kīrtana*) and each individual has his own unique experience of grace through the power of chanting.

Saṅkīrtana is singing God's name with feeling (*bhāva*), love (*prema*) and faith (*śraddhā*). In *saṅkīrtana* people join together and sing God's name collectively in a common place. *Saṅkīrtana* is one of the nine modes of *bhakti*. You can realize God through *kīrtana* alone. This is the easiest method for attaining God-consciousness in *Kaliyuga* or the Iron Age *kalau keśava-kīrtanāt*.

According to Paramhamsa Swami Satyananda Saraswati (1982: 36), *kīrtana* is an important aspect of yoga. Just as a sweet-dish is incomplete without sugar, so yoga is also incomplete without *kīrtana*. *Kīrtana* is not religious chanting, nor is it just singing one word many times. It is a part of *nāda-yoga* (the yoga of sound) in which you produce sound waves and follow them with your awareness. By singing *kīrtana* you are able to withdraw yourself from the body and your external environment. You are travelling by the jet of emotions, therefore, you do not confront the mind at all. In *rāja-yoga* you have to fight the mind, but in *kīrtana* you bypass the mind.

Kīrtana is not an intellectual yoga, but each and every sound that is produced in *kīrtana* goes deep into your consciousness. Intellectuals will try to understand *kīrtana*, but for them it is very difficult, because *kīrtana* is mainly concerned with the emotional personality of the individual. Although the emotions are not properly understood and utilized, they are very powerful tools in the hands of man. Through the intellect, you cannot go very deep; you cannot realize the consciousness. By means of the intellect you can know about God, truth and many things; but you can never experience them.

When several people join together and practise *saṅkīrtana*, a huge spiritual current or *mahāśakti* is generated. This purifies the heart of the aspirants and elevates them to the sublime heights of divine ecstasy (*samādhi*). The powerful vibrations are carried to distant places. They bring elevation of mind, solace, strength to all people and work as a harbinger of peace, harmony and concord. They annihilate hostile forces and quickly bring peace and bliss to the whole world.

Lord Hari says to Nārada,

नाहम् वसामि वैकुण्ठे योगिनाम् हृदये न च।
मद्भक्ता यत्र गायंति तत्र तिष्ठामि नारद।।

nāham vasāmi vaikuṇṭhe yogināṁ hṛdaye na ca ।
mad-bhaktā yatra gāyanti tatra tiṣṭhāmi nārada ।।

I dwell not in Vaikuṇṭha nor in the hearts of the *yogins*, but I dwell where my devotees sing my name, O Nārada!

Kīrtana destroys sins, *vāsanās* and *saṁskāras*, fills the heart with *prema* and devotion, and brings the devotee face-to-face with God. The harmonious vibrations produced by the singing of the names of the Lord help the devotee to control the mind easily. They produce a benign influence on the mind. They elevate the mind at once from its old ruts or grooves to magnanimous heights of divine splendour and glory. If one does *saṅkīrtana* from the bottom of one's heart with full *bhāva* and *prema* (divine love), even the trees, birds and animals will be deeply influenced. They will respond. Such is the powerful influence of *saṅkīrtana*. *Ṛṣi*s and *siddha*s visit the place where *saṅkīrtana* is held. You can see brilliant lights all round the *paṇḍāla* where it is held.

The mind is purified by constant *saṅkīrtana*. It is filled with good and pure thoughts. Daily *saṅkīrtana* strengthens the good *saṁskāras*. The mind of a person, who trains himself to think good and holy thoughts, develops a tendency to think good thoughts. His character is moulded and transformed by continuous good thoughts. When the mind thinks of the image of God during *saṅkīrtana*, the mental substance actually transforms into the form of the image of God. The impression of the object is left in the mind. This is a *saṁskāra*. When the act is repeated very often, the *saṁskāra* gains strength by repetition and a tendency or habit is formed in the mind. One who entertains thoughts of divinity actually becomes transformed into the divinity by constant thinking and meditation. The *bhāva* and disposition are purified and divinized. The meditator and the meditated, the worshipper and the worshipped, the thinker and the thought become one and the same. This is *samādhi*. This is the fruit of *saṅkīrtana*.

Svādhyāya: A Cognitive Therapy

All human activities, spread over the entire life span, are governed by the mind. The subtle and imperceptible thoughts and feelings arising in the mind determine the nature and direction of human actions. The end-results of these actions are also accordingly determined. Together with other aspects of life, physical health too, is to a large extent subject to this power of mind. Our mind can either sap or strengthen the body's defences, depending on the nature of its frame. Inner malice and ugliness get reflected in poor health. Conversely, good physical health denotes a healthy state of mind.

If the mind is freed of unhealthy thoughts, the body, too, escapes their deleterious effects. Healthy mind is the foundation of physical well-being. Many bodily ailments have mental and psychological origin. Hence mental health is imperative for physical health. Only noble thoughts lead to a noble life. There should be a constant endeavour not to fall prey to ignoble thoughts and negative emotions of anxiety, etc.; and if such feelings do arise these must be thrown out of the psyche through constant mindfulness.

We should seek out the possible cause of mental agony. It could be anything — a loss in business, not finding a job, estranged marriage, failure in examination, a bad interview, and so on. If the mind does not resolutely break free of the particular agony, it exerts pressure on the body and adversely affects health. We should try to remove such causes of stress. Even some compromise with the situation is not too bad, but you must not remain entangled in this brooding for a prolonged period. If the problem defies solution, just stop worrying about it.

Loneliness is another cause of man's sorrow. This is especially so in times of crises when loneliness magnifies one's sadness and misery manifold. If a matter is kept repressed for a long time, it builds up pressure inside leading to physical and mental disorders. Like happiness, loneliness, too, is a condition to be shared; it gets lessened this way. Occasional consultations with the spouse, kins and friends on troublesome matters act as pressure outlets. Their sympathy and co-operation give courage and comfort, and prevents emotional problems. When the mind feels buoyant, health acquires extra glow.

So a good prescription for sound health is *svādhyāya*. Etymologically it means one's own analysis, or study, but it is used for studying scriptures such as the *Bhagavad-Gītā*, or Bible. Sage Patañjali gives lot of importance to *svādhyāya*, as he mentioned it three times in his *Yoga-Sūtras*. One of the three *sūtras* in which the same meaning of *svādhyāya* reflects is:

श्

śauca-santoṣa-tapaḥ-svādhyāyeśvara-praṇidhānāni niyamāḥ ||

— *Pātañjala Yoga-Sūtras* 2.32

> Cleanliness, contentment, austerity, self-study and resignation to God are the five *niyamas*, i.e. basic codes of conduct to start yoga.

The urge of human self to evolve in consciousness is a natural expression of its spiritual nature. Evolution is the fundamental and eternal objective of the *jīvātmā* (the soul manifested in the individual self). This is what drives one towards progress. We may differ in regard to the true meaning of progress or the ideal path to be followed, but it is true that each one of us always wants to change, to ascend in the scale of consciousness. The thinkers and sages of all ages have affirmed that there is no place for weak, inactive creatures in this world. Nature also favours the survival of the fittest. Only the courageous and capable ones succeed in the stiff and stormy struggle of life. Power, energy and strength are essential, in some form or the other, for the sustenance of life.

The Śāstras elucidate this fact as:

या विभ्रति जगत् सर्वं स्वेच्छायालौकिका हि सा।

शैव धर्मो ही शुभगे नेह कश्चन् शंसया:।
योगता वच्छिन्न धर्मिना: शक्तिरेव धर्मा:।।

ya vibhrati jagat sarvaṁ svecchāyā-laukikā hi sā ।
śaiva dharmo hi śubhage neha kaścan śaṁsayāḥ ।
yogatā vacchinna dharmināḥ śaktireva dharmāḥ ।।

God has manifested this world through His supernatural power. It is also the duty of a human being (the crown prince of that Almighty) to enhance his abilities and attain greater strength. By "power" is meant here the zeal, vibrancy and will-power for ascent and success in life. As such, possession of wealth, physical might, human or other resources, etc. also make one powerful in the worldly sense. However, if we look at the glorious lives of great personalities, we find that presence of these resources is not necessary for *samunnati* (enlightened progress).

Gautama the Buddha became truly powerful after renouncing all his royal comforts, prosperity and princely powers. The power of enlightenment that he accessed on attaining Buddhahood proved to be immeasurably superior to that of thousands of emperors and the rich and the mighty across the world. Even the ever-victorious emperor Aśoka had to dedicate himself, his children, along with the resources of his empire for the spread of the Buddha's message of enlightenment and compassion. Mahatma Gandhi did not have anything that could be materialistically significant. He was even weak physically. But, this lean and thin man of 96 pounds shook the foundations of the grand British Empire, which at that time was the unchallenged superpower from one end of the globe to the other. These immortal examples illustrate that there is some other "supreme" power, which supersedes and controls all the worldly powers.

The pre-eminent power bestowed upon human beings is that of thoughts. The power of thoughts shapes the external as well as the internal realms of personality and drives our life accordingly. It is the flow of one's thoughts that generates and propels the triple currents of his qualities, nature and actions. If one wants to become different from what the nature of his thought is, he will not succeed. In fact, it is the flow of decisive thoughts that generates the constructive power to enable corresponding actions of the body. For example, whatever be one's end-goal, unless there is the will-power-charged thought of becoming healthy and physically fit, he would not be inspired to carry out the laborious physical exercises and devote the necessary time and efforts in adhering to a balanced diet. The energy of his powerful thoughts about *satyāgraha* had motivated Mahatma Gandhi to launch in right earnest the non-violent freedom struggle. The irresistible thought waves generated by his selfless, devoted endeavours thereafter had gradually inspired the whole nation to participate in this noble movement and make it a unique success. The force of focused thoughts is certainly mightier than everything else. In the views of the great philosopher Emerson (1860: 258):

> Spiritual power is superior to the materialistic or physical powers; (therefore) thoughts rule over our world. Our thoughts are the architects of our future. Righteous thoughts and their concordant actions always bring good results.

The eminent sages and thinkers of all ages have stressed and also demonstrated that thoughts are the source of immense power. Refinement and focused orientation of thoughts are the foremost requirements of higher-level accomplishments. We should give greatest importance to thoughts, as our thoughts shape our lives. The predominant role the power of thoughts plays in the materialistic, intellectual and spiritual evolution of human life is self-evident. However, we should not forget that the principal cause of one's perversion, decline and fall also happens to be his thoughts. Evil, immoral, heinous thoughts lead to depraved, sinful actions. Because of his wrong thinking one drains out all his powers and talents or wastes them in evil activities. Therefore, we need the power of elevated, enlightened, discerning thoughts for awakening and rising. Good literature is a rich source of good thoughts.

As we all know, literature plays a crucial role in setting the trends of rise or fall in human society. Concurrent literature is said to be the mirror of the psychological state of a society at a given time. In other words, the collective thoughts and hence the inclinations, nature and character of a society are reflected in its literature. The first step towards individual as well as collective growth in the brighter direction is certainly achieved if the literature that inspires prudent, progressive and illuminating thoughts is available to and extensively accessed by the people. By good literature we mean the writings or collection of thoughts, reading or hearing of which can inspire inculcation of virtuous tendencies; which can improve one's character. We need literature that has a purifying impact on the inner cores of our emotions for cultivating noble values and thus creation of a dignified life.

School or college books, cultural plays, devotional songs and poems and the scriptures propagating religious traditions alone are not sufficient for this purpose. What we require is a lively literature that is scientific and rational in its approach, that inspires moral and ethical values which bring about a positive transformation in people's attitudes and presents prudent solutions to the multidimensional problems of human life. A thoughtful person would hesitate in calling it good literature if a literary work is unable to awaken refined interest, positive thoughts, or if it can't satisfy our inner emotional, mental and spiritual aspirations. The literature, which cannot generate creativity, awakening and zeal in individuals and the society, is nothing more than a mere intellectual or linguistic exercise. By good literature is meant the literature, which can produce the strength, courage and determination that enable us to face and overcome the adversities with steadfastness, boldness and far-sightedness.

Good literature is that which bestows the inner self of the reader (or listener) with wisdom and enlightenment and fills it with spiritual fragrance. History is replete with examples of how an erotic, perverting and valueless literature could degenerate and destroy the vision and strength of individuals, societies and nations and put them into the abysmal tunnel of darkness and downfall. Today again, we can see it happening around us. Be it in the name of modernity, entertainment or because of crass sensuality and base commercial motives, propagation of literature and related arts and culture pertaining to vulgar, erogenous inclinations, valueless luxuries and immoral activities appear to have flooded all facets of our personal and social life. It is frightening to imagine the ultimate end-result of this cultural corruption and declining trajectory of the average individual and the society as a whole. It is high time the savants and awakened minds do something constructive to protect our present and future generations from the dreaded octopus of debased and misleading literature, and arts and culture.

Search, review, creation and dissemination of good literature and initiation of thought-revolution thereby have become the dire needs of the day. It is all the more vital in the present times when we hardly find the saints, seers and reformers who, because of the strength of their spiritual thoughts and high character, could provide the necessary support and guiding light to the society. Good literature and artistic and cultural works derived from the lives, thoughts and works of the visionaries and great personalities could spark the revolutionary change in people's thinking if propagated in the right spirit.

Sysaro (2003) has mentioned at one place:

> Reading (good) literature is a source of (mental) nourishment for the youth and entertainment and happiness for the old; it opens up the doors of hope and gives patience and courage in moments of difficulty. Literature keeps one healty inside and humble outside the home.

All the literary works that help refinement of thoughts and emotions; that present prudent analysis of the facts and provide far-sighted directions, should be brought under the category of good literature. Just reading the printed words or cramming them is not what corresponds to the study of (good) literature. Howsoever, small portion of it we take up, reading it, understanding its implications, contemplating over its teachings or guidance, and adopting it in our behaviour and conduct are what complete the study of good literature.

Once we develop this habit, good literature will indeed provide us the guidance, intimate support and inspiring light like a divine mentor. It should be noted that it is not the high literary standard of the language or intellectual complexity, which counts here. Rather, it is the universality, relevance, virtuous level, and emotional and mental impact of the teachings and their implications, which matter in such literature. Let us consider the *Rāmacaritamānasa*, for instance. It describes the divine odyssey of Lord Rāma in a simple, folk language in a narrative style. However, so spontaneous and intensive is its effect on those who read or listen to it with serenity, that, even in moments of great dilemma, doubt or influence of accumulated evil tendencies, they experience instant guidance and mental purification from whatever page they read from.

If we could set such an intimate linkage of our mind and heart with an inspiring literature, nothing can stop the empowerment of our thoughts and inculcation of inner strength and righteous intellect thereby. We ought to be ever mindful to enhance the purity and power of our thoughts for the dual purposes of protection from untoward diversions, attractions and confusions of mind, and for dignified growth towards the path of mental and spiritual evolution. *Sādhanā* (devout endeavour) and not *sādhana* (resources) is required here. Good literature holds the key to our real empowerment and progress. The roots of our talents, our strength, our morality, our majesty, our divinity are hidden here. These could be nurtured by enlightened thoughts emerging from our *sādhanā* of the study of good literature.

Satsaṅga: A Cognitive Therapy

Satsaṅga is made up of two Sanskrit roots: *sat* (truth) and *saṅga* (company). Thus *satsaṅga* means the company of the "highest truth", or the company of a *guru* or the company with an assembly of persons who listen to, talk about, and assimilate the truth. That means "gathering together for the truth" or, more simply, "being with the truth". Truth is what is real, what exists. So all there is, is truth. Whenever something increases your experience of the Truth, it opens your heart and quiets your mind. Conversely, whenever something, such as a thought, fear, or judgement, limits or narrows your experience of the truth, the heart contracts and the mind gets busier. We are all equally endowed with this capacity to discriminate and experience the truth. Thus, the true teacher (*satguru*) is within you, and *satsaṅga* (being with the truth) is endless.

In the words of Paramhamsa Swami Satyananda Saraswati (1982: 36), the_psychotherapist and the *guru* both have important roles to play. Where the work of the psychotherapist finishes, the work of the *guru* begins. Therefore, instead of comparing the two, let us connect them. Of course, the *guru* can act as a psychotherapist, but that is not his primary motive. A psychotherapist is a person who helps you through a particular crisis in your life, but in the relationship with *guru*, psychotherapy is spontaneous and ongoing. The *guru*'s relationship with the disciple, his own personal life experience, and his knowledge of the nature of the mind are such that after relieving his disciple of certain mental problems, he is then able to give him spiritual life.

That is why, right from the beginning, certain rules and regulations have been fixed. Not everybody can become a *guru*. In order to become a *guru* you must first have had a perfect discipleship. How can you become a lecturer or a professor in a university unless you have been a student? If you have only read some of the yoga *sūtra*s and yoga books and attended a few seminars here and there, you should not think that you are a qualified *guru*. That is a very dangerous situation; such *guru*s need a psychotherapist.

If you treat someone's mind, and then leave him at that point, he will continue to have problems. Of course, at a certain level, sickness of mind has to be treated, but there is no end to it. In my opinion, it has to be transcended rather than treated. The mind is a composition of three *guṇa*s, which keep on assaulting it all the time. Therefore, a disciple should develop new tools of knowledge and experience with which to deal with the problems of the mind.

Similarly, we cannot really equate *satsaṅga* with group therapy, even though many a time we try to explain *satsaṅga* in these terms. The Sanskrit root *sat* means reality, divinity and purity; it represents Self or God. *Satsaṅga* does not mean being in the company of many people; that is known as *saṅgha*, which means company or association. *Satsaṅga* is being in the company of truth.

There are various types of *satsaṅga*. You can close your eyes and practise *satsaṅga* all alone. When you are reading a spiritual book which deals with the topics of reality that is also a form of *satsaṅga*. *Satsaṅga* happens when you are with a group listening to the glory of divine being or the ways of purity and self-evolution. Hearing about the lives of those people who have had divine experiences and who have suffered or lived for the higher experience, is also one of the most inspiring types of *satsaṅga*.

In *satsaṅga* you may practise *kīrtana* (meditation) but these are not *satsaṅga*, they are only ways of conducting *satsaṅga*. In *satsaṅga* the most important thing is the constant movement of ideas related to the ultimate reality, divinity or highest being.

There are certain groups which I have come across in recent years where people join together to do some practices and to help each other. There is a very simple, scientific explanation for this. If you put a grandfather clock in with many other small clocks, you will find that initially, the movement of their pendulums does not coincide, but after some time all the clocks will be following the grandfather clock. This experiment has been repeated many times. Similarly, when you play a violin, all the other violins in the room begin to resonate. If you listen carefully, you will find that the vibrations from the first violin are being transmitted through the inactive violins. The same thing happens in a group also, when people get together to help each other.

In India, there is not much need for these group sessions, because the social situation is still very well organized. If a group of people live together in a joint family or in an *āśrama* situation, they begin to understand the nature of human psychology. They have an opportunity to see where they stand with one another. They are able to assess their own minds, their limitations, and faults, which is a great change from the modern culture.

In the West, particularly in this century, group therapy has become an important phenomenon. In the eighteenth or nineteenth centuries, the situation was different. There was a more compact and well-knit family and community life. But in the last 150 years, the social structure has deteriorated bit by bit, and so the need for group therapy has arisen.

However, we must remember that mind is not the ultimate reality; there is something beyond the mind. We only talk in terms of mind because mind seems to be a barrier for many people. Actually, whatever we do in spiritual life is not done for the sake of the mind, but for the discovery of the universal spirit. Therefore, the path of psychotherapy can only be followed to a certain extent; then there comes a point where it must be left behind. Psychoanalysis can definitely be of great use at a certain stage of development, but eventually it becomes a barrier and then you have to transcend it.

Worship: A Faith and Emotion Therapy

A human being does not receive complete satisfaction from sensual pleasures. He always feels that he is in want of something and is restless and discontented. Then he longs to come into conscious communion with the Lord of the universe, and to attain immortality and everlasting peace. This ultimate craving of man finds its satisfaction in worship. The individual soul desires to unite himself with his father, the Supreme Soul. This is done through worship. Love and devotion naturally arise in the heart when you hear the glory and greatness of the Lord.

An object of worship is therefore necessary for you to pour forth your love and devotion. Worship helps spiritual evolution and eventually brings the devotee face-to-face with God. As the Absolute cannot be comprehended by the limited and finite mind, the concept of the impersonal God in His lower, limited form came into existence. It is an external symbol of God for worship. It is a reminder of God.

Practice of divine worship and devotion is of paramount importance for spiritual refinement and elevation. Depending upon one's intrinsic faith, conviction, mental make-up and religious training his/her mode of might varies. It begins with a simple practice of worshipping and praying to the Almighty. With the piety and depth of emotions and surrender of the devotee to the Deity of worship, could gradually become a sublime source of living linkage between the *upāsaka* (worshipper, devotee) and the *upāsya* (the divine object of reverence or worship, God). These majestic effects are not just mythological, occult or mysterious magic; rather, these are natural outcomes of the scientifically affirmed immense potentials of, in relation to human psychology, intrinsic tendencies and the inner mind.

What kind of *upāsya* one would select naturally depends upon his intrinsic tendencies and psychological make-up. It transforms the devotee's personality as per the nature and qualities of *upāsya*. This is a natural psychological effect, as also pointed out in the *Yoga-Sūtras;* what becomes of one depends upon what he thinks and does (one's thoughts and deeds make him what he is).

सत्त्वानुरूपा सर्वस्य श्रद्धा भवति भारत।
श्रद्धामयोऽयं पुरुषो यो यच्छ्रद्धः स एव सः।।

sattvānurūpā sarvasya śraddhā bhavati bhārata ।
śraddhāmayo 'yaṁ puruṣo yo yac-chraddhaḥ sa eva saḥ ।।
— *Śrīmad Bhagavad-Gītā* 17.3

One is attracted towards the characters or objects according to his own values and inner inclinations. This is what accounts for his compatibility with the colleagues, his selection of friends and ideals in life. As the above *śloka* points out, one's devotion to the object of natural reverence depends upon his inner sentiments and nature. The deeper this *śraddhā* (intrinsic reverence and faith) is, the more intense and effective will be the influence of devotion in one's psychological transformation. That is what is implied by *yo yac-chraddhaḥ sa eva saḥ* (one is what one's *śraddhā* is).

Pūjā is the common term for ritual worship of which there are numerous synonyms such as *arcanā, vandanā* and *bhajana,* though some of these stress certain aspects of it. The object of worship is the *iṣṭa devatā* (guiding deity or the particular form of the deity) whom the devotee worships.

By the performance of *pūjā,* the deity is pleased. The idol is made up of the five elements; they constitute the body of the Lord. The idol remains an idol, but the worship goes to the Lord. If you shake hands with a man, he is highly pleased. You have touched only a small part of his body and yet he is highly pleased. He smiles and welcomes you. Even so, the Lord is highly pleased when a small portion of His *virāṭ* (cosmic) body is worshipped. An idol is a part of the body of the Lord.

The worshipper superimposes on the image the Lord and all His attributes. He performs *śoḍaśopacāra* (worship with sixteen kinds of offerings) such as *pādyam* (water for washing the feet), *arghyam* (water offered in a vessel), *āsana* (seat), *snāna* (bathing), *vastra* (clothes), *ācamana* (water for sipping), *puṣpa* (flowers), *dhūpa* (incense), *dīpa* (waving of lights and camphor), *naivedyam* (food), etc. The wandering mind is fixed now in this form of worship. The aspirant gradually feels the nearness of the Lord. He attains purity of heart and slowly annihilates the ego.

To the worshipper who believes in the symbol, any kind of image is the body of the Lord under the form of stone, clay, brass, picture, etc. Such worship can never be idolatry. All matter is a manifestation of God. The very act of worship implies that the object of worship is superior and conscious. This way of looking at things must be attained by the devotee. The untutored mind must be trained to view things in the above manner.

Amongst the founders of modern psychology, Carl G. Jung had strongly advocated incorporation of devotional practices as part of psychological healing and personality development. He also opined that the positive effects of devotional practices in mental healing far outweigh what even all the psychotherapists and psychiatrists of the world together might provide. His views indeed prove insightful if we analyse the real nature of human life.

A human being is not just a psychosomatic system of the mind and the body. Neither are the dimensions of human life confined only to the individual self, family, society, nation or the visible world. Its emotional and spiritual existence is most consequential and pre-eminent. Emotional depth and spirituality are the distinct keys to the fulfilment of the quest for peace and joy in human life. These alone can satisfy the natural aspiration of the inner self for ultimate bliss and beatitude. Without realizing this origin, we remain driven by the cravings of the conscious mind and keep searching for happiness in the illusive mirage of worldly pleasures and egotist satiation. This is the reason why, despite the amazing advancement of science and technology and the plethora of comforts gained thereby, most of us are most often trapped in the feelings of insecurity, skepticism, fear, anger, jealousy, gloom and despair. Happiness remains a dream, a mirage for us.

According to the *Indian Vision of Spirituality* by Pranav Pandya (2004: 27), the human self is endowed with all the attributes of divinity; the source of immense knowledge, power and beatified bliss is hidden deep within the inner self. Realization, awakening and expansion of this inner light are the keys to resolve all the problems, howsoever daunting they might be, of life in a scientific mode to accomplish this. It is suitable for all men and women in all circumstances of life. It gradually induces spiritual progress, which begins from within and also encompasses all dimensions (including the worldly spheres) of life.

Whatever be one's faith and religion, emotionally dedicated endeavour leads to the projection of the entirety of the soul in the *upāsya* god (ideal of reverence). The process of inner awakening, enlightenment and spiritual transmutation begins with the devotee's deep faith, emotional and harmonious consonance (of the devotee's inner mind) with the *upāsya*. Daily practice of devotion intensifies one's faith and accelerates the pace of progress. It fulfils the otherwise unnoticed void in one's life and bestows unique strength and sense of security and optimism; and gradually it awakens the otherwise dormant folds of the inner mind and eventually fulfils the eternal quest of the inner self.

The practice of worship differs according to the growth and evolution of the individual. There is nature worship. The Parsis worship the element of fire. Hindus worship the Ganges, the cows, the *aśvattha* tree and the *tulasī* plant. In the Vedas there are hymns to Indra, Varuṇa, Agni and Vāyu. This is nature worship. There is also hero worship. Great heroes like Shivajī and Napoleon are worshipped even today. In hero worship the individual imbibes the virtues of the person whom he worships. Birthday celebrations of great persons and their anniversary celebrations are also forms of worship. There is also the worship of *gurus*, *ṛṣis* and different deities.

As one evolves, one passes from one stage of worship to another. The lower stages drop away by themselves. However, a person at a higher stage should not condemn another who is at a lower stage. One should not forget the underlying, indwelling, interpenetrating essence or intelligence when one performs any kind of worship. The fundamental object in worship is union with the Lord who permeates all names and forms. This has to be achieved by developing intense love.

It is not possible for most people to fix the mind on the Absolute or the Infinite, to behold God everywhere and to practise the presence of God. The external symbol of God is necessary for worship in the beginning and is a support for the aspirant during his spiritual childhood.

A symbol is absolutely indispensable for fixing the mind. The mind wants a prop to lean upon. Without the help of some external aid, in the initial stages, the mind cannot be centralized or have a conception of the Absolute. In the beginning, concentration or meditation is not possible without a symbol. Steadiness of mind is obtained by *saguṇa* (worship with form). The worshipper will have to associate the ideas of infinity, omnipotence, omniscience, purity, perfection, freedom, truth, omnipresence in the form.

Saguṇa worship makes concentration of mind simpler and easier. You can bring before your mind's eye the stories the Lord has played in the specific *avatāras* in which you view Him. This is one of the easiest modes of self-realization. Just as the picture of a famous warrior evokes heroism in the heart, a look at the picture of a form of God will elevate your mind to divine heights. Just as the child develops the maternal feeling by playing with its imaginary toy-child made up of rags, so also the devotee develops the feeling of devotion by worshipping the image and concentrating on it.

While all things may be objects of worship, choice is naturally made of those objects which, by reason of their effect on the mind, are better fitted for it. An image or one of the useful emblems is likely to raise in the mind of the worshipper the thought of a deity. The *śāligrāma* stone easily induces concentration of mind. Everybody has got a predilection for a symbol, emblem or image. An idol (*mūrti*), the sun, fire, water, the Ganges and a Śivaliṅgam are all symbols of the Absolute which help the aspirants to attain one-pointedness of mind and purity of heart. They refer to personal inclinations in the worshipper due to his belief in their special efficacy for him.

Psychologically, all this means that a particular mind finds that it works best in the desired direction by means of particular instruments, emblems or images. The vast bulk of humanity has impure or weak minds. Therefore, the object of worship must be pure for these people. The objects that are capable of exciting lust and dislike must be avoided. However, an advanced *sādhaka*, who has a pure mind and sees the divine presence everywhere and in everything, can worship any kind of object.

Worship goes to the indweller through the form which is being worshipped. It is sheer ignorance to think that one form is superior to another. All worship goes to the one basic reality, the Supreme *Brahman*. The differences are only differences in name and form, on account of differences in the worshippers. There is no difference in the essential object of worship. It is only out of ignorance that different religions and sects fight and quarrel among themselves. Therefore, be tolerant and have a broad outlook on life because the basic essentials of all religions and paths leading to God are the same.

The image in a temple, though it is made of stone, wood or metal, is precious for a devotee as it bears the mark of his Lord, as it stands for something which he holds holy and eternal. A flag is only a small piece of painted cloth, but for a soldier it stands for something that he holds very dear. He is prepared to give up his life in defending his flag. Similarly, the image is very dear to a devotee. It speaks to him in its own language of devotion. Just as the flag arouses martial valour in the soldier, so also the image arouses devotion in the devotee.

The devotee superimposes on the stone statue his Beloved and all His attributes. When your devotion and meditation become intense and deep, you do not see the stone image. You behold only the Lord in it.

The divinity of the all-pervading God is vibrant in every atom of creation. There is not a speck of space where He is not. Why do you then say that He is not in the idols? There are others who would glibly say, "Oh, God is the all-pervading formless being. How can He be confined to this idol?" Are these people ever conscious of His omnipresence? Do they always see Him and Him alone in everything? No. It is their ego that prevents them from bowing to the idols of God and with that motive puts this lame excuse forward.

Prāṇa Cikitsā or Prāṇic Healing

Prāṇa cikitsā is a unique ancient Indian method of treating pain without medicines. It is more than a "Healing Touch". Nowadays it is very common among complementary therapists and popularly known as prāṇic healing. It works through the principles of omnipresent cosmic energy and the healer becomes the instrument to transfer that energy to the aspirant. Sometimes it looks like magic in a scientific and rational manner. It is holistic in approach and explores the reasons of pains, and after finding them out physically, it rectifies them. This therapy needs no medicine and has no side effects.

There is a lot more to prāṇic healing than just healing part. It also heals the patients psychologically. It not only makes us aware of the aura around the human body — the *cakra*s (energy centres) and their effects on our health, but also teaches us how to feel or scan the aura and determine which parts of the *cakra*s may be affected. By learning about energy, we become more conscious about its ubiquitous presence, be it in people, buildings or even objects.

What is *prāṇa*? *Prāṇa* is the name of the vital force or the life-force. It is the subtlest form of the breath that pervades the entire human body. It is more than the normal breath and the essence of life. It keeps every tissue of the human body alive and flows throughout the body.

How *prāṇa* helps in healing? Whenever there is obstruction anywhere in the free flow of *prāṇa*, there is pain. Pain is mainly a manifestation of the obstruction in the free flow of the *prāṇa*. This obstruction is caused by bad food habits, abnormal lifestyles and defective postures. *Prāṇa* therapy tackles these obstructions and set the flow of *prāṇa* in the right direction. The Centre for Practice and Research in Indian Prana Therapy deals with the diseases by manipulating the flow of *prana*. In *prāṇa* therapy, it is possible to discover the obstructions and compressions merely by touching the body by hands. It is not only a physical act, nor is it possible to tackle *prāṇa* by a mere physical touch. It is a highly spiritual method of treating pain and calls for an absolute oneness with the patient. It also calls for a perfect rapport with one another. It is not merely a practice of developing faith in one another, but is basically a sublimity of submission. This sublimity brings poise and inner peace.

THE SCIENCE OF PRĀṆIC HEALING

The term *prāṇa cikitsā* (*prāṇa* therapy) has been mentioned in the Vedas, ancient literatures on therapy and Āyurvedic scriptures like *Suśruta Saṁhitā*. It appears in many variations and definitions, but the *prāṇa* therapy is not based on any literature, book knowledge and theoretical technique. It is based on the patient. A relationship of identification is established with the patient to absorb his pain, to immerse one in the intensity of the anguish felt by him and feeling his pain, to see and understand what causes the pain. This is possible only when one will assimilate vital force, dissolve ego and surrender to serve him. In fact, the process of surrender is mutual, and in this process *prāṇa* (vital force) plays the main role. This force helps in diagnosis and acts as medicine. In the *prāṇa* therapy, medicines are used very rarely, and only for external application. This therapy does not depend on modern scientific tests.

In order to arrive at a complete and comprehensive diagnosis, the patient's current physical condition, his psyche and personal nature, and the symptoms of his disease are considered. A treatment based on such comprehensiveness can alone be truly effective. The treatment should be holistic, comprehensive and involve all the organs of the body. A disease cannot be understood properly and intensely if you look at it only in parts. Treatment should cover both the body and the mind. The causes are psychic, spiritual and physical. Therefore, *prāṇa* therapy basically works on the *prāṇa* within the patient's body, so that the body becomes active on its own, and proceeds towards being free of the malady.

This process of treatment by *prāṇa* therapy requires not only establishing a wavelength with the patient, but also activating his body. This activation has to be health-oriented, which is possible through pure and dedicated touch. The patient's body is probed with a feeling of God's grace in your hands in order to find out which part or organ of the body or which nervous system has a block or obstruction and how much is the intensity of such obstruction. It is believed that if the blockage is removed, the disease will also go. So on the basis of this belief, the nervous system is probed in order to identify the obstruction. This health-oriented touch, made with Śiva *saṅkalpa* (holy vow), in order to feel the obstructions, is the basic foundation of *prāṇa* therapy.

Today, the human touch has almost disappeared. Now, there is no one anywhere who inquires about patient's disposition with complete affection. Machines, computers and super-specialists have taken over the treatment. In this situation, if any practitioner of treatment probes and gets at a hidden area of pain, the patient gets enormous satisfaction, and his confidence develops into strong faith. Thousands of patients have now developed faith and confidence in *prāṇa* therapy and surrendered themselves. This health-oriented touch is a science itself and has a grammar of its own. This is not a magic nor the miraculous touch of holy nature. The grammar develops through a deep all-round understanding of the disease, and varies with each person. The touch is given according to the individual grammar that tingles his sensitive spots, activates them and puts life into them. The spread of new energy removes the obstacles, dislodges foreign fluids, etc. in the areas concerned and thus sets off a new flow of the blood and the new life to the nervous system. The revival of the nearly dead cells gets the patient rid of the malady.

The origin of this grammar of touch can be seen in the Vedas and in other ancient literature. In some literature, some sensitive spots are also described. But, this grammar is totally subjective, and keeps varying. This kind of touch is not confined to touching. Looking at the patient's condition and body, different vital spots are given different degrees of pressure with different duration, according to the malady and personality of each individual in order to activate them. These vital spots are spread like a network from head to toe. While applying pressure on the vital spots, the patient feels pain for the time being, but the result is unimaginable comfort and satisfaction. The spine is the most crucial part among all the vital spots. It is also known as *mūlādhāra* (basic foundation). According to modern science, the spine is the root-foundation of our nervous system. The vital force also spreads out through the spine. Therefore, in *prāṇa* therapy, the attention is mainly paid on the spine and it is found out that which nerves emerging from the spine are strong and active, and which are weak and need to be activated. The activation of these nerves not only helps in curing the disease, but also enhances and nourishes the *prāṇa* of the patient and makes his attitude positive to help him release from illness.

Vrata, Anuṣṭhāna and Upavāsa for Behavioural Control

The essence of *sādhanā* is self-discipline. The main purpose of any such spiritual activities like *vrata*, *anuṣṭhāna* or *upavāsa* is purification of the *citta* (mind) and behavioural control of the aspirant. When the mind is completely pure, it can attain worldly peace and freedom from several psycho-complexities and at the same time spiritual experiences can be attained very easily.

VRATA

The concept of *vrata* dates back to the *Ṛgveda*. Many commentators have tried to establish a definition for the word *vrata*, and what exactly it pertains to. However, these descriptions are varied. The general description used for *vrata*s as portrayed in the Dharmaśāstras is that of the religious vow or religious rite. They generally have to do with restraint and refraining from certain activities, though according to some commentators, it may also be a positive vow (i.e. "I must do this"). *Vrata*s may be used for many different reasons. Like pilgrimages, it can also be expiatory, placing it within the realm of *prāyaścitta*, but it can also be used for other means, such as a voluntary vow or the obligatory ones commonly practised by householders. *Utsava*s (religious festivals), share some elements with *vrata*s. They may contain elements often difficult to distinguish from the practice of *vrata*s.

*Vrata*s can consist of many different activities. Many *vrata*s had to do with the feeding of brāhmaṇas, a very auspicious activity, as well as giving to the poor and destitute. Other examples of *vrata*s can include fasting. The Smṛtis go into great details on the subject of *vrata*s, discussing even the details pertaining to what type of flowers should be used in worship.

Events such as death and birth, which can cause one to become impure, prevent a practitioner from observing his vows. A vow cannot be undertaken if one is impure. However, if one is in the middle of a *vrata* when impurity comes over him, he may continue with the *vrata* without any loss of merit, however there are still activities a person observing *vrata* must avoid. It is considered a grievous sin to abandon a *vrata* once one has undertaken it. Like pilgrimages, if one is unable to perform a *vrata*, he may have a representative to do it for him, though this is only if the vow is obligatory or has to do with a special event. One may not have a representative if the vow is undertaken out of desire for something.

ANUṢṬHĀNA

What is *anuṣṭhāna*? It is composed of two words *anu* and *sthān*. *Anu* means firm. *Sthān* means place or residence the original place of residence of the Lord. When one performs the following activities with firm conviction, that is an *anuṣṭhāna*. Become aware of the qualities of the place of the Lord; adopt as many qualities of the Lord as you can while simultaneously cutting yourself off from worldly activities. Make an independent place to perform good deeds of divine nature or to establish a relationship between your soul and the Lord. Sit with a firm determination to worship any form of the Lord or do *japa* (read the scriptures), etc. Do these for a period of time you have fixed beforehand. It is very critical to select a spot from where the *āsana* cannot be moved. Only then is the *anuṣṭhāna* accepted.

By the practice of *anuṣṭhāna*s, the negative, external, worldly factors that influence the mind and create obstacles on the spiritual path are forgotten. The mind flows toward the Lord and toward your *iṣṭa devatā* (a favourite form of the Lord). The mind becomes one with Him more easily and you gradually begin to forget yourself. You experience that the body is becoming more pure and divine, able to enjoy divine bliss, which many call *samādhi*. You can alter your mental attitudes in accordance with the qualities of Rāma as described in the scripture (and) begin to experience Rāma Himself.

In this manner, as the practice of *anuṣṭhāna* increases, it becomes very easy, even at the time of death, to meditate on the Lord and leave the body. Through *anuṣṭhāna,* you can experience the world through the physical body, yet divine bliss and divine body are not destroyed. In order to reach this state, you must follow the proper guidelines required for specific practices.

If in your current life there are few negative *saṁskāra*s (tendencies) and you have adopted some spiritual practices, and have faith and devotion, you may negate all *saṁskāra*s in twelve years or less. If you have created many positive *saṁskāra*s and your mind is tired of worldly affairs and your mind is drawn predominantly toward the Lord, at least four years of regular *anuṣṭhāna* are necessary to remove the *saṁskāra*s. Depending on the individual, this may take two to six more years. Even if you die before completing the required *anuṣṭhāna,* it is not wasted but is taken into account in the next life. Hence, you can attain realization in a shorter time in the next life.

Many perform a *saṅkalpa* (statement of intention) for short *anuṣṭhāna*s of one month or seven, eleven, or twenty-one days. When this is completed, they continue for shorter periods. In this way, they are doing continuous *anuṣṭhāna*. For those who expect no obstacles, the duration of an *anuṣṭhāna* could be from one to four months or even one and one-fourth to four years. The regular and continuous practice of an *anuṣṭhāna* is an austerity itself. If you start an *anuṣṭhāna* but cannot finish it due to some obstacles that come along the way, that is not wasted. At the first opportunity, you should resume the *anuṣṭhāna* and complete it.

In order to obtain the grace of God and *guru*, whatever *anuṣṭhāna* is being performed for a specific period of time is likely to encounter several obstacles. If you pay no attention to these, disregard them and continue the *anuṣṭhāna* as planned for the set time, only then is the *anuṣṭhāna* complete. The ultimate state of *Para-Brahman*, of bliss, is very stable and firm. There are no changes, no imbalance or modification in the degree of bliss.

UPAVĀSA

Fasting for a spiritual purpose is called *upavāsa*. The spiritual significance of fasting is being forgotten today as man is losing contact with his inner being. Nevertheless the science of fasting, as preserved in the Vedas and Śāstras, is a method of purification which can help man in his mundane and spiritual life. These ancient texts are inherited from our ancestors who understood and were in tune with the law of nature and man. The systems they devised came from their profound knowledge and enable man to raise his consciousness into the higher realms.

It has been scientifically proven that fasting makes the mind calm and serene. In yogic terminology this is known as the sāttvic element. Because the mind becomes predominantly sāttvic and more receptive, the scriptures advise the worship of certain deities during these fasting periods. This is called *vrata*, a specific type of purifying austerity or *tapa*. In the *tapovanśānt paras* fasting is referred to as *parama tapa* or supreme austerity.

When the positive aspects of a particular deity are concentrated on, those qualities are ultimately evoked in the individual. The deities are not actually separate beings; they are aspects of the dormant mind waiting to be awakened and utilized in man's consciousness. Worship can arouse these potential faculties so that the low, sensual consciousness can be elevated to super-consciousness.

The systems propounded in the Vedas and Śāstras co-ordinate man's biological rhythms with the cycles of nature. One of nature's most fundamental rhythms can be observed in the phases of the moon. Scientifically it is known that the tides of the ocean rise during full moon and by dark moon they have completely ebbed. These phases must therefore affect the human body, considering it is approximately 70 per cent water. The systems of fasting are based on the different stages of the moon's waxing and waning. The cycles of the moon influence women in particular through the menstrual cycle, so fasting is practised more extensively by women.

There are two phases in the moon's monthly cycle. The first part consisting of fifteen days as the moon waxes, is known as *śukla pakṣa* (the white fortnight). On the fifteenth day, *pūrṇimā* (full moon) occurs. Then the second half begins as the moon wanes. The next fifteen days are referred to as *kṛṣṇa pakṣa*. By the fifteenth day or *amāvasyā*, it is completely dark. The days specified for fasting are calculated according to the intensity of the moon's influence during these two phases. Fasting can be done on the fourth days of either fortnight. This is known as Saṅkaṣṭa Caturthī. This is a time for the worship of Gaṇeśa, the remover of obstacles and troubles. From this comes the name Saṅkaṣṭa (obstacles).

The eighth day of each fortnight is called *aṣṭamī*. Although fasting is not normally practised on every *aṣṭamī*, it is of importance on special occasions, such as the birthday of Kṛṣṇa, Gokula Aṣṭamī. On this day the divine qualities of Kṛṣṇa are remembered and revered. Navarātra Aṣṭamī, in the *śukla pakṣa* of Āśvin, during September–October, is devoted to the aspects of Devī, and fasting is done with respect to Durgā and Kālī. The ninth day, *navamī*, is the next significant date. The birth of Rāma, Rāmanavamī (in March–April) is especially noted.

The eleventh day of either fortnight, *ekādaśī*, is one of the more important dates for fasting. According to *Skanda Purāṇa* fasting on *ekādaśī* serves as a preventive medicine. This is of most relevance during *cāturmāsa* (the four months of monsoon). At this time maximum fasting is done because the weather is not conducive to digestion and the quality of available food also degenerates as a result of the climate. From the first *ekādaśī*, Hariśayanī Ekādaśī, in Āṣāḍha (June–July) up till the eleventh day in Kārttika (October–November) some people eat only once a day. It is said that the God Hari goes to sleep during this period; it is like a time of hibernation. Nirjalā Ekādaśī is observed in Jyeṣṭha. As the name indicates, no water is to be drunk on this day.

The monsoon period of fasting is not only exclusive to India. In the Islamic religion, during Ramadan, in the ninth month of the Arabian year, food and drink are prohibited in daylight hours. Obviously, in countries where monsoon does not occur, maximum fasting will not be so essential at this time. One has to adapt the rules to the conditions of the climate in which he lives.

The most relevant and popular periods for fasting are *pūrṇimā* and *amāvasyā*. These times are recommended for young and unmarried youths in particular. On Buddha Pūrṇimā in Baiśākha (April–May) fasts are done by devotees of Buddha. Guru Pūrṇimā is for all disciples to offer homage to their *gurus*. Mahā Śivarātri, which falls on the *amāvasyā* in March, is noted as the time when Śiva, consciousness, was married or united, with Pārvatī (energy). This particular *amāvasyā* is very significant, because it is supposed to be the darkest night of the year. However, any *amāvasyā* falling on a Monday is also noted with special reverence to Śiva.

Other fasts which do not fall on particular dates can be done weekly on one specific day. Monday fasting is done in reverence of Śiva. Tuesday is for pleasing Gaṇeśa or Devī. Thursday is in worship of Guru Dattātreya, the tri-headed form of Brahmā, Viṣṇu and Maheśa. On Friday Santoṣī Mā is worshipped and on Saturday blessings from Hanumān can be granted. One specific day is taken by an individual in accordance with his personal being. This is often allotted under the guidance of a *guru*.

On various fasting days different types of fasts are specified. When one meal is taken in the afternoon this is called *eka bhukta*. Eating once at night is called *nakta vrata*. To fast completely or take only a little fruit is *upavāsa*.

India, of course, being divided into many sects and religious groups, supports systems of fasting depending on local beliefs and climatic conditions. Jains, for example, will fast for one day, one week, one month, or even until the final *samādhi* occurs. Only boiled water can be taken twice a day. The fasts are done to induce a state of non-violence (*ahiṁsā*) in all acts. By fasting the aim is to rise above the influence of the five senses. Therefore, these fasts are very strict. Other groups fast on a single food, depending on climate and availability, some eating only wheat at certain times, others only rice. For some, grains are forbidden, and only fruit and/or dairy products are allowed. The whole of man's external and internal conditions are taken into consideration.

Person having psychological symptoms can adopt these systems of fasting to help us in our daily lives no matter what our profession is, where we live, or which religion we have faith or no faith in. These systems were formulated and recorded to enable all people to go beyond individual consciousness and experience the real essence of life. Fasting is systematically advocated in the scriptures in order to align the physical and subtle bodies with the whole cosmos, enabling sustained equilibrium in every aspect of life.

Prāyaścitta Sādhanā: Penance

The word *prāyaścitta* came from two Sanskrit roots: *prāya* and *citta*. Meaning of *prāyaścitta* is nothing but (*prāya* — sin) (*citta* — destructions) destructions of sins. *Prāyaścitta* is a personal attempt for atonement for wrongs committed against another. It "denotes an act or rite, intended for the destruction of sin. It can be considered a different sphere of the law. Penance is the English term used for the same. Generally it refers to repentance or contrition for sin. It refers, more particularly in the Orthodox and Roman Catholic traditions, to a sacrament, or an outward sign of an inward grace. In the area of psychotherapy it can be used to treat the patients suffering with guilt.

The concept of *prāyaścitta* can be traced back to the Vedas. Though in the Indian Purāṇas it is held that mere remembrance of Lord Nārāyaṇa is capable of removing all sins, *prāyaścitta* in *Nārada Purāṇa* enumerates five despicable crimes and how one can compensate for it. The word *prāyaścitta* also comes from *prāya* meaning *tapas* and *citta* meaning "resolve". The *prāyaścitta* is so called because of the firm belief that it will be a means of the sin removal. Sage Nārada, in *Nārada Purāṇa*, states that murderer of a brāhmaṇa, a drug intoxicant, gold thief, violator of teacher's bed and one who links with the above-mentioned evil acts needs to *prāyaścitta*.

In the Code of Manu, we find various kinds of *prāyaścitta* for the destruction of various kinds of sins. *Prāyaścitta* is of two kinds — extraordinary (*asādhāraṇa*) and ordinary (*sādhāraṇa*). Extraordinary penances are those which are prescribed in the Code of Manu for the destruction of particular sins. If anyone repents and openly admits his minor offences, the sin is washed away. In doing *prāyāścitta* the offender actually suffers, he punishes himself by long fasting and other ordeals as described above. Action and reaction are equal and opposite.

The five sinners counted as the equals of a murderer of a brāhmaṇa are: *paṅktibhedī* (one who defiles a society of persons), *vratapākī* (one who cooks for one's own use), *nityam brāhmaṇadūṣaka* (one who kills brāhmaṇas often), *ādeśī* (one who does acts forbidden by the king) and *veda-vikretā* (a seller of the Vedas). Again, an obstructer of a brāhmaṇa on his way to bathe or worship, a liar, one who is unrighteous, one who hurts others or speaks ill of others, etc. also are considered as a killer of brāhmaṇa.

One, who kills unknowingly a brāhmaṇa as expiation, should wander in the jungle for twelve years wearing bark as a garment and with a human skull. While doing this he should bathe, worship Lord Viṣṇu and take food once a day only. A gift of 10,000 *mudrās* given to a virtuous brāhmaṇa is also considered to expiate the sins of murdering of a brāhmaṇa. In order to redress the sin of liquor drinking one has to drink boiling milk, ghee or cow's urine.

Sins like theft of fruits, musk, jewels, metals like zinc and iron, honey, sandalwood are also equal to stealing of gold also. For pilfering gold belonging to a brāhmaṇa the offender has to undertake *brahma-hatyā vrata* for twelve years. By stealing the same thing belonging to his teachers, sacrificers, after coating his body with ghee he should burn himself in fire.

A person consigning intercourse with his own mother, step-mother or teacher's wife mistakenly can compensate the sin by killing himself. Accidental contact with four of the above types of offenders requires the performance of *kāyakracra vrata.*

Punishments are also mentioned for killing frog, crow, mouse, cat, dog, cow and some other animals. Donation is also prescribed as *prāyaścitta.* Reparation also differs according to *varṇa* also. If a brāhmaṇa kills a sacrificer, kṣatriya, he should endure *brahma-hatyā vrata, agnipraveśa* or throwing oneself into the air and ending life. If the slayer is a kṣatriya or a vaiśya, the same expiations recommended above should be performed twice and three times respectively. If the killer is a śūdra he is put to death and punished by the king. This shows that the punishments for misdeeds depended upon the *varṇa.*

These sins can be removed by the expiations said to be prescribed by the prophets, there are some sins which are called complete sins leading the sinner to hells as no penance has been recommended. An offence which has no remedy include lack of sympathy to brāhmaṇa, betraying the trusted, ingratitude, contact with a śūdra woman, living on śūdra's food, offending Vedas and noble stories, and entering a Buddhist temple.

*Prāyaścitta*s are not necessary only for the cleansing of one's own soul, but also for the satisfaction of the society, as they are not permitted to have social contact with one who has sinned and not completed their penance.

There are some rituals performed in Hindu traditions to reduce the severity of or eliminate the effects of bad or prohibited deeds. *Prāya* is austerity and *citta* is firm resolution; a firm resolution to take up austerity and following through with it is *prāyaścitta*. It includes austerities like fasting, chanting of *mantra*s, giving away gifts or going to pilgrimage. It is a ritual which is performed to eliminate the effects of bad deeds. Human beings are bound to make mistakes. However one has to repent and resolve, so that the sin is not repeated.

If one commits a sin he has to commit expiation to get over the guilt. *Prāyaścitta* depends on the type of sin committed. There are two types of sins: *mahāpātaka*s and *upapātaka*s. *Mahāpātaka*s include killing a person of knowledge, drinking intoxicating liquids and smoking. *Upapātaka*s include neglect of sacred fire, offending one's teacher, theft, non-payment of debts, selling banned articles, cutting down trees or killing animals that are not dangerous.

Some particular procedures a sinner must undergo: take the form of paring his nails, shaving his head, bathing with clay, cow dung, and holy water, drinking clarified butter, and making a declaration of performing the penance indicated by the assembly of the learned brāhmaṇas, all on the day prior to commencing his penance. On the next day, he is to bathe, perform *śrāddha* and *homa*, and give gifts to the brāhmaṇas and feed them. Also during the time of *prāyaścitta*, the sinner must observe certain rules on food and other matters. This includes that the sinner refrain from taking food at another's house, from sexual intercourse, from speaking at an improper time, and from everything that might cause him to feel strength or sexual passion. It is customary that when undergoing a penance, the sinner begins with a *mantra* — "O Fire! Lord of *vrata*! I shall perform a *vrata*". In the same way, when one has finished his penance, he recites a *mantra* — "O Fire! Lord of *vrata*s: I have performed the *vrata*, I had the strength to do it, may it be propitious for me". There are also particular virtues that should be practised while doing penance such as honesty. These are known as *yama*s.

Two kinds of *prāyaścitta*s exist: one which is done openly, *prakāśa*, and one which is done secretly, *rahasya*. Many Smṛtis lay down rules about performing secret *prāyaścitta*s. One reason a man would perform a secret *prāyaścitta* is because no one but himself knows about the sin he has committed. A general rule exists that secret penances are meant for those who have consecrated the Vedic fires, who are disciplined, old or learned, and that the open penances are meant for other people. It is even said that women and śūdras can perform secret penances because they too can give gifts and *prasāda*. While some Smr̥tis prescribe the enactment of a penance immediately as needed, some other place restrictions on the time (i.e. the *prāyaścitta tattva* says that a penance should not commence on the 8th or 14th *tithi* of the month). If one is in mourning, he may also wait to perform penance until the period of mourning has been completed.

Bibliography

Akiskal, H.S. and F. Benazzi, 2006, "The DSM-IV and ICD-10 Categories of Recurrent [major] Depressive and Bipolar II Disorders: Evidence that They Lie on a Dimensional Spectrum", *J. Affect Disorder*, **92(1):** 45-54 (May).

Allport, Gordon Willard, 1937, *The American Journal of Psychology*, **50**: 141-56.

Ansel, Woldt and Sarah Toman (eds.), 2005, *Gestalt Therapy: History, Theory, and Practice*, Gestalt Press.

Anthony, Roth and Peter Fonagy, 2005, *What Works for Whom?: A Critical Review of Psychotherapy Research*, Guilford Press.

Aung, Steven K.H. and Lee, Mathew H.M., 2004, Music, Sounds, Medicine, and Meditation: An Integrative Approach to the Healing, *Arts, Alternative and Complementary Therapies*, October, 10(5): 266-70.

Aurobindo, Sri, 1993, *The Integral Yoga*, Sri Aurobindo Ashram Publication Department.

Austin, James, 1998, *Zen and the Brain*, Cambridge: MIT Press, Boston.

Aziz, Robert, 2007, *The Syndetic Paradigm: The Untrodden Path Beyond Freud and Jung*, a refereed publication of The State University of New York Press.

Bateman, A. and J. Holmes, 1995, *Introduction to Psychoanalysis: Contemporary Theory and Practice*, Routledge.

Bateman, Anthony, Dennis Brown and Jonathan Pedder, 2000, *Introduction to Psychotherapy: An Outline of Psychodynamic Principles and Practice*, Routledge.

Belsare, K.V., 1989, *Santanche Atmacharitra*, 2nd edn., Mumbai: Tridal Publishers.

Benson, Herbert, 1972, "The Physiology of Meditation", *Scientific American*, **226**(2): 84-90.

Bhogle, S. and I. Jai Prakash, 1993, "Indicators of Subjective Well-being in a Non-clinical Sample", *Psychological Studies*, **38**(3): 135-41.

Bhole, M.V., 1981, "Yogic Treatment of Bronchial Asthma: A Medical Report", *Yoga Mīmāṁsā*, 1981; **20:** 1-12

Bhushan, L.I., 1994, "A Yogic Model of Mental Health", *Indian Journal of Psychological Issues*, 1(3): 1-5.

Birkenholz, Robert, J., 1999, *Effective Adult Learning*, Interstate Publishers.

Bodhananda, Swami, 1939, *The Bhagavad Gita*, Vedanta Society.

Cattell, Raymond Bernard, 1957, *Personality and Motivation Structure and Measurement*, New York, World Book.

Clark, L.A., 2007, "Assessment and Diagnosis of Personality Disorder: Perennial Issues and an Emerging Reconceptualization", *Annu Rev Psychol*, **58:** 227-57.

Crocker, Sylvia, 1999, *A Well-Lived Life, Essays in Gestalt Therapy*, Sage Publications.

Daftuar and Sharma, 1997, *Psychology of Well-being*, New Delhi: Global Vision Publishing House.

Dalal, A.S., 2001, *Psychology, Mental Health and Yoga*, Sri Aurobindo Ashram Press, Pondicherry.

Dalal, A.S., 2001, *A Greater Psychology: An Introduction to Sri Aurobindo's Psychological Thought*, Jeremy P Tarcher/Putnam.

Datey, K.K., 1978, Yoga: Prevention and Management of Hypertension, *Swasth Hind*, **22:** 56-58.

Davidson, R.J. et al., 2003, "Alterations in Brain and Immune Function Produced by Mindfulness Meditation", *Psychosomatic Medicine*, July-August, **65(4):** 564-70.

Davies T., 1997, "ABC of Mental Health: Mental Health Assessment", *BMJ* (May) **314(7093):** 1536-39.

Davis, K.L. (1989), *Serotonergic Studies in Patients with Affective and Personality Disorders*, Arch. Gen. Psychiatry, 46: 587-599.

Divekar, M.V., 1982, "Yoga Therapy for Diabetes and Obesity", *Yoga*, **20(6):** 19-29.

Ellenberger, Henri F., 1970, *The Discovery of the Unconscious: The History and Evolution of Dynamic Psychiatry*, Basic Books.

Emerson, Ralph Waldo, 1860, *The Conduct of Life*, Boston: Ticknor and Fields.

Eysenck, Hans, 1991, "Dimensions of Personality: 16: 5 or 3? Criteria for a Taxonomic Paradigm", *Personality and Individual Differences*, **12**: 773-90.

Fiske, D.W., 1949, "Consistency of the Factorial Structures of Personality Ratings from Different Sources", *Journal of Abnormal Social Psychology*, **44:** 329-44.

Frank, Jerome, 1988 (1979), "What is Psychotherapy?", in Sidney Bloch (ed.) *An Introduction to the Psychotherapies*, Oxford: Oxford University Press.

Freedman, J., 1978, *Happy People*: What Happiness is, Who has it, and Why, New York: Harcourt Brace Jovanovich.

Funder, D.C., 2004, "Personality and Life Satisfaction: A Facet Level Analysis", *Personality and Social Psychology Bulletin*, **30:** 1062-75.

Gamma A., J. Angst, V. Ajdacic, D. Eich and W. Ro'ssler, 2007, "The Spectra of Neurasthenia and Depression: Course, Stability and Transitions", *Eur Arch Psychiatry Clin Neurosis*, **257**(2): 120-27 (March).

Gazzaniga, M.S. and T.F. Heatherton, 2006, *Psychological Science*, New York: W.W. Norton & Company.

Goldberg, L.R., 1981, "Language and Individual Differences: The Search for Universals in Personality Lexicons", in L. Wheeler (ed.), *Review of Personality and Social Psychology*, vol. 2, Beverly Hills, CA: Sage.

Heuer, Richard, 1999, *Psychology of Intelligence Analysis*, Centre for the Study of Intelligence.

Hostman, Judith, 2005, *The Scientific American Brave New Brain*, Scientific American.

Jangid, R.K., J.N. Vyas and T.R. Shukla, 1988, "Effect of Transcendental Meditation in Cases of Anxiety Neurosis", *Indian Journal of Clinical Psychology*, **15:** 77-79.

Joshi, Rajani R. (2006), *The Integrated Science of Yagna*, Mathura: Yug Nirman Yojna, Gayatri Tapobhumi.

Kashner, T.M. et al., 2003, "Impact of Structured Clinical Interviews on Physicians' Practices in Community Mental Health Settings", *Psychiatric Service*, **54**(5): 712-18 (May).

Kaul, H. Kumar, 1993, *Yoga and Drug Addiction*, Delhi: B.R. Publishing Corp.

Kaur, P., and A.K. Sinha, 1992, "Dimensions of guna in Organizational Setting", *Vikalpa*, **17:** 27-32.

Kinderman, P. and F. Lobban, 2000, "Evolving Formulations: Sharing Complex Information with Clients", *Behavioral and Cognitive Psychotherapy*, **28**(3): 307-10.

Korchin, Sheldon J., 2004, *Modern Clinical Psychology*, New Delhi: CBS Publishers and Distributors.

Kotbagi, Harish, 1997, *Human Capabilites (Memory)*, Georgia Technology College of Computing.

Larsen, R.J. and D.M. Buss, 2005, *Personality Psychology: Domains of Knowledge About Human Nature* (2nd edn.), Boston: McGraw-Hill.

Lawton, M.P., 1983, "The Varieties of Well-being," *Experimental Ageing Research*, **9:** 65-72.

Linton, Ralph, 1936, *The Study of Man: An Intoduction*, D. Appleton-Century Company.

Lundberg, Gary, 1999, *I dont have to Make Everything All Better*, Amazon.com.

Mayer, John D., 2007, "Asserting the Definition of Personality", *The Online Newsletter for Personality Science*, Issue 1, Spring 2007, pp. 1-4.

McAdams, D.P., 2006, *The Person: A New Introduction to Personality Psychology* (4th edn.), New York: Wiley.

McCrae, R.R., and P.T. Costa, 1987, "Validation of the Five-factor Model of Personality across Instruments and Observers", *Journal of Personality and Social Psychology*, **52:** 81-90.

MacIver, R.M., 1915, " Personality and the Suprapersonal", *The Philosophical Review*, September, **24**: 48.

Motoyama, H., 1979, "Yoga and Oriental Medicine", *Kundalini*, **3:** 9-15.

Nagarathna, R. and H.R. Nagendra, 1980, *Therapeutic Application of Yoga: A Report*, Kanyakumari: Vivekananda Kendra Yoga Therapy and Research Centre.

Naug, R.N., 1975, "Yoga Therapy in Neurotic Disorders," *Indian Journal of Clinical Psychology*, **2:** 87-90.

Newberg, Andrew et al., 2001, "The Measurement of Regional Cerebral Blood Flow during the Complex Cognitive Task of Meditation: A Preliminary SPECT Study", *Psychiatry Resource*, **106:** 113-22.

Norman, W.T., 1967, *2,800 Personality Trait Descriptors: Normative Operating Characteristics for a University Population*, Department of Psychology, University of Michigan.

Ogburn, William F., 1964, *On Culture and Social Change*, Phoenix Books, University of Chicago Press.

Okun, M.A. and W.A. Stock, 1984, "Correlates and Components of SWB", *Journal of Applied Genetology*, **61:** 95-112.

Ornish, D., 1990, *Reversing Heart Disease*, New York: Ballantyne Books.

Pandya, Pranav, 2004, "The Occult Science of Upasana", *Akhand Jyoti*, September–October, p. 27.

Pandya, Pranav, 2005, "Science and Spirituality: Awaken the Hidden Powers of Hearing by Nada Yoga", *Akhand Jyoti*, **3:** 23.

Park, Robert and Ernest Burgess, 1921, *Introduction to Science of the Sociology*, University of Chicago Press.

Paul, Richard, 1992, *Critical Thinking Defined*, Handout given at Critical Thinking Conference (November), Atlanta, GA.

Paul, Richard, 1992, "Critical Thinking: What, Why and How", *New Directions for Community Colleges*, **77**: 5-24.

Pervin, L.A., D. Cervone, and O.P. John, 2005, *Personality: Theory and Research* (9th edn.), Hoboken, NJ: John Wiley & Sons.

Rajvanshi, A.K., 2002, "Palliative Effect of Good Music", Editorial article in *Times of India*, 15 April.

Ramamurthi, B., 1977, "Yoga and Neurology", *Journal of Rehabilitation in Asia*, **18:** 16-17.

Robert, E. Park and Ernest W. Burgess, 1921, *Introduction to the Science of Sociology*, Chicago, p. 11.

Salovey, Peter, and John D. Mayer, 1990, "Emotional Intelligence", *Imagination, Cognition and Personality*, **9**(3): 185-211.

Saraswati, Swami Karmananda, 1982, "Yoga Averts Heart Attack", *Yoga*, **20(5):** 11-17.

Saraswati, Swami Muktananda, 1982, "Yoga Nidra: Yoga, Brain and Consciousness", National Symposium Conducted at NIMHANS, Bangalore.

Saraswati, Swami Niranjanananda, 1993, *Yoga Darshan*, Deoghar, Sri Panchdashnam Paramahamsa Alakh Bara, Rikhia, Bihar.

Saraswati, Swami Niranjanananda, 1996, "The Impact of Yoga Practices on Jail Inmates: A Report from 24 Jails in Bihar", unpublished paper, Bihar Yoga Bharati, Munger.

Saraswati, Swami Satyananda, 1976, *Four Chapters on Freedom*, Munger: Bihar School of Yoga.

Saraswati, Swami Satyananda, 1980, *Yoga from Shore to Shore* (3rd edn.), Munger: Bihar School of Yoga.

Saraswati, Swami Satyananda, 1981, "Satsang and Psychotheraphy", *Yoga Magazine*, Bihar School of Yoga, Munger, July, p. 6.

Saraswati, Swami Satyananda, 1982, "Kirtan: Rocket to Self-realization", *Yoga Magazine*, Bihar School of Yoga, Munger, September, p. 36.

Saraswati, Swami Satyananda, 1996, *Asana Pranayama Mudra Bandha*, new edn., Munger: Bihar Yoga Bharati.

Sethi, B.B., J.K. Trivedi, and R. Anand, 1981, "A Comparative Study of the Relative Effectiveness of Biofeedback and Shavasana in Tension Headache", *Indian Journal of Psychiatry*, **23:** 109-14.

Sharma, Acharya Shriram, 1976, *Dhyāna Yoga kā Vyavahārik Kriyā Paksha*, Mathura: Yug Nirman Yojna Press, p. 27.

Sharma, Acharya Shriram, 2001, *Music: The Nectar of Life*, Mumbai: Gayatri Parivar Yug Nirman Yojna Trust.

Sharma, Acharya Sriram, 2003, *Yagya, ek Samagra Upchar Prakriya*, vol. 26, Akhand Jyoti Sansthan, Mathura.

Sharma, I. and S.S. Agnihotri, 1982, "Preliminary Observations on the Effect of Controlled Breathing in Anxiety States: Yoga, Brain and Consciousness", National Symposium conducted at NIMHANS, Bangalore.

Shear, M.K., et al., 2000, "Diagnosis of Non-Psychotic Patients in Community Clinics", *Am J Psychiatry*, **157**(4): 581-87.

Shelvamurthy, W., 1996, "The Influence of Yogic Practices on Defence Scientists", *The Times of India*, Patna.

Silverman, D.K., 2005, "What Works in Psychotherapy and How Do We Know? What Evidence-Based Practice Has to Offer", *Psychoanalytic*

Psychology, **22**(2): 306-12.

Singh, R.H., R.M. Shettiwar and K.N. Udupa, 1978, "The Role of Yogic Practices in the Prevention and Treatment of Hypertension", *Swasth Hind*, **22:** 63-65.

Skinner, B.F., 1953, *Science and Human Behavior*, New York: Macmillan.

Smith, G.M., 1967, "Usefulness of Peer Rating of Personality in Educational Research", *Educational Psychological Measurement*, **27:** 967-84.

Strupp, Hans and Jeffrey Binder, 1984, *Psychotherapy in a New Key: A Guide to Time-limited Dynamic Psychotherapy*, New York: Basic Books.

Sysaro, S., 2003, *Occupational & Environmental Medicine*, **60**: 3-9.

Udupa, K.N., *Stress and its Management by Yoga*, Delhi: Motilal Banarsidass.

Udupa, K.N., 1977, "Pathogenesis and Management of Stress Disorders", *Quart. J. Surg. Sci.*, Banaras Hindu University, **13**(2): 56.

Varma, L.P., 1979, "Yoga, Meditation and Mysticism", *Indian Journal of Psychiatry*, 21: 293-304.

Verma, S.K., 1988, "Measurement of Positive Mental Health: Some Theoretical and Practical Considerations", *Indian Journal of Clinical Psychology*, **15:** 6-11.

Vrinte, Joseph, 2002, *The Perennial Quest for a Psychology with a Soul*, Delhi: Motilal Banarsidass.

Yinger, J. Milton, 1965, *Towords a Field Theory of Behaviour*, New York: McGraw Hill Book Company.

Index